Jim Crow Nostalgia

Jim Crow Nostalgia

Reconstructing Race in Bronzeville

Michelle R. Boyd

University of Minnesota Press
Minneapolis • London

Portions of chapter 3 have been previously published as "Reconstructing Bronzeville: Racial Nostalgia and Neighborhood Redevelopment," *Journal of Urban Affairs* 22, no. 2 (2000): 107–22; copyright 2000 Urban Affairs Association. Portions of chapter 5 have been previously published as "The Downside of Racial Uplift: The Meaning of Gentrification in an African American Neighborhood," *City and Society* 17, no. 2 (2005): 265–88; copyright 2005 by the American Anthropological Association.

Published by the University of Minnesota Press
111 Third Avenue South, Suite 290
Minneapolis, MN 55401-2520
http://www.upress.umn.edu

Library of Congress Cataloging-in-Publication Data

Boyd, Michelle R.
  Jim Crow nostalgia : reconstructing race in Bronzeville / Michelle R. Boyd.
    p. cm.
  Includes bibliographical references and index.
  ISBN 978-0-8166-4677-7 (hc : alk. paper) — ISBN 978-0-8166-4678-4 (pb : alk. paper)
  1. Bronzeville (Chicago, Ill.)—Social conditions. 2. Bronzeville (Chicago, Ill.)—Politics and government. 3. African Americans—Race identity—Illinois—Chicago. 4. African Americans—Segregation—Illinois—Chicago—History. 5. Community life—Illinois—Chicago—History. 6. African Americans—Illinois—Chicago—Politics and government. 7. African American leadership—Illinois—Chicago—History. 8. Nostalgia—Social aspects—Illinois—Chicago. 9. Nostalgia—Political aspects—Illinois—Chicago. 10. Chicago (Ill.)—Race relations. I. Title.
  F548.68.B76B69 2008
  305.8009773'11—dc22

                                                                                              2008004244

Printed in the United States of America on acid-free paper

The University of Minnesota is an equal-opportunity educator and employer.

15 14 13 12 11 10 09 08   10 9 8 7 6 5 4 3 2 1

Contents

Acknowledgments

The most delightful moment in writing this book came when I drew near enough to the end to begin contemplating the composition of this thank-you letter.

My first debt is to the residents of Douglas/Grand Boulevard, men and women who opened their lives to me and gave unstintingly of their time, kindness, and insight. Promises of confidentiality prevent me from calling them by name, but my silence does nothing to diminish my gratitude. While they gave me lessons in race and community, my dissertation committee helped me make sense of all I was learning. My advisor, Adolph Reed, challenged my thinking about race, pushed me beyond my self-doubt, and insisted I continue taking my own intellectual route, even when it was uncomfortable to do so. He and Henry Binford undid the damage of several years of K–12 history courses and taught me to respect the past, especially that of the city of Chicago. Susan Herbst kept me grounded in political science when my interdisciplinary leanings threatened to run away with me. And Mary Patillo jumped merrily on board during last-minute committee restructuring and responded to my work with an engagement unusual for a reader. The tasks they set me to were made easier by funding from the National Science Foundation, the Northwestern University Graduate College, and the Illinois Consortium for Educational Opportunity Program; time to write up the findings was generously provided by the Institute for the Humanities at the University of Illinois at Chicago.

One would have thought I'd used up my life's portion of good luck with that committee, but I apparently had some leftovers. Imagine an academic department in which your colleagues constantly challenge you to give your best rather than prove your worth; where intellectual engagement and professional mentorship are the norm rather than the exception; and where you count your colleagues among your closest friends. Now click your heels three times and you'll be in the African American Studies Department at the University of Illinois at Chicago. As the head of the department while I was writing this book, Beth Richie repeatedly took time out of her overloaded schedule to help me think through my professional goals and work through intellectual and practical dilemmas. Kerry Ann Rockquemore is perhaps the only person I know whose love of order and organization surpasses my own. She has used those gifts to help me boost my productivity as both a writer and a teacher. There is absolutely no limit to Amanda Lewis's energy, attention, and commitment to her colleagues, and I'm lucky to be one of them: she is a one-stop shop for professional advice, rides home, critical feedback, and wacky e-card support. Cynthia Blair's mellow demeanor masks an effortless habit of razor-sharp reflection; this project has been improved by long conversations in which we tussled with both the intellectual and emotional challenges of my writing it. Helen Jun's spot-on analyses of my writing and my writing failures are as hilarious as they are insightful. I'm indebted to these women and other writing group members (Dave Stovall, Corey Capers, and Badia Ahad) for helping me complete this work.

The gifts given me by these men and women were enhanced by the support I received from colleagues in the city of Chicago and beyond. I am particularly indebted to Gina Pérez, whose friendship is a lighthouse that has guided me through this and countless other storms. An ethnographer by training and by nature, she helps me see what is true about me and my work. She, along with Regina Deil, Deborah Parédez, and Heather McClure, helped me maintain my center during graduate school and shepherded this project through its infancy. Larry Bennett has for years managed to deliver unflinching criticism of my work along with unyielding support for it. Although he has never formally been my teacher, I consider him among the most significant of my mentors. John Jackson read several versions of this work and asked pressing, pointed questions that required me to reach even further past disciplinary boundaries. Long talks with Ellen Berrey reminded me why this work is important and fun, but ultimately not the center of the universe. The good-humored and sharp-eyed editing of Erin Starkey caught the worst of my writing errors, while the professionalism of the University of Minnesota Press staff helped me navigate the multiple and mysterious stages of book publishing. None of these good works would have meant a thing had it not been for a family who maintained a sometimes puzzled but always enthusiastic support for me, as well as outright disbelief in any uncertainty I had about this project. My parents, Sandra and Woody Boyd, and my big brother, Marc Boyd, are proud of me whether or not I finish this book, which is of course the very thing that made me able to do it at all.

Everyone I've mentioned has—at least once—picked me up, dusted me off, and set me back on the path to completing this project. For every time they have done so, my husband, David Stevens, has done it twice. At 3:38 in the morning. Amid tears of frustration. A book is a wretched thank-you gift after all he's done. But finishing it seemed the most likely path to ending his suffering—so here it is.

Introduction: Race, Nostalgia, and Neighborhood Redevelopment

As we pulled away from the corner of Forty-third Street and King Drive, Steven Anthony stood up and began narrating our tour of the Douglas/ Grand Boulevard neighborhood. The bus was filled with approximately twenty-five men and women, members of a community leadership class designed to mobilize residents around the revitalization happening in the neighborhood. Our tour stopped at more than three dozen buildings, homes, and lots between Twenty-second and Fifty-first Streets on Chicago's South Side. Mr. Anthony, gripping a seat back and swaying with every turn of the bus, provided a commentary juicy with gossip, personal anecdotes, and descriptions of well-known community figures. But though the trip took place in early January 1998, the vibrant portrait he painted was of black life during Douglas/Grand Boulevard's segregation era.

Mr. Anthony first sketched in the physical landscape, pointing out various commercial streets and indicating which structures had been built or used in the early 1900s. Where no physical traces remained, he vividly described the buildings that had stood there. State Street, we discovered, was the business and entertainment district, and the strip south of Thirty-fifth Street was home to "the most important vaudeville houses" of the day. At Forty-seventh Street and King Drive he stopped the bus driver and, as no buildings remained, he asked us to imagine when "these vacant lots here on Forty-seventh were the Savoy and the Regal Theaters." Mr. Anthony then fleshed out the bare bones of this physical inventory with proud descriptions of the institutions these buildings had once housed—the churches, businesses, political groups, and voluntary organizations that had played such an important role in the lives of migration-era blacks. At the corner of Twenty-fourth and State Streets he gestured to Quinn Chapel, "one of the most famous of urban developments. . . . It is one of the oldest religious buildings built and constructed by blacks, and it was a station on the Underground Railroad. If my grandparents, for example, had escaped from slavery and run north to Chicago, this is a place they might have come." He drew our attention to buildings like Quinn because they represented both important moments in African American history and the accomplishments of blacks themselves. A few blocks east, at Twenty-fourth and Michigan, for example, he pointed out the original Defender Building, which "housed the most influential newspaper in America." It was not the architectural detail of this building that merited comment, but the success and influence it represented. "At one time," he claimed, the *Chicago Defender* "had a subscription of three hundred thousand. But for every one subscription, there were two to three people who read the paper. That's almost a million readers."

Finally, against this backdrop of land, buildings, and institutions, Mr. Anthony described the people who had lived in this black community and the characteristics that had made them so successful. He admitted that blacks endured racism, but he depicted Douglas/Grand Boulevard as a racial refuge, an independent island to which African Americans had retreated to attend to their economic, social, and political needs. According to him, the neighborhood was filled with visual and musical artists, elected officials, business owners, and race activists. These were people whose contributions had made community life so rich that "you didn't want to go outside the neighborhood." Because these community members had displayed a strong sense of racial solidarity, they served as leaders and role models for the rest of the residents. As Mr. Anthony claimed, "in that day, you didn't have to be important to know important people . . . to *become* like those people. It was just a matter of waiting, of preparing. We'd look at them and say 'They look like us; they walk like us; they talk like us. Why can't we be them?'"

Mr. Anthony's commentary was noteworthy in part because it expressed such strong nostalgia for the Jim Crow era—a yearning for and a celebration of black life during the period of legalized racial segregation. His description of the Douglas/Grand Boulevard of the early twentieth century conveyed a clear admiration for black life during this time period and made no mention of the more brutal aspects of racial segregation. Perhaps most telling was an exchange between Mr. Anthony and one of the leadership class members that took place toward the end of the tour. "Do you think that integration was what ruined the neighborhood?" she asked. "Yes!" he exclaimed. "Now how to fix that is your task." With this statement, he established himself as part of a larger wave of longing for the past that is now a common element of contemporary political rhetoric, popular and literary culture, and public policy (Reed 1996; Williams 1988, 2002). Yet his commentary constituted more than a wistful walk down memory lane. Mr. Anthony's reimagining of black life is also significant because it is the basis for a specific understanding of contemporary black identity—of the values, characteristics, and behaviors that defined the African American residents of this neighborhood. As many scholars have pointed out, a sense of common history is one basis for a sense of racial identity. Thus, in describing the history of the neighborhood, Mr. Anthony was also describing the common roots and shared culture that bind together the black residents who now live there.

Understanding the emergence and political significance of this particular racial identity is the aim of this book. I examine first how community leaders in Douglas/Grand Boulevard came to reimagine contemporary black identity through nostalgia for the Jim Crow past. This conception of blackness constitutes just one of the many available notions of blackness that Douglas/Grand Boulevard leaders could cultivate and draw on in their community leadership class. Yet it has become more and more popular in the last twenty years, not only in Douglas/Grand Boulevard, but in similar neighborhoods across the country. Leaders and residents of urban black neighborhoods increasingly argue that the communities formed in the wake of the Great Migration represented a more authentic, successful expression of blackness, one that would have remained intact had it not been for the unfortunate experience of integration. My first objective, then, is to explore how particular notions of black identity surface within African American communities.

Most remarkable is the way this specific, nostalgic vision of black identity is being expressed and institutionalized in urban development policy and politics today. Not only do blacks make increasing public reference to the segregation era in their depiction of black identity, but in cities like Chicago, Philadelphia, New York, and Washington, D.C., the articulation of this identity is accompanied by neighborhood revitalization strategies designed to recreate the black communities that existed during the early twentieth century (Boyd 2000; Moore 2002, 2005; Prince 2002; Taylor 2002; Williams 1999). These strategies include the creation of racial tourism districts, mixed-income housing developments and black gentrification. Proponents assert that these strategies will benefit all neighborhood residents by revitalizing the economies of poor black neighborhoods and reasserting the social and moral structures of the migration era. This expression of Jim Crow identity is taking place within a very specific set of political projects; therefore, my second aim is to explore how the emergence of specific racial identities is related to the pursuit of particular notions of racial group advancement.

What I show is that neighborhood elites in Douglas/Grand Boulevard constructed Jim Crow racial identity as they pursued their political preferences, and in ways that framed those preferences as intrinsic to blackness. They then drew on this understanding of racial identity to legitimize their pursuit of an economic development strategy that ultimately privileged homeowners over low-income and public housing residents. What happened in Douglas/Grand Boulevard illustrates how the *meaning* of racial identity is crucial to black elites' efforts to legitimize the pursuit of their political preferences. My point here is not just that African American leaders seek support with appeals to a shared racial identity. Rather, I contend that they first specify the characteristics of that common identity—defining their own values, characteristics, and preferences as its central components—and then adopt those characteristics as the standard by which political legitimacy is judged.

This argument diverges from current work on the political significance of racial identity, most of which emphasizes the factors influencing the strength with which that identity is felt and its salience relative to other identities. With this book, I try to explain how the *content* of racial identity, rather than its salience, plays a role in political actors' efforts to set the political agenda in black urban communities. Doing so helps to explain how Jim Crow, a period of violent, repressive, state-sanctioned racism, has come to be popularly understood as a racial utopia, a haven from the uncertainty, disappointment, and inadequacy of the contemporary period. Promoters of Douglas/Grand Boulevard's revitalization have defined identity through Jim Crow nostalgia—in other words, they have defined contemporary black identity by describing it as an extension of a reimagined past. Their vision of that past, like all visions of the past, is a partial one—gilded by fond memory, embroidered by fable, and tinged by contemporary concerns. Thus, it depicts the segregation period generally, and the Great Migration era in particular, as characterized by class harmony, collectivist middle-class leadership, and vibrant black culture. Douglas/Grand Boulevard leaders have attempted to revitalize the neighborhood without sparking racial displacement, and in doing so, they have institutionalized Jim Crow nostalgia, both in their organizations and in the built environment. This reinterpretation of the segregation era is therefore not an accident; nor is it the natural result of the passage of time. Rather, it is a political artifact, a strategic rendering of race, space, and history that political elites have used to both challenge and reproduce contemporary racialized urban inequality.

Nostalgia and Anxiety in the Post–Civil Rights Era

While nostalgia for the segregation era may seem puzzling to members of the post–civil rights generation, it reflects a growing public anxiety over the existence and stability of collective black identity. These concerns surfaced in part because of the widening economic polarization of the black population. In the 1970s, the African American middle class began to penetrate national job markets and as a result became more secure, prosperous, and integrated than the preceding generation (Kilson 1983; Landry 1987).

Yet its successes coincided with the impoverishment of the country's poorest blacks, who, in contrast, began to experience increasing insecurity, destitution, and marginalization. As this polarization became harder to ignore, activists were faced with the challenge of organizing around race in ways that account for intraracial divisions and conflicts. Similarly, academics have reignited the debate over the relative significance of racial identity among African Americans (Brashler 1978; Clark 1978; Clark and Gershman 1980; Dawson 1994; Kilson 1983; Marable 1981; Simpson 1998; Tate 1994; Warner and Bedell 1974; Wilson 1980). At the heart of this public and academic discussion is the fear that the class concerns of the black middle class will undermine their commitment to racial advancement.

The dilemma of intraracial division is important, but not new. Economic and other distinctions have always marked the black population (Cannon 1984; Sites and Mullins 1985). Not only has intraracial economic stratification existed since Reconstruction, it has also been the basis for substantial variation in black public opinion and behavior (McBride and Little 1981). In the North, and in southern cities like New Orleans, Mobile, Savannah, and Charleston, free mulatto populations were the basis for the formation of a black upper class (Drake and Cayton 1993; Foner 1990; Meier 1962). This entrepreneurial and professional stratum initially lacked the stability and influence of its white counterpart, but it soon became the core of urban black political leadership, particularly after the Great Migration (Gosnell 1935; Meier 1962; Spear 1967). While it has not been uncommon for this leadership class to join forces with lower strata blacks, neither has it been unusual for them to distance themselves. Black elites have consistently attributed the problem of white racism to the improper social behavior of the poor and have even gone so far as to suggest that poorer blacks were undeserving of the rights of citizenship. Clearly, intraracial conflict has been a hallmark of black politics, even during the much-applauded civil rights period (Greenberg 1991; Valocchi 1996; Waite 2001). Diversity of experience among blacks—class-based or otherwise—has therefore been a recurring element that political entrepreneurs have constantly and repeatedly had to overcome to garner the "black vote." Contemporary manifestations of black political diversity are the result, not just of the growing numbers of middle-class blacks, nor of a sudden increase in the significance of class identity; rather, they reflect a number of political and economic shifts that have changed the relationship between middle-, working-, and lower-class blacks. Thus, the concerns about intraracial conflict are best considered against a wider view of the post–civil rights political landscape.

The principal feature of this landscape is the attendant move "from protest to politics," the transition in which the main locus of black political efforts shifted from the field of protest to the electoral arena (Rustin 1965; R. Smith 1981). Following the passage of the Voting and Civil Rights Acts of 1964 and 1965, black voter registration and participation rates rose to unprecedented levels, and new black voters wasted no time using their newfound power to elect African American candidates (Browning, Marshall, and Tabb 1984). Moreover, the War on Poverty and other programs of the 1960s installed a leadership class of black bureaucrats to administer social services to poor blacks. These changes led to a dramatic improvement in the quality of life for African Americans generally (Owens 1997). Yet this entrance into the formal mechanisms of decision making, important as it was, resulted in the limited political incorporation of African Americans. As many scholars have noted, privileged blacks are now integrated into institutions in ways that constrain their ability and incentive to expand poorer blacks' access to and power within governing institutions (Brown and Erie 1981). The black public officials whose electoral success depends on black votes are limited by political economy and growth coalition ideology in how they can respond to the needs of their black constituents (Bennett 1993; Reed 1988). Similarly, the ability of community organizations to make demands on city administrations is diminished by the fact that many skilled leaders have left neighborhood organizations to participate in governing coalitions (Clavel and Wiewel 1991). As black elites become increasingly dependent on mainstream resources, "the goal of maintaining and expanding integration into the dominant society often becomes [their] primary concern," one which "may come at the expense of more radical transformation and redistribution of dominant institutional resources" (Cohen 1999, 64).

As scholars have already noted, the entrance of blacks into politics was also accompanied by changes in the black class structure. What was significant about these changes was not the increase in the *numbers* of individuals in the middle class, nor the increase in the *income* of individual blacks; rather, it was the change in what kinds of jobs placed them in that class bracket and how it changed the relationship between poor and middle-class blacks. The latest shift in the black class structure added a new element to the relationship between the black elite and the rest of the black population: through job acquisition, middle-income blacks have "increasingly assumed administrative control of the institutions of urban governance, the public apparatus of social management" (Reed 1999a, 119). Black city and state employees are more likely to be managers in public welfare, corrections, and housing departments than are whites. And according to Brown and Erie, Great Society public employment policies created a new social welfare economy "of publicly funded middle-income service providers and low-income service and cash transfer recipients," especially among blacks (1981, 311). A similar trend existed in private industry, where black managers and workers were routed into racialized fields such as personnel, labor relations, public relations, and social welfare—jobs that were designed to serve and exploit black markets and "calm disruptive elements of the population" (S. Collins 1997, 30). In these positions, the black elite more blatantly exhibited their previous role as mediators of interracial conflict and watchdogs of poor blacks' behavior (Cohen 1999). Thus, while social scientists have emphasized the impact of class status on individual identity and consciousness, the structural features of class position have had equally, if not more, significant implications for intraracial relations.

These changed relationships are related to a third and final component of the postsegregation political landscape—the liberal retreat from an agenda of racial equality. In response to the political demands of the black power era, the liberal elements of the civil rights coalition have pointed to the successes of the black middle class as proof that contemporary racial inequality should be blamed on the culture of poor blacks (Steinberg 1995). This response is part of a larger pattern of neoliberal rhetoric that claims that overt and excessive capitulations to blacks have destroyed the traditional

New Deal coalition, and therefore hurt the chances of the Democratic Party (Reed 1999b). The proposed solution is to shun "special interests" and pursue race-neutral policies. Rather than responding with a critique of the racism inherent in white backlash, or organizing blacks against its unequal consequences, black leadership as a whole has remained strangely and disappointingly silent. Many black academics have supported the strategy of promoting universal remedies for the problems facing blacks (W. Wilson 1980; West 1993). At the same time, both conservatives and liberals now argue that civil rights legislation has eliminated racial discrimination, that contemporary racial inequality is a function of African American culture rather than white racism, and that public policy should therefore be "color-blind" (Brown et al. 2003; Bonilla Silva 2003). This context provides reduced political support and incentives for making race-based demands, thus altering the political calculus that black leaders use to determine which interests they will pursue and with what strategy.

Assuming that intraracial differences reflect the sudden significance of African American class identity obscures important features of this dilemma. Questions about black identity are surfacing in a context that highlights not just the differences in how individuals in the same racial category experience race and racial power, but more important, how the black elite's privileges and success often come at the expense of poorer African Americans. The very benefits that the black middle class has accrued depend in part on the political behavior of the black majority, and on the claim that the policies that produced them would lead to an inclusive racial dividend (Omi and Winant 1994, 28). These conditions have provoked both activist concern and academic curiosity about the nature of black racial identity, and the extent to which it is politically meaningful in the contemporary period.

Race and Identity in Political Science

Political scientists have offered a number of competing theories to address this question. The social cohesion tradition asserts that the importance of race is a function of the group's economic homogeneity. This tradition predicts that the salience of race will decrease over time with integration, and it is the seat of the debate over whether race or class is the most significant interest in black American life. In his classic articulation of this perspective, Robert Dahl argues that class stratification will make race-based political appeals "embarrassing or meaningless" for the black middle class (1961, 35). This framework has gained a new following, however, as a result of the publication of William Julius Wilson's *The Declining Significance of Race* (1980), which argues that with the expansion of economic opportunity, "black life chances became increasingly a consequence of class affiliation" (153). The second strand of the literature challenges the pluralist notion that group cohesion springs forth naturally from shared circumstances. Instead, it posits that the influence of race is a function of associations and communication with group members. This social interaction theory regards the significance of race as dependent on the individual's ties to and interaction with their surrounding social context (Dawson 1994; Evans 1992; Gay 2004; Miller 1956; Putnam 1966; Weatherford 1982; MacKuen and Brown 1987). Once isolated from those networks, its proponents argue, blacks are unlikely to feel either a sense of connection with other blacks or a commitment to furthering black interests. This emphasis on the importance of context also exists in the third tradition, the racial conflict literature. This body of work argues that it is not the social but the political environment that determines the significance of racial identity and suggests that the influence of race depends on the level of intergroup conflict in the political environment. Within this framework, racial identity is more likely to become salient when individuals perceive their group interests to be threatened by other racial groups (Dollard 1957; Davis, Gardner and Gardner 1941; Matthews and Prothro 1966; Fosset and Kiecolt 1989; Glaser 1994; Knoke and Kyriazis 1977; Key 1949; Wright 1977; Bobo 1983, 1998; Kaufmann 1998, 2004).[1]

Although these three perspectives differ in significant ways, they are unified by three important presumptions: the first is that the political significance of race lies in the relative salience of racial identity for the individual. That is, each assumes that political outcomes depend on the extent to which one identity stands out from and dominates others. The second shared assumption is that cohesive racial identities predate political interaction. In other words, these approaches understand racial identity as a fixed orientation that may vary in strength, but whose content is stable. Finally, all three strands of the race politics literature assume that racial identity is best understood in affective, relational, and individual terms: that is, these frameworks define identity as the depth of feeling and degree of commonality that one individual feels toward other members of the same group (Conover 1984, 1989). In the most influential treatment of the question to date, Dawson argues that black racial identity may be understood as a feeling of "linked-fate," or the sense that the destiny of the individual is tied to that of other blacks (1994).[2] He understands identities as necessarily competing with one another for dominance. The idea is that the stronger one's sense of identity, the more salient or prominent that identity is in the opinion-formation and decision-making process.

While race politics research says much about racial *identification*, it reveals less about racial *identity*. That is, this line of inquiry illustrates a great deal about the strength of individual attachment to the group and how that attachment shapes political attitudes. Yet it indicates little about what might be called the "content" of that attachment—the understanding of what makes someone a member of the group. While it is important to understand how *strongly* individuals cleave to their group, it is equally important to understand how the group to which they cleave is characterized and represented. Across the social sciences, scholars have demonstrated that individuals feel attachment not to a generic, all-purpose blackness, but to specific understandings of the behaviors and values that characterize the racial group (Simpson 1998). These understandings vary across time and space and by social location. Not only are they historically contingent, but at any given moment or location, racial identity is constructed by different actors at different levels of social organization: it may therefore take a different form depending on whether it refers to the world (member of the black Diaspora), the nation (African American), the city (black Chicagoan) or even the area of the city (South Side blacks). Political scientists readily admit that racial identities are malleable and can take an infinite variety of forms, yet our study of identity traditionally has not reflected this fact. Because understandings of black community are so varied and contingent, any explanation of the contemporary significance of race must explain how particular understandings of racial identity emerge, how they are constructed, and to what end they are used by political actors.

These questions have been more directly addressed by the constructionist approach to race and identity. This theory emphasizes how groups and group identity are constructed through material and ideological process that are linked to one another. In their classic account of racial formation theory, for example, Omi and Winant (1994) argue that the notion of race itself is maintained and transformed through racial projects in which elites offer explanations of the social world that both assert the existence of racial groups and seek to distribute resources along racial lines. As Kim points out, these discursive and material processes not only reproduce racial categories, they reproduce a multiaxis racial hierarchy as well, positioning groups "differently and relationally so that one group's misfortune becomes another's opportunity" (2000, 37–38). More recently, Rogers Smith (2003) has called on political scientists to give greater attention to the discursive element of this process. He argues that elites help create a sense of political membership by articulating narratives of "peoplehood" that are institutionalized in law and policy. Particularly useful is his description of how racial identity becomes the basis for a sense of peoplehood. Smith argues that certain kinds of stories

> proclaim that members' culture, religion, language, race . . . or other such factors are constitutive of their very identities as persons, in ways that both affirm their worth and delineate their obligations. These stories are almost always intergenerational, implying that the ethically constitutive identity espoused not only defines who a person is, but who her ancestors have been and who her children will be. (64–65)

Constructionist theories differ from traditional race politics approaches in a number of ways. First, they conceptualize identity not as a strong sense of commonality, but as a set of characteristics that identify someone as a member of the group.[3] They concur with the race politics argument that the strength of identity influences political opinion and behavior. Yet they move beyond that argument by arguing that the meaning of identity itself has political consequences. A second important distinction between these two literatures lies in their theorization of the relationship between multiple identities. Constructionists argue that understandings of black community are constituted by other social identities and are therefore explicitly and implicitly classed and gendered (Jackson 2001; Moore 2002, 2005). Research using this approach therefore examines not the degree to which racial identity "trumps" another identity, but the mechanisms through which classed and gendered notions of racial identity are constructed. Finally, the constructionist framework differs from traditional race politics literature in its conceptualization of the relationship between politics and identity. Rather than seeing politics as a function of preexisting identity, this approach focuses on the construction of identity, understanding it as a *form* of political behavior. Within the constructionist paradigm, the focus is on specifying the manner and mechanism through which identity construction itself achieves certain political goals, rather than the way it shapes political attitudes.

This book draws on the constructionist approach to examine the emergence of Jim Crow identity in Douglas/Grand Boulevard and its relationship to community leaders' neighborhood revitalization agenda. In the late 1980s, several community organizations in Douglas/Grand Boulevard began collaborating to form the Mid-South Planning and Development Commission (Mid-South), a community-based planning organization. Over a three-year period, they worked with the city to develop a land-use plan for the two neighborhoods called "Restoring Bronzeville." As the name of the plan suggests, leaders of community-based organizations sought to re-create the neighborhood as it existed in the past, using a combination of mixed-income housing development, black gentrification, and racial heritage tourism. By developing tourist-oriented, black-owned businesses, preservationists hoped to market the neighborhood as another of Chicago's many ethnic neighborhoods and thus attract the ethnic travelers who now constitute a growing portion of the tourism market.

In promoting the neighborhood as a heritage tourism destination, leaders of Douglas/Grand Boulevard's community-based organizations reinvented the neighborhood's history in ways that sanitized the most brutal elements of the Jim Crow era. Their depiction of the neighborhood, captured so neatly by Mr. Anthony, minimized the extent and nature of white control over the neighborhood, exaggerated the size and impact of the black elite, celebrated its leadership, and minimized its disdain for and conflict with lower-status blacks. More important, development advocates also reimagined contemporary black identity through this nostalgia for the past, depicting it not just as the history of the neighborhood, but as the shared history of the race, one that bound and unified its current black residents. This vision of racial identity frames middle-class leadership and business investment as intrinsic to the Bronzeville racial identity. It also defines collectivism—the degree to which one prioritizes group over individual advancement—as the defining characteristic of the Douglas/Grand Boulevard racial community. Neighborhood residents and organization leaders clashed over the nostalgic vision of the neighborhood, as well as the redevelopment agenda it was designed to bolster. Yet collectivism still operated as a powerful standard of racial authenticity and political legitimacy, one that both leaders and participants drew on to make claims and arguments about who could participate, what their role should be, and what constituted group preferences. In Douglas/Grand Boulevard, nostalgic identity has been politically consequential because its elements have constituted the terms in which conflicts are carried out, as well as the criteria for making political judgments.

In the course of elaborating this argument, I repeatedly touch on two important themes. The first is that black elites pursue agendas that reflect their class status. Not just in the current period, but throughout the twentieth century, black politicians and business leaders have understood racial advancement and community development in terms that prioritize their particular needs and preferences. Thus, one implication of this book is that it reframes the long-standing question about the relative significance of race and class identities in contemporary politics. That debate casts the period prior to the civil rights movement as one in which black elites displayed an extraordinary commitment to collective racial goals, a commitment assumed to reflect either the minimal existence of class identity or its absorption within racial identity. This book, on the other hand, highlights the consistency with which black elites pursue preferences that reflect both their race and class status. The second theme that arises throughout the book is that elites' pursuit of class-based racial agendas always takes place within a context confined by specific forms of racial subordination. In other words, black elites are confronted by both the opportunities of increased economic mobility and the limitations that continue to be imposed by racialized political subordination. This point is important to note, not because it excuses their class bias, but because it helps explain both the pursuit of black elite preferences and the reason elites are able to depict that pursuit as an avenue to group advancement. Because black elites themselves remain constrained by white political elites, their claims to common cause with low-income blacks are both plausible and compelling. For this reason, it is impossible to make sense of racial politics in Douglas/Grand Boulevard without paying attention to two important dynamics: the *inter*racial contestation through which black neighborhood leaders and their constituents struggle to gain leverage over white economic and political elites, and the *intra*racial conflict in which black leaders work to construct competing visions of black interests, to mobilize residents around those visions, and to vie for the right to represent them to those outside their communities.

Urban Ethnography and the Study of Black Politics

The Douglas/Grand Boulevard neighborhood has been an important source and center of nostalgia about pre–civil rights era black communities, in part because it was the subject of Drake and Cayton's 1945 ethnography, *Black Metropolis*. This classic text provides a fine-grained picture of black life prior to desegregation and is often selectively cited by scholars and neighborhood residents to make claims about the character of urban black communities of the segregation period (Ehrenhalt 1996; Wilson 1996). The neighborhood is located just two and a half miles south of the Loop, Chicago's central business district. The northern border of Douglas/Grand Boulevard lies at Twenty-sixth Street, and it stretches south for twenty-five blocks to Fifty-first Street. The Dan Ryan Expressway forms its western edge, while to the east lies Lake Michigan. The contours of the neighborhood closely approximate those of the city's "first ghetto," the outlines of which were initially determined by white resistance to black migration (Drake and Cayton 1993; Philpott 1991; Spear 1967). While racial hostility shaped its original outlines, after World War II urban renewal and public housing programs were the biggest factors in neighborhood development. These state-sponsored strategies not only helped to confine blacks to the neighborhood, but they packed the neighborhood with low-income public housing residents while displacing uncounted homes and businesses (Hirsch 1983).

The consequences of this disinvestment were still being felt by residents when I began my research in 1997.[4] The median family income in 1990 was just over $10,500 in Douglas and just over $8,300 in Grand Boulevard. Forty-nine percent of Douglas and 64 percent of Grand Boulevard residents earned incomes below the poverty line. Unemployment in Douglas area census tracts ranged from 20 to 50 percent. In addition, Douglas had a large nonworking population: 35 percent of its inhabitants were under the age of eighteen, and residents aged sixty-five years or older constituted 15 percent of the community. While several enclaves in the neighborhood contain historic or distinctive single-family homes, the residents who inhabited them had only slightly higher incomes than their neighbors. The effects of such low income were evident in the composition of the housing stock, of which single-family homes made up a mere 6 percent in Grand Boulevard and 8 percent in Douglas. The two neighborhoods were also home to a significant amount of public housing. In 1990, the Prairie Avenue Courts, Dearborn Homes, Ida B. Wells projects, Stateway Gardens, and Robert Taylor Homes made up half of the community's housing units. Such broad strokes, however, hide the significant variation to be found within this community. In the northern and central areas of Douglas, median income in 1990 was as high as $67,000, while in census tracts containing public housing, median income barely reached $5,000. The most affluent census tract in Grand Boulevard had a median income of just over $24,000, and less than 5 percent of the total population earned an income over $50,000. In addition, while women outnumbered men only slightly, there were a significant number of female-headed households in the area. Indeed, the concentration of such households is only one example of how the spatial organization of the neighborhood combined with population variation to produce significant intraracial diversity. Female-headed households were among the poorest in this neighborhood and, along with unemployed households, were concentrated in public housing. Likewise, elderly households, although spanning the area, were concentrated in a few spots that include senior housing projects. Yet despite their spatial concentration, these residents were within walking distance of the enclaves of relatively affluent home-owning professionals. In addition, the neighborhood was dotted with "white" health and educational institutions, such as the Illinois Institute of Technology, De La Salle High School, the Illinois College of Optometry, and Mercy and Michael Reese hospitals.

I began attending Mid-South meetings in March 1997 and continued for two years until February 1999. I participated first as a general member of the Mid-South Planning and Development Commission and then as the co-chair of the Economic Development Committee for the last eight months of fieldwork. After several months I became active in the Bronzeville Organizing Strategy Session, which acted as the political arm of Mid-South, as well as their organizing subcommittee, the Bronzeville Organizers' Alliance. In this capacity, I was involved in the planning and execution of several events designed to mobilize and educate the community. I also attended meetings of the group that eventually became the Bronzeville Community Development Partnership, an umbrella organization of seven community stakeholders that sought to acquire money for neighborhood community development corporations. In addition to attending regular organizational meetings, I also attended events as they arose, including a twelve-week organizer's class, planning charettes, informational sessions, and aldermanic meetings.

Participation in these events provided an avenue for consistent involvement in the Douglas/Grand Boulevard community, which was particularly important given that I did not live in the neighborhood. The fact that I traveled to meetings from the northernmost neighborhood in Chicago marked me as a permanent outsider throughout my two years of research.[5]

The significance of this was clarified for me on my first trip to the neighborhood, when I visited the office of Fourth Ward alderman Toni Preckwinkle to ask about neighborhood organizations. The staff member behind the desk insisted that the alderman had no such information and that in any case, it would be hard to find any organizations willing to talk to me because people are so suspicious of "spies" who just come and "learn all they need to learn and then leave." This reply was a blunt introduction to the importance of residence, not just to me as a researcher, but to anyone associated with the neighborhood's revitalization. As chapter 4 illustrates in detail, residence played a strong role in establishing both one's trustworthiness and one's racial authenticity. This response also reflected a longstanding pattern that I struggled with while researching and writing this book and of which I remain painfully aware: residents of Douglas/Grand Boulevard specifically, and poor blacks generally, are the constant, sometimes unwilling subjects of research that demonizes them. As scholars, we rely on these communities for our personal and professional success, and as resident Althea Lane told me, many who live there "have a problem with these universities who just come into communities to do their papers or their theses and then they just leave. They don't leave anything behind for the community."

Ever mindful of this sentiment, I undertook my participant observation in Douglas/Grand Boulevard with one eye on data collection and the other on possibilities for making at least some limited contribution to the organizations with which I was involved. These groups held monthly, bimonthly, and weekly meetings, and whenever possible I offered to take minutes, run errands, make phone calls, and staff community events.[6] In resource-poor communities and organizations, where residents and staff do not always have the time or energy to attend meeting after meeting, my consistent and reliable involvement served to solidify residents' trust in me and to mitigate the negative effects of my status as a North Sider. Over time, I was often introduced as an "intern" who was "helping out" with the organization in question. This access was facilitated as well by my gender, race, youth, and student status, producing the familiar insider/

outsider status that both eases and confounds ethnographic research. Older black residents in particular were gratified to meet a "young person" who was working on her doctorate, and I was often praised for representing the race by going so far in my education. These relationships and activities "[did] not so much disrupt or alter ongoing patterns of social interaction as reveal the terms and bases on which people form social ties in the first place" (Emerson, Fretz, and Shaw 1995, 3). They either engendered, or gave me access to, interactions that revealed the criteria upon which membership in the local black community was based.

I supplemented these data with twenty formal and dozens more informal interviews and document analysis, reviewing government reports, minutes from community meetings and planning forums, newsletters, press releases and flyers, city and neighborhood newspapers, and the personal archives of neighborhood activists. These sources provided a rich supply of interactions, written accounts, and verbal utterances that illuminated how, and to what purposes, notions of blackness are constructed. Yet my focus on the activities of community development organizations gave me access mostly to homeowners, rehabbers, developers, and community development activists, rather than public housing residents or low-income renters. Thus, this is necessarily a work about black neighborhood elites: those whose work or economic status increased their ability, inclination, or opportunity to participate in and influence the course of community change. The study does not aim to obscure the location of this analysis, but to maintain confidences, I have changed the names and at times the identifying features of the informants who so graciously opened themselves to yet another researcher.[7]

The Road Ahead

To round out nostalgic visions of African American life during the segregation era, the book begins with an analysis of neighborhood life in the late nineteenth and early twentieth centuries. Chapter 1 focuses on the Black Belt elite from 1890 to 1950 and its response to various forms of political and spatial containment. Chapter 2 examines the establishment of a new cadre of black community development elites and its initiation of neighborhood revitalization. Both chapters illustrate how over time, black elites responded to racial threats with strategies of racial advancement that privileged their own preferences. Together the chapters historicize contemporary debates over the relative significance of race and class preferences and anchor subsequent analysis of the reimagination of local black community.

Readers who are less invested in that particular dispute may wish to skip ahead to chapters 3 through 5, which detail how Douglas/Grand Boulevard's community development leaders have constructed and deployed Jim Crow identity in the contemporary era. Chapter 3 describes how the new civic elite reimagined both people and place through nostalgia for its segregated past. Despite the fact that community elites used this history to portray the neighborhood as a unified racial bloc, the process of collaborative neighborhood planning was marked by intraracial class divisions and leadership conflicts. Chapter 4 analyzes those conflicts and describes how community leaders and residents conducted those conflicts through the rhetoric of authenticity. Chapter 5 examines how black civic leaders used claims of common racial identity to frame their particular preferences as beneficial for all black residents. Chapter 6 concludes by considering what this case suggests about broader patterns of black politics in the post–civil rights era.

Neighborhood development conflicts are extremely useful for examining identity construction because they are contests over the appropriate boundaries and meaning of community. It is through such political struggles that residents actively consider, negotiate, and articulate both the character and the interests of black community. Redevelopment conflicts also contain a physical and spatial dimension that helps to highlight and make more concrete the ways that racial meanings are constructed and used. Much of the existing work on racial group identities relies on national survey data, which produces a broad view of black behavior and opinion but is divorced from the settings within which those opinions and identities are cultivated. This study seeks to supplement that view with a portrait of the contingent meanings of blackness, one grounded in the internal politics of a specific community, as they emerge from conflicts over space. In offering this account, I remain aware—as Althea so pointedly reminded me—that I am a guest in this house. I have therefore tried to give a faithful portrayal of my hosts, one that elaborates and clarifies the intricacies of race and class in their lives and politics.

CHAPTER 1

The Way We Were: Political Accommodation and Neighborhood Change, 1870–1950

In the 1990s, the public discussion of Douglas and Grand Boulevard's restoration was marked by fanfare and praise. While some pundits objected to the estimated cost of the revitalization plan, most were supportive of the project and the history on which it was premised. Residents, politicians, and observers repeated the assertion of the Mid-South Planning and Development Commission: Bronzeville had been a crucible of black economic and political success and would be again after its revitalization. Only very rarely did a dissenting view disrupt the public consensus: one such view was that of former resident William Simpson, who in a lone editorial offered a less-than-rosy view of the neighborhood's past. In contrast to the celebratory recollections that filled the public discussion, Mr. Simpson remembered a Forty-seventh Street that

> was dominated commercially by white owned businesses, even though there were black stores. The police and firemen were almost all white. Ditto the streetcar drivers, conductors and bus drivers. And the utility companies' service people and office workers. The Bronzeville area is a shining example of blacks accommodating ourselves to white repression and subordination; but unable to sustain the area once the whites moved away, which they were doing back 50 years ago. (W. Simpson 1996)

According to Mr. Simpson, the segregation era was not a period of black accomplishment, nor were the Douglas and Grand Boulevard communities independent and self-sustaining. Instead, they were neighborhoods in which whites were ubiquitous, powerful, and repressive, and black residents adjusted themselves to those facts.

Mr. Simpson's criticism highlights two important features of the nostalgic interpretation of black neighborhoods like Douglas and Grand Boulevard. The first is that nostalgia portrays the history of urban black neighborhoods as a "rise and fall" narrative. That is, it portrays the Jim Crow period as a golden era in black history, a high point from which the community descended as the twentieth century wore on. Second, nostalgic interpretations posit *cultural explanations* for that rise and fall: they suggest that racial solidarity was an "ironic" or "unanticipated" benefit of segregation; that such unity was responsible for the growth of neighborhood institutions; and that desegregation destroyed those institutions— and thus the communities as a whole—by seducing away the black middle class. Such interpretations are offered, not only by proponents of Douglas/ Grand Boulevard's restoration, but by more far-flung commentators as well (Ehrenhalt 1996). Thus nostalgic interpretations mirror those analyses that attribute urban poverty and decline to the deterioration of black cultural practices.

Certainly, these nostalgic understandings provide an important corrective to existing analyses of early twentieth-century black communities, which—though they rightly emphasize the devastating impact of racial discrimination on black neighborhoods—also tend to portray African Americans as passive rather than active agents. Nostalgists counter this tendency by emphasizing how blacks shaped neighborhoods through their response to racism. Yet their interpretation masks two key features of urban black life in the segregation era. The first is the unevenness of African Americans' experience across class and gender. There is no doubt that the migration to Chicago and other northern cities represented an improvement over life in the Jim Crow South. Yet it is also the case that only a tiny proportion of blacks fell into the category of elites whose business successes and political leadership are the basis for the sunny interpretation that Mr. Simpson criticizes. The tendency to miss such details is inherent in the notion of a golden era itself. It is an idea fundamentally bound to the backward glance from the present, one that sees the past not on its own terms, but only in relation to perceived contemporary failings.

The second factor missed by Jim Crow nostalgia is the role that racial politics played in shaping the emergence, development, and deterioration of the neighborhood. In Douglas/Grand Boulevard, as in many urban black neighborhoods across the country, racial politics in the first half of the twentieth century was decidedly accommodationist, accepting of limited and individual political favors as evidence of racial progress (Branham 1981). Accommodationism was not a random choice, nor was it the only choice. Rather, it was a strategy that Douglas/Grand Boulevard's black elites turned to when their other sources of power and influence were threatened. From the 1870s to the 1910s, when blacks first began moving to the area, Chicago's black and white elites worked together to advance a racially egalitarian agenda at the state and local levels. But during the Great Migration, between 1915 and 1930, several factors combined to diminish whites' commitment to integrationism, and black elites found themselves in a political context that increasingly rewarded active and passive participation in the racial hierarchy. The second period of accommodationism took place between 1930 and 1965, when black elected officials reestablished clientage ties with the Democratic machine, which similarly provided neighborhood leaders with access to party patronage while minimizing their influence in decision-making processes. Bearing those two features in mind recasts the progression of neighborhood development in Douglas/Grand Boulevard. What we see over the course of the twentieth century is not the rise and fall of community life that results from the decline of racial solidarity and social organization. Rather, we witness the continued isolation of blacks within the borders of a neighborhood facing continual disinvestment from white political and economic elites, a process that was itself partly shaped by the emergence and transformation of multiple forms of black political accommodationism.

Brokerage Relations and the Politics of Equality, 1870–1900

Black Americans were some of Chicago's earliest migrants, having reached the city on the Underground Railroad throughout the 1840s and 1850s.

In 1861, approximately one thousand blacks lived in Chicago's "sinkhole of abolition," most of whom were fugitive slaves (Drake and Cayton 1993, 33, 39). Until the 1870s, they lived clustered along the south branch of the Chicago River, a location whose only advantage was that it proved unattractive to the insatiable Chicago Fire of 1871. Having been spared once, the city's blacks got their comeuppance only three years later, when a second fire destroyed their small enclave and caused them to relocate along the northern edge of the Douglas community.

Race relations in the late nineteenth century were harmonious enough that black and white elites pursued an integrationist agenda. This was the case for at least three reasons. The first was the number and distribution of blacks in the city. In 1870, Chicago held just under 300,000 inhabitants, and at a little more than 3,600, black residents were a barely noticeable 1.2 percent of the city's population. Even twenty years later, when Chicago's 1890 population reached more than one million, Chicago blacks remained only 1.3 percent of the total population, and "no large, solidly Negro concentration existed" (Spear 1967, 12). Instead, blacks "clustered in a number of small colonies, usually close by, but separate from, the white residential districts where so many of them worked as domestics" (Philpott 1991, 117, 120–21; Spear 1967, 12). By the early 1900s, African Americans occupied "a good portion of the houses west of State and south as far as Thirty-Fifth Street," a fact that proved alarming to the white and ethnic residents who remained nearby, but provoked no violence (Holt and Pacyga 1979, 52; Spear 1967, 20). As a small, barely noticeable portion of the city's population, African Americans attracted less hostility than they would in the following century.

A second determinant of black–white relations in Chicago was labor market segmentation, which eliminated racial job competition by confining blacks to positions that were unwanted by whites. African Americans were concentrated in the domestic and personal services as barbers, porters, servants, launderers, and seamstresses (Drake and Cayton 1993, 433–44, 543; Meier 1962, 263). They were virtually excluded from better-paying trade, manufacturing, clerical, and secretarial positions. The 1890 census revealed there "were but 16 colored among the city's 7,847 machinists, 3 among 2,959 cabinetmakers, 2 among 3,679 plumbers and pipe fitters, and 37 among over 20,000 carpenters and joiners" (Pierce 1957, 237). Similarly, there were very few blacks in the professions, and those that were tended to be "concentrated in the professions that required relatively little formal training—music, the theater, and the clergy" (Spear 1967, 29). This confinement in the personal service trades kept blacks out of competition for white ethnic jobs and largely isolated them from the city's increasingly tense labor conflicts (Drake and Cayton 1993, 50). The combination of demographic trends, residential patterns, and employment discrimination helped blacks maintain a low profile and kept native-born and immigrant populations from seeing them as a threat to their homes or jobs (Drake and Cayton 1993, 224).

A third factor shaping interracial relationships in the nineteenth century was blacks' inability to compete for political power in the city. While the instability and competitiveness of Chicago's early machine system encouraged candidates to seek votes from all available factions, black Chicago's small voting population could make only a miniscule contribution to local candidates' winning coalitions (Kantowicz 1995; Pierce 1957, 349–51, 356). African American leaders instead pursued their political goals by relying on a variety of client-patron relationships—personalized ties to powerful whites that gave them the resources they needed to claim leadership status.[1] Black men developed these ties through both their business dealings and their social networks (Spear 1967, 54). One of the most influential nineteenth-century leaders, for example, was John Jones, a popular tailor with a large and prosperous white clientele. Among his fellow black leaders at the state level were two barbers, a hominy manufacturer, a minister, and the owner of a confectionery store—men whose occupations and associations brought them in frequent contact with white elites (McCaul 1987, 17, 19).

By nurturing these associations, African American elites cultivated allies "among Republican politicians, civic-minded liberals, and the wealthy" and they depended on them to press an integrationist agenda in legislatures and public forums (Drake and Cayton 1993, 50). In these struggles, blacks wrote letters, authored pamphlets, made speeches, and held conferences. But they relied on white legislators to introduce bills, they sought out white newspapermen to print editorials, and they depended on white property owners to provide them with meeting halls. John Jones and his colleagues, for example, were responsible for writing and selling the influential tract *The Black Laws of Illinois and a Few Reasons Why They Should Be Repealed* and for canvassing the state for signatures (Glizzio 1975; McCaul 1987, 41). But lacking elected positions themselves, they ultimately "enlisted the support of such powerful white allies as the former Free Soil journalist and editor of the *Chicago Tribune* Joseph Medill, Cook County Senator Francis Eastman, and Illinois Governor Richard Yates" to publicize and support their proposal (Branham 1981, 7).

Few of these black leaders were professional politicians. Most were what James Q. Wilson (1960) refers to as "lay civic leaders," citizens who were employed in other jobs but saw public leadership on racial issues as an extension of their civic activities (Spear 1967, 77). Yet some of them also developed client-patron relationships with members of the Republican Party and as a result were able to gain both appointive and elective positions at the county and state levels. These black officials were also dependent on white leadership figures such as Martin Madden, who "carefully cultivated the delegates from the areas inhabited by Negro voters" (Gosnell 1935; 1937, 66). With help from these leaders, blacks were elected as state representatives and county commissioners as early as the 1870s (Gosnell 1935, 1937). These elections took place not in spite of, but because of, the support of the white electorate. At both the state and the local levels, the African American population went largely unnoticed by white and immigrant voters (Gosnell 1935; 1937, 83). In addition, the use of the Australian Ballot meant that "any person, white or colored, who voted the straight Republican ticket in a senatorial district where a colored man had been nominated for representative, automatically cast one, one and a half, or three votes for that colored representative, depending on whether the Republican convention had nominated three, two or one candidates" (Gosnell 1935; 1937, 67). At the state level at least, the structure of the voting system gave blacks the opportunity for formal representation.

While African Americans were able to gain patronage and elected positions at the county and state levels, they were unable to do so at the city level. The highly coveted aldermanic seats of the Second and Third Wards were beyond their reach and would remain so until blacks had something more to bargain with than the mediation of potentially volatile or uncomfortable racial interactions (Gosnell 1935). Instead of pursuing elected office, black elites focused on using their ties to whites to bring resources to the burgeoning Black Belt. Through the end of the nineteenth century, these community-building strategies were used to try to achieve racial equality. From the 1870s through the 1890s, black leaders were particularly focused on repealing the Illinois black laws, winning black male suffrage, and desegregating schools (Spear 1967, 52). Black elites in Douglas/Grand Boulevard sought to institutionalize integration as well, establishing interracial social and political organizations to meet the needs of the emerging Black Belt. The best example of this is the 1891 establishment of Provident Hospital, the nation's first interracial hospital and one of Grand Boulevard's oldest institutions. Well-known black physician Daniel Hale Williams helped found the hospital, which was distinguished not only by its willing treatment of black patients, but by its employment of both black and white medical and nursing staff. Likewise, the advisory board of Provident Hospital was all white, and "its major support in the early years came from wealthy white Chicagoans, such as Philip Armour, H. H. Kohlsaat, and Florence Pullman" (Spear 1967, 98). So strong was black elites' opposition to separatism that many viewed even this deliberately interracial effort with suspicion. This response followed a general pattern evident at the time, in which any effort to establish services for blacks could be "met with stiff opposition from those who regarded it as a form of self-segregation" (Spear 1967, 53).

The strategies and ideologies adopted by this early black elite—the "old settlers," as they called themselves—were grounded in their structural position. Their fervent interracialism and dedication to desegregation reflected the opportunities available to them given their access to white elites. The financial and political support of whites

> enabled the Negro client leadership to obtain positions in community and government institutions reasonably commensurate with their leadership-claimant status. It permitted the Negro client leadership to control or at

least influence some part of the political process that allocated services to the Negro urban subsystem, especially welfare and settlement services. (Kilson 1971, 172)

Yet African American elites were not chosen by other blacks for their ability to represent their views and desires. Instead, they were designated as leaders through white decision making and selective resource distribution and thus they lacked a true constituent–leader relationship. They were, in other words, given the appearance of having power and exerting it on behalf of the black populace, when they in fact held positions that encouraged them to act with at least partial attention to the interests of whites. Because white elites were the source of their power, black elites were beholden to their patrons rather than to the black populace they claimed to represent. This fact limited the degree to which elites could press for the needs of their constituents. As a result, they "structure[d] their leadership role in a manner presumed to be acceptable to white patrons" by minimizing racial conflict and regulating black social behavior (Kilson 1971, 172).

Despite its limitations, clientage politics was key to the low profile required to prevent racial conflicts and maintain relative racial harmony. Along with demographic and residential patterns, client–patron politics kept native-born and immigrant populations from seeing blacks as a threat to their homes, jobs, and political standing (Drake and Cayton 1993, 224). Most important, this political arrangement provided a space within which the city's African American population could push for what was then the radical notion of integration.

Self-Help Politics, 1890–1930

This early black challenge to de jure and de facto segregation was in great contrast to the accommodationism that became prevalent during the migration years. During that era, the lay leadership and its integrationist agenda were replaced by a professional leadership class that focused on developing—rather than dismantling—the ghetto that was growing in Douglas/ Grand Boulevard. Between 1890 and 1910, Chicago's black population more than tripled, growing from 14,000 to 44,000. At first, Chicago absorbed its new black residents "without any serious difficulty" (Drake and Cayton 1993, 61). But between 1910 and 1920, the black population more than doubled its size, ballooning to more than 100,000 (Philpott 1991, 117). One factor compelling blacks to migrate north was the atmosphere of political and social deterioration in the South. Equally important was the unemployment experienced by sharecropping blacks as a result of a massive boll-weevil infestation and the mechanization of agricultural production. Black workers attempting to find jobs in southern cities faced competition from similarly displaced rural whites, who pressed for and won passage of laws to exclude blacks from jobs they had previously considered beneath them (Marks 1989, 57–60, 64). Yet the jobs that blacks could not secure in the South were plentiful in the North. When wartime arms production and declining immigration increased northern labor demands, southern blacks heeded the call en masse.

After 1915, Chicago's African American population became more noticeable, not only because of the rapid increase in migrants, but because blacks began competing for resources from which they had been previously excluded. Black men, once confined to service positions, increasingly secured industrial work with machine manufacturers, such as International Harvester; metal foundry and metal product companies, like National Malleable Castings Company; and slaughtering and meat-packing companies, such as Armour, Morris, and Swift (Chicago Commission on Race Relations 1968, 361). According to Carole Marks, packinghouses in Chicago employed 67 blacks in 1910 and "nearly 3,000 in 1920. In steel, black representation increased from 6 percent in 1910 to 17 percent in 1920" (1989, 121). As these positions opened up to them, black men gained the attention of working-class ethnics and became more prominent figures in labor disputes (Spear 1967, 36–41).

Migration also prompted blacks to push beyond the borders of the neighborhoods in which they were concentrated. Prior to World War I, African Americans had been able to find decent housing in the Black Belt (Spear 1967, 148). But after 1914, housing in Douglas/Grand Boulevard became overcrowded, scarce, ill-maintained, and expensive (Drake and Cayton 1993; Spear 1967). As the number of residents overwhelmed the housing capacity of the city's black enclaves, black elites began pushing against those boundaries, attempting to distance themselves physically and socially from newer, poorer migrants. African American elites had long complained about being forced to live in such close proximity to blacks they considered beneath them. In a 1904 speech at the Frederick Douglass Center, Dr. George Cleveland Hall expressed the feelings of many blacks when he complained that those

> who are desirous of improving their general condition are prevented to a great extent by being compelled to live with those of their color who are shiftless, dissolute and immoral. . . . Prejudice of landlords and agents render it almost impossible for [the Negro] to take up his residence in a more select quarter of the city . . . no matter . . . how much cultivation and refinement he may possess. (Spear 1967, 73)

This sentiment intensified as the postwar housing shortage reduced blacks' options for housing space. As African Americans increasingly inhabited both the eastern and the western borders of the Douglas/Grand Boulevard neighborhood, the area between the two was fast becoming mixed. At the same time, housing construction dropped during World War I, and "white people found it increasingly difficult to abandon whole streets to the advancing blacks, for there were fewer and fewer places to run to" (Philpott 1991, 162). The group that had been the city's wallflower during the late nineteenth century had, by war's end, become its most well-known pariah.

Whites responded to blacks' visibility and quest for economic and spatial resources by increasing segregation. As both native-born and ethnic whites became aware of and hostile to African Americans, they began reversing their previous support for integrationism, and blacks found themselves unwelcome in all spheres of social and economic life. Segregation and discrimination had always existed in Chicago, but "as Negroes became more numerous and conspicuous, white hostility increased and Negroes encountered an ever more pervasive pattern of exclusion" (Spear 1967, 48; Pierce 1957, 48–50). Residents of nearby white neighborhoods began an intense campaign of racial containment: Kenwood, Woodlawn, and Hyde Park residents sought to keep blacks from spilling over into their neighborhoods, while in Douglas/Grand Boulevard whites tried simply to slow the rate of racial transformation. The Hyde Park–Kenwood Property Owners' Association, for example, organized their members against blacks by establishing a network of block captains, who were instructed "to apply pressure to any property owners who considered selling or renting to Negroes" (Spear 1967, 211). In 1917, the Chicago Real Estate Board, alarmed by the decrease in property values that followed black residency, agreed not to sell or rent to blacks unless the area was already three-quarters black, and threatened the ouster of those members who defied the agreement (Philpott 1991, 164; Spear 1967, 210). An equally popular tool was violence. From July 1917 to March 1921, black homes were bombed at least fifty-eight times in an attempt to terrorize blacks and persuade them to leave white neighborhoods (Spear 1967, 211).

The Building of the Black Belt

In response to this increasing segregation, the older civic elite fought back by trying to more concretely institutionalize their integrationist agenda. In 1903, for example, a number of prominent men protested against the segregation of the city's public schools by establishing the Equal Opportunity League (Spear 1967, 84).[2] Two years later, two members of the league founded a local branch of the Niagara movement, the organization established by W. E. B. DuBois to challenge the accommodationist philosophy of Booker T. Washington (Spear 1967, 85). Though it failed by 1907, many of its allies reconnected in the Chicago branch of the NAACP, established five years later in 1912 (Spear 1967, 58).

Despite these efforts, the Black Belt's pro-integration leaders were defeated by both the hardening Jim Crow line and the ascendancy of a new black elite—a group of political and race relations professionals whose job it was to manage and represent blacks to the broader white population (J. Wilson 1960, 10). In the face of shrinking political opportunities, these new leaders emphasized developing Black Belt institutions rather than challenging segregation (Spear 1967, 71–89). The concentration of so many African Americans in one space created a captive market for this burgeoning group of economic and political professionals. As migration continued, segregation hardened, and wages rose, this elite responded by establishing a wide range of organizations and institutions to serve blacks' needs, attract their dollars, and win their votes. Unlike their predecessors, who had maintained an integrationist standpoint, the new elite adopted a racial self-help philosophy and strategy "centered on the development of Negro business enterprise through a combination of thrift, industry and racial solidarity, or Negro support of Negro business" (Meier 1962, 258). Faced with a growing black market and excluded from others, the black elite worked to institutionalize and enhance whatever aspects of community life they could control. They advocated self-improvement and self-help methods for advancing racial justice, strategies that relied on individual black elites' relationships to whites rather than on collective demands for improvement. These organizations, which became staple elements of the Black Belt, were much like those that had previously drawn fire for endorsing "self-segregation" (Spear 1967).

These new institutions included adjustment organizations that sought to smooth African Americans' transition to urban living and working conditions through education, self-improvement, and moral suasion. Primary among these was the Chicago Urban League, founded in 1917. Although the league was established with interracial support and funded largely by white industrialists and philanthropists, it focused on coordinating welfare and employment services for new southern migrants (Strickland 2001, 32–39). It acted as an information "clearinghouse," administering or funding the work of smaller welfare agencies in Douglas/Grand Boulevard, such as the South Side Soldiers' and Sailor's Club (Strickland 2001, 46–47). The league also functioned as an employment broker, attempting to create job opportunities for blacks and mold newly arrived migrants into compliant workers. The efforts of the Chicago Urban League and its satellite organizations were complimented by the work of a host of religious and community centers, women's clubs, and fraternal organizations that responded to increasing segregation by providing housing, job training, recreation, and welfare services for newly arriving Douglas/Grand Boulevard residents (Chicago Commission on Race Relations 1968, 147–50; Spear 1967,

91–110). The Black Belt's numerous women's clubs, for example, "banded together to form the Colored Women's Conference of Chicago. The clubs operated kindergartens, mothers' clubs, sewing schools, day nurseries, employment bureaus, parent-teacher associations, and a penny savings bank" (Spear 1967, 102).

Black leaders' stance on these self-help ventures was in sharp contrast to the one the older elite had held at the end of the century. In 1889, for example, African American leaders' attempts to organize a black YMCA dissolved in the face of protest. Yet twenty years later, as blacks were excluded from locations serving whites, "the voices that had protested in 1889 were now almost mute," and well-known integrationists came to support the building of another YMCA exclusively for blacks (Spear 1967, 100). Even community organizations initially designed to be beacons of integration were eventually transformed into all or mostly black institutions: in the case of Provident, the interracial hospital established by Daniel Hale Williams, the opportunities for integrationism were diminished as much by the lack of alternatives for medical staff and patients as they were by the changing attitudes of blacks who "came to regard it as their hospital [and] . . . expected the hospital to provide positions for Negroes as a matter of duty" (Spear 1967, 99). Thus, despite its optimistic beginnings, the hospital was increasingly funded, staffed, and patronized by blacks, and "by World War I, Provident was for all practical purposes a Negro institution" (Spear 1967, 100).

The number of business elites catering to Douglas/Grand Boulevard residents also grew during this period. Not only did the neighborhood see an increase in the absolute number of businesses, but older companies that had once catered to white clients instead turned greater attention toward the black market.[3] In 1905, there were 566 black-owned businesses in Chicago. By 1916 that number had jumped to well over 1,200, and in 1924 it reached its migration-era peak of almost 1,400 (Drake and Cayton 1993, 434). The most numerous were small service and retail establishments: barbershops, hair salons, groceries, and restaurants were among the most popular (Drake and Cayton 1993, 434; Chicago Commission on Race Relations 1968, 140–41; Spear 1967, 112). Fewer in number but equal in significance were the black newspapers established during migration, including the *Fellowship Herald* in 1916, the *Chicago Enterprise* in 1918, the *Chicago Whip* in 1919, and the *Chicago Bee* in 1926 (Drake and Cayton 1993, 399). The *Chicago Defender*, founded in 1905 by Robert Abbott, eventually eclipsed these smaller papers to become one of the largest and most successful black publications in the country (Spear 1967). The neighborhood also experienced an expansion of larger-scale financial businesses. In 1908, Jesse Binga established the first black-owned bank in the city. Moreover, four insurance companies and two banks were established in Douglas/Grand Boulevard during the migration period. The most successful of these eventually became the Supreme Life Insurance Company, one of only a few insurance companies financially stable enough to survive the Depression (Drake and Cayton 1993, 436; Spear 1967, 181–83). Not only did business owners see themselves as providing a valuable service product, they also regarded patronage of their stores as a method for racial advancement. In "its most extreme form, the dream of controlling the Negro market visualizes a completely separate Negro economy: 'The idea is to be able to support ourselves instead of being wholly dependent on the white race'" (Drake and Cayton 1993, 439).

Douglas/Grand Boulevard's business expansion included a blossoming leisure economy. As wages grew and they experienced a rise in disposable income, African Americans both opened and frequented new entertainment businesses in the Black Belt. Some of these establishments provided amusements regarded as family oriented, or at least suitable for women, including sports competitions, vaudeville acts, film screenings, and musical performances. The first notable music space was the Pekin Theater, opened by Robert T. Mott in the early 1900s; it was quickly followed by venues such as the Dreamland Café and the Elite Club (City of Chicago 1994). This growing leisure economy also included extralegal businesses, such as gambling saloons, cabarets, after-hours clubs, and brothels. Sites such as Johnnie Seymore's Saloon and Hugh Hoskins's club provided patrons with the opportunity to supplement their musical or theater experiences with prostitution (Blair forthcoming). While both "respectable" and illicit businesses were geographically concentrated on State Street between Thirty-first and Fifty-first Streets, even residential and public space became sites for this growing informal economy (Chicago Commission on Race Relations 1968, 343).[4] Black sex entrepreneurs established buffet flats—private apartments in which they sold food and alcohol, featured musicians and singers, and provided clients with prostitutes or sex shows (Blair forthcoming). Eventually the street itself became a place for business, as the shortage of brothels led prostitutes to ply their trade outside.

The growth of community and business institutions was complimented by the development of client-patron links at the city level. While blacks had seen some success in the state Republican Party in the pre-migration era, they had "struggled in vain to secure an alderman of their race" since 1910 (Gosnell 1935, 74). Edward H. Wright and Oscar De Priest both caught the attention of party officials by producing black support for white candidates, but they were initially unable to receive the party nomination for office (Gosnell 1935, 154). After 1915, however, blacks established client-patron relationships with the city's Republican Party leadership. Participation in the machine was facilitated by two factors: the first was residential segregation, which funneled black migrants into sizable voting blocs in the Second and Third Wards, where Douglas/Grand Boulevard was located. The "political balance of power in Chicago—both between the parties and between warring factions within the Republican party—was precarious enough to give the leaders of any sizable voting bloc considerable leverage," and blacks became the swing vote that determined electoral outcomes (Spear 1967, 120).

The second factor encouraging black machine participation was the mobilization of this newly concentrated electorate. The Alpha Suffrage Club, a women's political organization established by Ida B. Wells Barnett in 1913, was central to the election of the city's first black alderman. In 1914, the club canvassed vigorously for a black aldermanic candidate, who, although he did not win, received 45 percent of the vote (Tompkins Bates 2001; Spear 1967, 123). Recognizing the growing power of the Alpha Suffrage Club and black voters in general, Republican machine leaders pledged to support a black candidate in the next election if the club would promise not to mobilize voters in opposition to their candidates (Knupfer 1996; Tompkins Bates 2001). As a result, Oscar De Priest became Chicago's first black alderman in 1916. With the election of Robert R. Jackson in the Second Ward two years later, African Americans had "race men" to represent them in both black wards (Spear 1967, 190; Gosnell 1935, 75–76). In 1920, machine regular Edward Wright won the election to ward committeeman, thus "cement[ing] Negro control of the Republican party in the black belt" (Spear 1967, 191). The relationships between local black elected officials and the Republican Party mirrored those established at the state level during the pre-migration era. Both engaged in individualized ties that required a white patron and took place within the machine. What distinguished them was the politics practiced by each: while the former sought equal treatment and access to resources, the latter sought the receipt of spoils within the confines of the ghetto.

This new professionalized elite was primarily concerned with the management of the ghetto. They were, as Drake and Cayton argue, "primarily administrators and not mass leaders" (1993, 741). Because of this focus, they emphasized the establishment of the neighborhood's social, economic, and political organizations, building what historian Allan Spear calls the "institutional ghetto" (1967). The accomplishments of this generation are significant: beyond establishing an impressive array of institutions in the face of severe economic deprivation, they provided the base for future economic success and political organization among black Chicagoans. The development of a separate space is often attributed to the growing political radicalism of blacks: institution-building can therefore be seen as one factor that contributed to blacks' decreased tolerance of racism in the North. Black elected officials provided descriptive and at times substantive representation to the residents of Douglas/Grand Boulevard and the rest of the Black Belt. Their political successes, combined with the financial accomplishments of black business owners and professionals, stood as proof against racist assumptions of black inferiority. The concentration of money in South Side financial institutions also helped blacks obtain loans to purchase homes and build wealth, both in the migration era and after (Drake and Cayton 1993, 436). By nurturing and developing the Black Belt to which they were confined, Douglas/Grand Boulevard residents were able to endure the conditions of urban racial subordination. Yet as Drake and

Cayton suggest, the focus on the management of Douglas/Grand Boulevard's institutions meant that black elites "were 'uplifting the masses'—not leading them" (1993, 733). In attempting to capitalize on their misfortune, black community leaders responded in ways that reproduced, rather than challenged, racial subordination.

The Limits of Self-Help

The first and most obvious drawback to the self-help strategy was that it was "inadequate to meet the needs of the growing Negro community" (Spear 1967, 106–7). The social service and welfare agencies that dotted the South Side did not have the financial or organizational capacity to service the more than 200,000 black migrants that came from the South between 1900 and 1930. Similarly, while the number of black businesses grew significantly during the migration period, they never matched the number of white-owned businesses in the area; as a result, Black Belt residents were never able to create an independent, self-sustaining business sector to serve African American residents. Throughout the migration period, white business owners dominated Douglas/Grand Boulevard and the rest of the Black Belt. Not only did they stay in the area during the wave of black entrepreneurship, but they enjoyed decided advantages in location and capitalization (Drake and Cayton 1993, 436). Racial discrimination meant that black business owners began their enterprises with less capital than whites did. They also had less access to the credit that would allow them to improve, expand, or relocate their businesses. As a result, whites controlled most of the business on major thoroughfares (Spear 1967, 181–84; Drake and Cayton 1993, 434–37). Even more important, white business owners received the lion's share of black business patronage, much to the consternation of African American business owners and self-help advocates. In the 1930s, "while Negro enterprises constituted almost half of all the businesses in Negro neighborhoods, they received less than a tenth of all the money spent by Negroes within these areas" (Drake and Cayton 1993, 438; Philpott 1991, 215). Thus, while black entrepreneurs insisted on the importance of economic self-sufficiency, "Negro business remained more a slogan than an actuality" (Spear 1967, 181).

The second limitation of self-help was that it was never really all that independent. As the experience of African American business owners illustrates, black neighborhoods were embedded in broader financial markets from which there was no escape. This was the case as well for Douglas/Grand Boulevard's social and political leaders, who also depended on the economic and political support of whites. For example, many of the community organizations that provided social and employment services to migrants were funded or run by white elites (Spear 1967). George Pullman, employer of the majority of the city's porters, gave significant sums of money to the Chicago Urban League, the Wabash YMCA, and Provident Hospital. He also supported prominent opinion makers such as religious leaders and newspapers, providing them with financial aid, personal favors, and symbolic status positions (Tompkins Bates 2001). This behavior was common among industrialists and philanthropists in the migration period, and in one sense was an extension of the client-patron relationships of the late nineteenth and early twentieth centuries. But because migration-era patrons sought racial containment rather than integration, their dependence led to a third limitation: it encouraged black social and political leaders to prioritize the concerns of whites over those of their black constituents. In deference to their patrons, for example, black elites sometimes ignored or cooperated with practices that helped maintain black economic and political subordination. The Chicago Urban League, for example, often found itself in the position of "serving at least two masters, the employer and the Negro worker" (Strickland 2001, 48). It sought to convince employers that hiring blacks was beneficial, yet in doing so, the organization "tried to insure him against inefficient, indolent and troublesome workers" (Strickland 2001, 48). Similarly, religious and business leaders who were supported by the Pullman company (including the editors of both the *Chicago Defender* and the *Chicago Whip*) opposed the unionization effort of Pullman porters in the mid to late 1920s (Tompkins Bates 2001). These responses reflected the fact that elites were concerned with the administration of the Black Belt, not political agitation.

Black elected officials' dependence on the white Republican machine also hampered their ability to press for black interests. While blacks gained entry into the Republican Party in 1915, the citywide Republican ward organization—the seat of the machine's power—was still controlled by whites. As late as 1935, no blacks had "won the headship of a city department and at no time ha[d] they received in the patronage positions as a whole rewards which were commensurate with their voting strength" (Gosnell 1935, 202). Thus, despite their incorporation into the machine structure, black politicians lacked the power to make demands on behalf of the residents of the Second and Third Wards. Even if they had achieved more influence, the structure of the machine did not encourage elected officials—black or otherwise—to make demands on behalf of their constituents. Machine politics is patronage rather than issue focused. Thus, African American politicians used their influence to obtain jobs and favors for voters and they sought high-paying positions for like-minded associates and allies (Gosnell 1935, 154–62).[5] Edward H. Wright, the black committeeman of the Second Ward from 1920 to 1927, was generally regarded as an "aggressive" and successful ward boss who was particularly well known for his ability to wrangle favors, high-level jobs, and elected or appointed positions from white party leaders (Gosnell 1935, 153–62; Drake and Cayton 1993, 350–51). Yet Wright distributed these benefits according to the contribution made to the party, and he "kept a card index of his followers, whom he rewarded with positions or money in accordance with their delivery at the polls" (Drake and Cayton 1993, 350). Like any good machine politician, Wright was more concerned with delivering the vote than with challenging racial inequities. Thus, his emphasis on the distribution of individualized benefits and privileges led him to be "accused of neglecting the unsanitary conditions, the growth of vice, the lack of police protection, and the lack of recreational facilities in the colored neighborhoods" (Gosnell 1935, 162).

A fourth shortcoming of self-help strategies was that they encouraged the exploitation of economically vulnerable African Americans by black political and economic entrepreneurs. The structure of electoral politics partially aligned the interests of black and white elites, as African American businessmen, professionals, and politicians came to rely increasingly on the concentrated black population for their financial and electoral success.

So while they opposed the measures used to confine blacks, they benefited substantially from segregation itself—a fact they were willing to own up to in their less guarded moments. Drake and Cayton, for example, quote one leader as saying "I don't want Negroes moving about all over town. I just want to add little pieces to the Black Belt. I'd never get re-elected if Negroes were all scattered about. The white people wouldn't vote for me" (1993, 201). As a result of these myriad influences, black elites did not attack the sources of their constituents' housing and employment problems head on. While building up the Black Belt provided some Douglas/Grand Boulevard residents with economic and political successes, it ultimately failed to protect blacks as a whole from racial subordination, as expressed through job discrimination, political exploitation, and housing segregation.

Particularly in the real estate industry, African American business owners eagerly adopted the same tactics used by whites to exploit other blacks. For example, both Oscar DePriest and Jesse Binga—prominent community members lauded for their contributions to the black community—built their personal and professional fortunes by exploiting black working-class renters (Gosnell 1935, 169). Binga managed property on the corner of Forty-seventh and State Streets that was known at the time as "the longest tenement row in Chicago" (Spear 1967, 113). He, DePriest, and other real estate developers handled

> slum properties, where they charged all the traffic would bear, and they leased large buildings in transitional areas and rented the flats to Negroes. They charged their "own people $10 to $15 more than the white renters had been paying." Their excuse was that the money was there to be made in Negro housing, and black businessmen should get some of the profit. As realtor William D. Neighbors said in self defense, "If the Colored real estate dealers did not charge the rent required by the owner, there would be found plenty of white agents who would." (Philpott 1991, 151–52)

It is important to realize that this sentiment—that black rather than white elites should be profiting from poor blacks—is not in contradiction to self-help; rather, it is its ultimate expression. Self-help ideology advocates black

businesses development as a strategy for "improving the economic standing of the Negro community as a whole and of indirectly obtaining citizenship rights by demonstrating the ability of Negroes to meet American
petty-bourgeois standards of respectability and success" (Meier 1962, 258).
In adopting these exploitative practices, African American property owners
embodied the self-help assumption that the success of black elites represents advancement for the entire race. In that sense, they were excellent
models of both the logic and the limitations of self-help strategies: they
achieved individual success, but the accumulation strategies they promoted
as universally beneficial actually promoted their own advancement at the
expense of poor and working-class blacks.

The final shortcoming of self-help strategies was that they facilitated racial segregation. When they chose self-help and adjustment over
a direct attack on racism, black leaders made the continued segregation of
blacks and the subsequent overcrowding and property disinvestment that
much easier. Drake and Cayton make an important distinction between
the existence and the expression of black elites' objection to migration-era
racism: they argue that community leaders "did not hesitate to voice their
disapproval of any attempts to infringe upon the rights of Negroes or to
deny them equal opportunity. Most of the community leaders had their
hands full, however, maintaining Bronzeville's institutional life. They were
the people who knew how to organize fund-raising drives and to make a
budget and stay within them. They were people who were 'uplifting the
masses'—not leading them" (Drake and Cayton 1993, 733). This was particularly the case in the late 1910s, when white elites turned their attention and resources toward the city's growing housing crisis.

The 1919 race riot served as a clear sign that blatant and forceful
racial discrimination was increasingly likely to provoke violent backlash—
thus, white elites began looking for alternative ways to "renounce 'segregation' and still respect the universal white phobia against integrated neighborhoods" (Philpott 1991, 212). Between 1917 and 1922, white real estate,
business, and social leaders began advocating a Black Belt construction
program as a way to both address the housing shortage and maintain the
racial integrity of the city's neighborhoods. The strategy was built on the

assumption that African Americans' entrance into white neighborhoods was a result of inadequate housing stock in the Black Belt: building houses in black areas would therefore encourage African Americans to stay in their own neighborhoods. Not only was the strategy advocated by the city's business community, it was ultimately adopted by the Chicago Riot Commission, a biracial organization whose overall stance was relatively critical of racism and discrimination. Yet as Philpott illustrates, their 1922 report "condemned segregation by 'force' or by 'proscription' . . . [and] then went on to recommend segregation without calling it by name" (1991, 225).

Black leaders' involvement in and response to this plan reflected their limited options, as well as their accommodationist response to those options. Many black community leaders were vehemently opposed to forced segregation, and they objected to plans whose baldly stated purpose was to contain African Americans within the Black Belt. In the years prior to the Riot Commission's report, they repeatedly pulled out of negotiation processes that cast them as having explicitly advocated segregation (Philpott 1991, 210–20). Yet in the face of shrinking opportunities for integration and the growing violence against blacks, black leaders became more concerned with securing housing and minimizing racial violence. Challenging the pattern of segregation became less important in comparison to these goals; as a result, black opinion makers and representatives ultimately gave approval—sometimes explicit, but more often tacit—to the plan of "voluntary" segregation advocated by white business and social elites. Charles S. Duke reflected the opinion of many black real estate professionals, for example, when he argued that the solution to the housing crisis was a Black Belt building plan led by African American developers and supported by white businessmen and industrialists (Philpott 1991, 215).

While not all blacks agreed with him, important opinion makers in Douglas/Grand Boulevard—including black dailies such as the *Chicago Defender*—"maintained a discreet silence" about the plan and its implications (Philpott 1991, 224). This response illustrates what can only be called a begrudging acceptance of the plan on the part of Black Belt residents. African American alderman Louis B. Anderson deftly articulated this sentiment in a statement in the *Defender*. In discussing the plan, he made the obligatory reference to Negro rights. The black man, he said, had "the same right" to live in a modern apartment building as the white man, provided he was "financially able." But the alderman went on to say that "most Negroes would prefer to live in a district exclusively inhabited by people of their own Race." Going further he said, "The Colored man has no desire to mix indiscriminately with the whites, but he must have a roof over his head." (Philpott 1991, 224–25)

Despite black leaders' willingness to accept segregation, the housing program never materialized. As the housing shortage eased up in the 1920s, developers realized that building and space restrictions prevented them from constructing new homes anywhere other than white neighborhoods—a move that would have undermined the very point of racial containment. The only construction that took place in Douglas/Grand Boulevard in the 1920s was the Michigan Boulevard Apartment Building.

Black leaders' overall response to the plan illustrates an important feature of accommodationism. Black elites accepted "improved housing, segregated though it was, without accepting the *principle* of segregation" (Philpott 1991, 265). Thus, self-help strategies, though not deliberately or even consciously accommodationist, were inherently so because they acquiesced to—rather than challenged—unequal power. In the wake of this accommodationist strategy, the Black Belt continued to grow, wider and longer, throughout the 1920s. Conflicts over housing were eased somewhat by a seven-year boom in citywide construction that began in 1921. During this period, racial hostility was diminished by whites' ability to move away from blacks. But the stream of southern black migrants increased the black population to more than 200,000 by 1930, leading to an increasing concentration of blacks in the Black Belt. By then, not only the eastern and western borders of the neighborhood but the blocks in between were largely black: 89 percent of Douglas's more than 50,000 residents were African American, and in Grand Boulevard, more than 82,000 of the 87,000 residents were black (Chicago Fact Book Consortium 1938; Holt and Pacyga 1979). In response, hostile whites "redrew their line at Cottage Grove," at the eastern edge of the Black Belt, and increasingly began to rely on restrictive covenants as a strategy of racial containment.[6] Previously available for use only on single plots, restrictive covenants were used in the 1920s to restrict black access to white communities. Desperate to contain the burgeoning black population, white neighborhood associations launched an extensive campaign to mobilize their members in support of these contracts. By the end of the decade,

> the *Hyde Park Herald* was pleased to announce that a "fine network of contracts" extended "like a marvelous delicately woven chain of armor" from "the northern gates of Hyde Park at Thirty-fifth and Drexel Boulevard to Woodlawn, Park Manor, South Shore, Windsor Park and all the far flung white communities of the south side." (Philpott 1991, 195)

While the containment of blacks within the borders of Douglas/Grand Boulevard was clearly the result of white racial hostility and organizing, its way was paved by black acquiescence. Trapped within these physical and political constraints, the new black elite sought not to rally their community against segregation, but to install themselves "as the dominant force in the Negro community, ready to lead the South Side into an era of hopeful expansion and consolidation" (Spear 1967, 192).

Client–Patron Politics and Neighborhood Decline, 1930–60

Despite this rosy outlook, the onset of the Depression dashed the hopes of migration-era black elites: as their economic circumstances deteriorated, Douglas/Grand Boulevard residents lost their faith in self-help and gave their support to organizations that challenged racial segregation at the local level and beyond. Chicago was particularly vulnerable to the ravages of the Depression, saddled as it was with "an antiquated revenue system and a chaotic government setup [that] were not equal to the emergency" (Gosnell 1937, 6). The dozens of governing authorities that operated in Cook County in the late 1920s all maintained a level of autonomy and independence that complicated any attempts at coordinated relief efforts. More important, the city was facing its own financial crisis even before the onset of the national Depression. A state-mandated reassessment of property taxes had resulted in the suspension of all tax collections from

1927 to 1929. City agencies continued spending, however, securing loans based on the anticipated tax revenue. When tax collection finally resumed in 1929, a group of large property owners extended the crisis by waging a three-year campaign in which they refused to pay their taxes and filed multiple suits challenging the constitutionality of the reassessment. The City of Chicago was unable to secure loans from area banks, had a backlog of unpaid taxes, and was unable to pay even the workers it employed. Providing relief to the casualties of the Depression was the last thing the city could handle (Biles 1984, 21–23).

Because of this economic crisis, 40 percent of the city's workers were unemployed by 1932, and the number of people needing assistance reached more than 2.5 million (Biles 1984, 22). Chicago's African American population suffered disproportionately from the effects of the disaster, largely because they had remained concentrated in vulnerable service occupations. Although significant numbers of black men had broken into the industrial labor market during the First World War, 25 percent of employed African American men and 56 percent of African American women were working as porters, domestics, personal servants, waiters, janitors, and elevator attendants in 1930 (Drake and Cayton 1993, 221). Because the services they provided were considered a luxury, these workers were often the first to lose their jobs. Black service workers also faced increased competition from whites and ethnics whose economic circumstances were dire enough to induce them to take lower-status work.[7] In 1935, blacks made up 22 percent of the city's unemployed, despite the fact that they were only 8 percent of available workers (Drake and Cayton 1993, 217).

Blacks performing service, unskilled, and semi-skilled labor faced the greatest economic hardship, yet even black elites suffered the consequences of economic crisis. In 1930, only 7,000 African Americans, or 3 percent of the city's black population, held professional jobs. Over the next five years, their numbers decreased by 15 percent, from 7,000 to 5,900 (Drake and Cayton 1993, 217). Moreover, the ripple effects of the Depression meant that

the banks on the South Side failed earlier than others in the city, resulting in the loss to Negro depositors of millions of dollars in savings. Business and

> professional interests dependent upon Negro patronage were in danger of
> impending bankruptcy. Investments in homes were lost; and landlords, many
> of whom were also in dire straits, had hundreds of impecunious families
> evicted and their possessions placed upon the streets. (Strickland 2001, 104)[8]

These problems were exacerbated by the fact that blacks continued to
migrate to Chicago during the 1930s, despite the turmoil of the Depression.
During that decade, the number of African Americans in the city increased
by 18.7 percent, from 233,903 to 277,731 (Hirsch 1983, 17). During the
same decade, the number of blacks living in Douglas/Grand Boulevard
increased by 24,170 to 151,143.[9] In combination, the "continuous squeez-
ing of Negroes out of industry and the tide of in-migration combined to
raise the proportion of Negroes on the relief rolls, until by 1939 four out
of every ten persons on relief were Negroes and five out of every ten Negro
families were dependent upon some type of government aid for their subsis-
tence" (Drake and Cayton 1993, 88). Douglas/Grand Boulevard residents
also continued to face a severe housing shortage, one exacerbated by inadequate city building programs. The only significant construction that took
place in Douglas/Grand Boulevard in the 1930s was the Ida B. Wells housing project, located in the southeast corner of Douglas, and it "destroyed
nearly as many apartments as it supplied. When the project finally opened
in 1941, 17,544 applications were received for 1,662 units" (Hirsch 1983,
18; Bowly 1978, 30).

These hardships weakened the power of self-help advocates in two
ways. First, they led to a temporary though significant loss of power among
black elected officials. Despite its deteriorating quality of life and its bud-
ding political restlessness, the black electorate "was the only group in Chicago that did not shift its allegiance, in either local or national elections,
to the new Democratic party of power at the outset of the 1930s" (Grimshaw 1992, 47).[10] When Black Belt favorite William Hale Thompson lost
his 1931 bid for reelection to Democrat Anton Cermak,

> the power of the Second and Third Ward machines was no longer felt, as
> they were in the wrong column. Without patronage the ward machines began

to disintegrate. On the other hand, without patronage—for that matter, without leadership—Negroes could not immediately build up a Democratic machine. (Drake and Cayton 1993, 352)

Although black politicians would eventually switch to the dominant party, this temporary loss of power diminished black Republicans' capacity to acquire benefits for Douglas/Grand Boulevard residents. Shortly after taking office, Cermak fired numerous black city workers, began harassing gambling and vice organizations in the Black Belt, and developed the bones of a black Democratic organization in the Third Ward (Biles 1984, 89–90). The point was not to destroy black political and economic power, but to bring it under Democratic Party control. By installing political flunky and policy insider Michael Sneed in the position of Third Ward committeeman, the Democratic leadership challenged the influence of black Republicans and assured itself the financial support of powerful South Side gambling concerns (Biles 1984, 90; Grimshaw 1992, 73).[11] In the meantime, migration-era political leaders were left to walk the fine line between Republican black voters, who had yet to realign their political loyalties, and Democratic Party leaders, who held the keys to their continued power.

The Depression also undermined self-help advocates by threatening the influence of traditional self-help race organizations. The combination of economic crisis and changing political fortunes made the city's blacks increasingly impatient with both the gradualist techniques of traditional advancement organizations and the economic nationalism of black business leaders. Beginning in the late 1920s, Black Belt residents were increasingly attracted to organizations that actively protested against segregation and unequal treatment, particularly in the housing and employment arenas. In some instances, these efforts were fairly traditional. The "Spend Your Money Where You Can Work" campaign—supported by the Chicago NAACP—pressured nearby white employers to hire blacks in positions from which they were excluded. This strategy was closely tied to the self-help ideology of the migration era. Because it portrayed patronage of black businesses as a political strategy that could advance the race, it was "the preferred objective of Negro businessmen" (Drake and Cayton 1993, 436).

Moreover, while some of these efforts sought to secure positions for laborers, many emphasized the attainment of clerical and professional positions (Drake and Cayton 1993, 743–44; Tompkins Bates 2001, 113). Overall, forced hiring campaigns acquired a small number of jobs, and thus tackled individual rather than structural sources of discrimination.

Yet other efforts were further from the self-help strategy. These focused on skilled and unskilled workers, and challenged the political economy that maintained racism rather than trying to develop blacks' position within it. The black union of the Brotherhood of Sleeping Car Porters, for example, experienced a sharp increase in its membership after 1935. That year, it became the first union to negotiate a contract with the powerful Pullman Company and was able to improve working conditions and compensation for many of the city's porters.[12] The brotherhood's victory did more than advance the welfare of individual Pullman employees, however. The union had long claimed that the porters' struggle for economic rights was but one element of the African American struggle for civil and economic rights, and in describing the porters' victory, the *Chicago Defender* agreed. The paper claimed that the union had "won 'respect' for all African Americans because they succeeded without 'begging'" (Tompkins Bates 2001, 127). Just as important as the symbolic victory was the way the struggle for unionization helped advance black Chicagoans' facility with new issues, alliances, and strategies. In the effort to secure support for unionization, the brotherhood's leaders educated black men and women on workers' rights, trained them in collective organizing, and helped them develop intra- and interracial coalitions. Throughout the 1930s, they were an active part of much of the city's left-wing politics, and their work "prepared the way for the rise of trade unionism and a prolabor point of view within the black community" (Tompkins Bates 2001, 127).

The work of the brotherhood was complemented by that of the Communist Party, which gained the support of black Chicagoans for its national and local activities. In 1931, the Communist Party established the Scottsboro Committee of Chicago, which organized around the Scottsboro case, in which nine black men were accused of raping two white women in an Alabama town of the same name. In the same year it established an

Unemployed Council, through which it protested the evictions of Chicago's unemployed blacks (Tompkins Bates 2001). The Communist Party's atypical commitment to interracialism and achieving concrete material gains won them the support of "an eclectic group [of African Americans], which included Republicans, Democrats, black fraternal orders, and some ex-members of the all black, Eighth Infantry regiment" (Tompkins Bates 2001, 112). In addition, the Communist Party boasted the support of the city's more elite blacks (Drake and Cayton 1993, 736). Although only five hundred black Chicagoans joined the party, it enjoyed widespread support of its mass actions, and those who were members made up half of all blacks in the Communist Party (P. Smith 2000).

These campaigns were distinguished not only by the challenge they posed to discrimination, but by their use of confrontational, collective action techniques. Particularly in the early years of the Depression, blacks used mass meetings, demonstrations, street-corner rallies, and even the threat of violence to express and press for their demands. As everyday African Americans became more fluent in and accepting of direct collective action, so did elites. Over time, these strategies were adopted by the more "safe" organizations—even the "Spend Your Money" campaign, conventional as it was, broke from the tradition of self-help in its use of boycotts and picketing of white businesses. Likewise, the Council of Negro Organizations, established by the conservative NAACP and "led by upper and upper-middle-class, middle-aged men and women, was itself organizing demonstrations in the proletarian style" (Drake and Cayton 1993, 738). The Chicago branch of the National Urban League and its affiliate organizations also led pickets and boycott campaigns against nearby dairies, tractor companies, theaters, and telephone companies that discriminated against black workers (Strickland 2001, 132). The widespread adoption of these tactics, by both traditional and more "radical" organizations, reflected the decreased popularity of self-help and adjustment strategies for racial advancement. While migration-era elites had sought to make the neighborhood a "city within a city" (Spear 1967, 91), economic hardship prompted them to challenge the discriminatory practices that maintained their separation.

While collective action strategies weakened the hold of self-help ideology, their influence was shortlived. The transience of leftist activism was partly a function of "the absence of organizational vehicles able to translate poor social conditions into a viable and accessible program" (P. Smith 2000, 135). While the radical tactics of communists and labor unions were used by conservative organizations, their adoption was a strategic move by groups seeking to maintain their legitimacy. Because they were "challenged on one hand by the communists and on the other by the racial radicals, the 'accepted leaders' [had] either to accommodate themselves to new techniques or give way to men who could do so" (Drake and Cayton 1993, 737).

The program of the Chicago Urban League exemplified this tendency: the league felt pressure to respond to the increasing radicalism of both Black Belt residents and some of its own staff.[13] Yet the organization had to bear in mind its more conservative white funders. To manage these competing concerns, the league adopted a dual strategy. When dealing with its white financiers,

> it placed the image of a social welfare organization using community organization, interracial cooperation, and education to better conditions within the Negro community and between the races. If pressure became necessary, it would be exercised through the time-sanctioned practices of petitioning. Among the restless Negro masses, on the other hand, the League wanted to be known as an organization in the forefront of the fight for racial advancement. (Strickland 2001, 122)

This strategy helps explain both the league's use of direct action techniques and its eventual return to the social adjustment agenda at the close of the decade (Strickland 2001, 134–35, 139). In its ambivalent approach to radicalism, the league represented the mood and direction of the 1930s, when radical language, ideology, and strategy were used haltingly and incompletely by institutions that remained conservative at their core. Whatever potential these organizations held for extending the protest tradition at the neighborhood level was further undermined by the organizational disarray they faced in the 1940s and 1950s. Both the Chicago Urban League and the Chicago chapter of the NAACP deteriorated during that time, as both faced internal conflicts that weakened their capacity to effectively address racial discrimination.

Machine Domination and Urban Renewal

At the same time that traditional and radical organizations turned their attention to internal issues, the Democratic machine was reaching its peak. After his 1933 election, Democratic mayor Edward Kelly began rebuilding his base among African Americans, ending the crackdown that the previous mayor, Anton Cermak, had orchestrated two years before. While Cermak had booted blacks from patronage jobs and thwarted the activities of neighborhood vice leaders, Kelly courted Douglas/Grand Boulevard residents with an increase in appointed and elected positions, government aid, and symbolic support for desegregation. The effectiveness of his strategy is evident in subsequent election returns: despite the fact that the city's blacks were still largely Republican at the time, they nevertheless supported Kelly's Democratic pick for First District congressman in 1934.[14] One year later, Black Belt residents affirmed their commitment to Kelly by giving him 80.5 percent of the vote in the 1935 mayoral election (Biles 1984, 94). African American politicians seriously reentered the city's electoral playing field in the late 1930s, when William Dawson began building his legendary submachine. Dawson had been the Republican Second Ward alderman from 1933 to 1939, when, in order to secure greater power, he switched to the Democratic Party and was awarded the post of ward committeeman (Grimshaw 1992, 74–78). Over the next few years, Dawson consolidated his rule by winning election to the U.S. House of Representatives, securing his allies' elections as Second and Third Ward aldermen and committeemen and gaining national prominence by playing a strong role in Truman's 1948 election (Grimshaw 1992, 79–80; Biles 1984, 96–102).

Dawson's submachine served the same function, and suffered from the same limitations, as did its Republican predecessor: it provided party supporters with symbolic benefits and personal favors instead of challenging racial power imbalances (Biles 1984, 91). Dawson had been vocal prior to his involvement with the machine, drawing on racial rhetoric to gain the support of voters. But "once Dawson entered the machine, he became strictly an organization man, working within the machine's narrow confines to achieve limited, concrete goals. His public silence on the race issue became nearly absolute" (Grimshaw 1992, 74).[15] Dawson himself readily admitted his aversion to pressing race advancement. When contrasting himself to Earl B. Dickerson, a fellow Democrat who lost favor with the party because of his outspokenness on race and labor issues, Dawson said that Dickerson "was always raising the race issue and antagonizing people. . . . Me, I never raise the race issue, even in Congress and I certainly didn't in the [Chicago City] Council" (quoted in Biles 1984, 100). Not only did the black submachine generally fail to make demands for racial equality, it used its resources to stifle or control civic and business organizations that might have challenged it (J. Wilson 1960).

Dawson's Democratic organization, like the Republican one that preceded it, owed its power to the machine. This was particularly the case in the late 1940s, when black Democrats lost two important resources. The first was the political protection of Mayor Kelly, who lost the 1946 election to Martin Kennelly. The second, related to the first, was the financial backing of the Black Belt underground. Like Anton Cermak before him, Martin Kennelly set out to undermine the power of Black Belt elites. He eliminated two popular, and by some accounts, necessary institutions in the Black Belt: the illegal jitney cabs, which catered to otherwise neglected blacks, and the policy wheel, or lottery, both of which were run by African Americans (Grimshaw 1992, 58–59). Not only did these moves make the lives of the average Black Belt resident more difficult, they also threatened the financial basis of black politicians, who relied on contributions from businessmen and policy operators to fund their organizations. As a result, the Dawson machine raised few challenges against racism.

In previous years, this accommodationist stance had helped to ease the way for segregation. In the late 1940s and early 1950s, accommodationism led to a different but equally devastating problem: it lubricated neighborhood disinvestment by failing to challenge urban renewal. Urban renewal, which took place primarily in Douglas, was the business elite's response to two shifts in the city's population. The first, an increase in black residents, was the result of a resurgence in African American migration. During the 1940s, the postwar economic boom buoyed the transportation and manufacturing industries in Chicago, including steel, heavy machinery, consumer appliances, and food production (Bennett 1989, 163). Attracted to the jobs offered by the city, blacks flocked to Chicago. From 1940 to 1950, the African American population increased 77 percent, from 277,731 to 492,265. A good portion of that increase showed up in Douglas/Grand Boulevard, which experienced a 23 percent increase, from 156,380 to 193,302. This growth in the black population was accompanied by a drop in the white population. Like other older industrial cities in the North and Northeast, Chicago suffered from the restructuring of the economy that had closely followed on the heels of postwar prosperity. Although blacks were drawn to the city by the promise of manufacturing work, whites were drawn away from it by manufacturers who began moving to the suburbs (Hirsch and Mohl 1993; Mollenkopf 1983; Squires et al. 1987). The decrease in white population was also augmented by federal highway and mortgage programs that encouraged white ethnic suburbanization, but prevented the movement of black residents (Hays 1985, 81). In the 1940s, the city's white population dropped from 3,118,000 to 3,110,000.

The exodus of whites to the suburbs, combined with the 1948 Supreme Court prohibition against restrictive covenants, opened up new areas of the city to black residents. Although the movement of blacks was ever farther south, the suburbanization of industries and population was nevertheless of great concern to white business elites in the Loop and the near South Side, who feared the loss of white middle-class consumers and the spread of "blight." The fear of blight was a highly racialized concern over the increased presence of African Americans in areas of the city traditionally dominated by whites. Business owners in the Loop dreaded the thought that black consumers and residents would push beyond the borders established by segregation, drive away middle-class white consumers, and diminish the value of their downtown property (Hirsch 1983). This sentiment was conveyed by one developer's comment that the Loop's trouble was really rooted in "people's conception of it. And the conception they have about it is one word: Black. B-L-A-C-K. Black" (quoted in Rast 1999, 31).

Two institutions that were particularly concerned with insulating themselves from these demographic and economic changes were located in the heart of the Douglas community. Michael Reese Hospital and the Illinois Institute of Technology had both made substantial investments in their facilities during the 1940s and were fearful of the impact of the surrounding community on their campuses. In 1946, the planning staffs of the two institutions united to form the South Side Planning Board and fight the spread of neighborhood "blight" in the surrounding Douglas neighborhood. The board fought for and won the passage of the Redevelopment and Relocation Acts of 1947, which authorized the use of public funds to acquire, clear, and then sell land at a reduced price to private developers. It used this authority to tear down supposed slum housing and expand both the university and the hospital campuses, as well as to build housing for their middle-class employees. The first such project was Lake Meadows, located in the northern end of Douglas at King Drive and Thirty-second Street. This was quickly followed by Prairie Shores, which like Lake Meadows housed a primarily middle-class population (Hirsch 1983, 259).

Some residents of Douglas objected to the projects on the grounds that the proposed sites of clearance could hardly be termed slums. Even more infuriating, however, was the failure of these projects to relocate the black residents whose homes they had demolished. Hirsch claims that "the most deep-seated, widespread and powerful opposition expressed the fear that blacks would be displaced from their traditional areas and left homeless in a city that was reluctant to house them" (1983, 125). And these fears were well founded, for the new developments were beyond the budget of most Douglas/Grand Boulevard residents and were planned by project managers to be fully integrated (Hirsch 1983, 125–27). Yet the response of neighborhood leadership to the threat of urban renewal was minimal and ineffective. Some business owners had even initially planned to invest in the Lake Meadows project, but fear of being associated with "Negro Removal" convinced them not to participate (J. Wilson 1960, 181). Yet the majority of Dawson's men remained painfully silent on the issue of displacement: the lone dissenter was Archibald Carey Jr., Republican alderman of the Third Ward, who proposed an ultimately unsuccessful ordinance to ban discrimination in projects aided by public subsidies (P. Smith 2000).[16] Although Carey's ordinance was supported by multiple civic organizations, including the Urban League and the NAACP, it was defeated in the city council thirty-one to thirteen.

The results of the urban renewal program had serious implications for the neighborhood, both immediate and long term. The activities of the South Side Planning Board fostered a good deal of residential and business displacement and population decline (Hirsch 1983, 122, 259). They also contributed to the concentration of poverty in Douglas/Grand Boulevard. Because of the inadequate relocation strategies, urban renewal advocates made the construction of public housing central to their plans. In attempting to house residents dislocated by South Side Planning Board projects, the Chicago Housing Authority was forced to violate its own admission rules, housing people and families who did not meet income requirements. From 1950 to 1954, "more than half of all public housing units constructed (2,363 apartments out of 4,636) were allocated directly to families displaced by government building programs" (Hirsch 1983, 124). Thus, by the time the projects were finished, Douglas/Grand Boulevard was home to the largest concentration of public housing in the country: Stateway Gardens and the Robert Taylor homes stood like a row of sentries along its western edge; Ida B. Wells guarded the northeast corner; and scattered-site reinforcements were spread judiciously throughout the community.

In addition, urban renewal helped prime the communities—Douglas especially—for subsequent rounds of redevelopment by reshaping both the physical and the demographic community. In generating only isolated and piecemeal reinvestment, urban renewal projects helped reproduce the conditions that encourage gentrification and racial displacement. By the project's end, huge portions of the two neighborhoods remained untouched by reinvestments, while pockets of affluence lay scattered about. As geographer Neil Smith points out, these arrangements facilitate gentrification by widening the gap between current and potential property values (N. Smith 1996). Thus, black elites' failure to effectively challenge the South Side Planning Board's project in the late 1940s and early 1950s laid the foundation for later conflicts over redevelopment. Just as important is how black accommodationism shaped the inter- and intraracial dynamics of those future conflicts. Urban renewal projects concentrated and sectioned off the poorest African Americans into distinct and highly visible parts of the neighborhood, while also creating enclaves of middle-income black elites. By the 1970s the middle-class enclaves of Prairie Shores, Lake Meadows, and South Commons stood in stark material and spatial contrast to public housing, despite their close proximity. These divisions had always been felt, but prewar residential segregation had reduced the degree to which they could be expressed spatially. By giving spatial articulation to the class cleavages within Douglas/Grand Boulevard, urban renewal helped to create a population of potential black gentrifiers—middle-income blacks who were concerned about maintaining the value of their property. Paradoxically, then, the same forces that maintained the segregation of blacks would also exacerbate class divisions within their community in the coming decades.

A Tarnished Golden Era

It is tempting to view the first half of the twentieth century as encompassing the rise and fall of black community—tempting, but misguided. The experience of Douglas/Grand Boulevard residents during this period was not one of unmitigated triumph followed by unfortunate demise; instead, it was a contradictory blend of expansion, progress, and stagnation. From 1910 to 1930 neighborhood residents produced and witnessed a remarkable growth in cultural, economic, and political institutions designed to serve their growing needs. While the development of these institutions was based in African American leaders' beliefs about the value of self-help, they were just as much a function of African Americans' decision to adjust to, rather than challenge, white Chicagoans' efforts to erect and maintain racial divisions. By adopting self-help—by accommodating themselves to white racism—Douglas/Grand Boulevard's leaders ultimately left their community open to continued racial subordination. Thus, the conditions commonly seen as a triumph were in themselves, if not their own kind of failure, at least limited in their success. Despite a significant shift in the form and focus of neighborhood politics in the 1930s, the radical tendencies of the era were funneled into organizations that were fundamentally moderate. The black Democratic submachine, emerging in the wake of the Depression, thus reestablished the accommodationist posture of the previous era.

Tracing the trajectory of black response to segregation illuminates how politics has shaped patterns of community building and neighborhood development. Since the Great Migration, white city residents and elites have worked to contain blacks within the borders of Douglas/Grand Boulevard and deliberately stripped the neighborhood of its resources. Unscrupulous real estate practices, landlord negligence, and dismissal by city authorities gave Douglas/Grand Boulevard a reputation for vice, social disorganization, and declining property values. In the postwar era, the same elements worked together with national urban policies to define Douglas/Grand Boulevard as an economic and social wasteland. In each case, the physical and institutional community was shaped by both white racism and black accommodationism.

In his letter to the editor, William Simpson provided contemporary developers with an important reminder of this pattern, highlighting both its existence and its role in shaping neighborhood conditions at the beginning of the twentieth century. As if it were not enough to have raised the awkward issue of the segregated past and insisted on its inadequacies, Mr. Simpson asks an even more pressing question about the purpose of idealizing such a stifling moment in black history. In his letter, he wonders

> what is the point in appearing to reincarnate Bronzeville—except as the fruition of some promoters' fantasies—when the most significant residents (in terms of power) were whites, and they will not be coming back? One can be all for revitalization of black communities such as Bronzeville without romantically recalling the past and making it appear to be what it was not. And what it was not was a time of freedom from segregation, exclusion and subordination of—and discrimination against—African-heritage people.

With this comment, Mr. Simpson moves beyond his pointed criticisms of historical memory to suggest that there is a political dimension to nostalgia. That is, romanticized reconstructions of black neighborhoods and those who inhabited them are not arbitrary creations; rather, they are visions of the past that have gained popularity and resonance because of the purpose they serve and the benefit they provide. When Mr. Simpson muses that real estate entrepreneurs are the primary beneficiaries of nostalgia, he has the story half-right. As the next chapter shows, nostalgia for the Jim Crow past, while exploited by developers, is the creation of contemporary black civic elites, neighborhood activists who, like their predecessors, seek to control their community's future.

CHAPTER 2

When We Were Colored:
Black Civic Leadership and
the Birth of Nostalgia, 1950–1990

In spring 1996, the Illinois Institute of Technology's (IIT) quarterly alumni newsletter, the *Catalyst*, was happy to report that despite the difficulty of finding "the right role for the urban university in its community," the institution had begun to foster a new relationship with the surrounding neighborhood of Douglas. Vice president of external affairs David Baker had recognized that remaining "an island in a deteriorating urban landscape" was a foolhardy strategy and he claimed to now understand the importance of "mutual interdependence" between neighborhood and university (Long 1996). To that end, the university had formally established a community relations department in 1989 and had hired longtime South Side resident and community activist Leroy Kennedy as its vice president. One of Kennedy's primary duties was to participate in a collaborative neighborhood planning effort between the university, area institutions, and the community's organizations and residents. The resulting organization, the Mid-South Planning and Development Commission, worked for three years in partnership with the city to develop a comprehensive neighborhood redevelopment plan entitled "Restoring Bronzeville."[1] The plan proposed that the foundation of Douglas/Grand Boulevard's economic revitalization should be historic preservation and heritage tourism development, which would both be pursued through a series of public–private partnerships. This strategy just happened to neatly complement those in the university's plan for campus enhancements, the ominously titled "Master Plan." Should the more cautious *Catalyst* readers suspect the university's motives, the executive director of Mid-South was happy to calm their fears. "The Commission," Pat Dowell assured us, "has had an excellent relationship with IIT. We have worked collaboratively on various projects. From my perspective, it bodes well for both the university and the community for IIT to extend itself beyond its walls" (Long 1996).

This alliance—between a black, member-based, community development organization and a private, white educational institution—represented a significant departure from previous patterns of community change. Since the beginning of the twentieth century, the development of the neighborhood had been shaped by white elites' efforts to contain black residents and black elites' accommodation to those efforts. The university had been a principal player in one of the more recent of these maneuvers, and both machine officials and traditional race advancement organizations had been loathe to challenge them on behalf of their constituents. Yet by the mid-1990s, Douglas/Grand Boulevard was home to hundreds of community groups and at least a dozen neighborhood development organizations (Kretzmann, McKnight, and Turner 1996).[2] Even more important, these organizations—like Mid-South—were beginning to pursue their goals through partnerships with city government and private institutions, some of whom had been the architects of past neighborhood disinvestment and racial displacement. This change in the focus and organization of neighborhood development reflected national trends in urban politics and organizing (R. Fisher 1994).

Were it not for neighborhood elites' long history of class-based leadership, this new willingness to work so closely with white elites could easily be read as a sign of the growing importance of class identity and interests. What changed, however, was not the relative significance of race and class identity, but the form of leadership and the institutions through which black elites pursued classed race goals. As this chapter details, Douglas/Grand Boulevard's political elite was reconfigured through two citywide and neighborhood struggles over racial equity in city resource distribution: the first, which took place from the mid-1950s to the 1970s, was a series of conflicts over segregation in housing and education that led to black voters' break with the machine; the second was a broadbased struggle by neighborhood residents to gain greater access to city development resources in the 1970s and early 1980s. This last set of conflicts precipitated the growth of a civic leadership cadre that was distinct from both elected officials and traditional race-relations leadership professionals of the early twentieth century. By the early 1990s, this leadership cadre had solidified its installation at the head of neighborhood organizations.

This new civic elite initiated a revitalization process from which Jim Crow identity would eventually emerge. Concerned that they would be excluded from the development process, black community leaders attempted to maintain both their political and physical presence by joining white elites in a "bottom-up" process of neighborhood planning. Far from opposing redevelopment, the "Restoring Bronzeville" plan advocated a form of it that emphasized the history and cultural heritage of the neighborhood's black population. Mid-South's "excellent relationship" with the university thus reflected, not a new class identity among black elites, but its contemporary manifestation within a particular set of political pressures. It also formed the basis for a vision of black identity rooted in the neighborhood's imagined past.

Rage Against the Machine: Civil Rights Organizing, 1955–70

As chapter 1 indicates, Chicago's Democratic machine maintained a stifling grip on neighborhood politics—and thus neighborhood development—from the 1940s to the mid-1950s. One result was the severe residential displacement and concentration of poverty at the northern end of Douglas, which local black aldermen had barely challenged, much less mitigated. Yet the same demographic shifts that prompted white business and political elites to develop and implement urban renewal also rearranged the racial makeup of the city's voter base. From 1940 to 1960, the percentage of white voters dropped from 87 to 72 percent, while the percentage of black voters more than doubled, from 8 to 20 percent (Kleppner 1985, 67). The significance of wartime demographic changes first became clear in 1955, when, voting as much against Kennelly as for Daley, the city's five black wards provided 60 percent of Daley's winning margin (Grimshaw

1992, 100; Hirsch 1995). Black support for Daley's Democratic machine only grew in the following decade. From 1955 to 1963, Daley had the support of a biracial coalition of white ethnics and blacks (Kleppner 1985, 66–69, 71; Grimshaw 1992), and black support was increasingly significant to Democratic Party victories.

Despite their growing importance, African Americans were unable to enhance their power in the Democratic Party. While black voters provided important majorities in Chicago Democratic victories, black elites continued to be excluded from the decision-making apparatus and were rarely consulted on important issues. Instead,

> the men upon whom Daley drew for advice, facts, and plans—the professional city planners, the businessmen-civic leaders, the downtown voluntary associations—were the kind of men who had opposed Dawson and the Negro machine and whom Dawson himself distrust[ed] and suspect[ed]. (J. Wilson 1960, 83)

Nor was the amount of patronage offered to black elected officials ever comparable to the contribution of the city's black population to Daley's electoral coalition. Changes in the electorate "made the old style of politics obsolete. New appeals [had] to be made to attract these [white] voters. . . . Blue ribbon candidates for important offices, and the development of a strong and attractive set of civic projects" (J. Wilson 1960, 83). Economic revitalization projects became the primary vehicle for rewarding allies, and their success "became integrally tied to the survival of the political machine, the source of Daley's substantial power" (Ferman 1996, 54, 28). These forms of patronage were not just unhelpful to blacks; they were detrimental to their very well-being. Despite the fact that "the Daley machine was a black machine" during the first half of his tenure, black constituents received far less than their fair share of benefits and arguably endured far more than their reasonable share of burdens (Grimshaw 1992, 115).

Over the last half of the Daley administration—from 1960 to 1976—a series of housing, education, and police conflicts drew attention to the administration's racism and ultimately spurred black voters to challenge the grip of the machine. One such battle was a four-year struggle by black community groups to desegregate the city's public schools. The Coordinating Council of Community Organizations formed in 1962, first to force the Chicago Board of Education to admit to segregation and then to push for integration. The council included traditional race advancement organizations like the NAACP and the Urban League, civil rights organizations like the Congress of Racial Equality and the Student Non-Violent Coordinating Committee, church and professional organizations, and newly forming community organizations from the south and west sides (Anderson and Pickering 1986, 90, 114). To publicize their opposition to segregation, the council organized school boycotts and visitations, sit-ins at the board of education headquarters, and public seminars. The board of education finally agreed to create a desegregation program in 1963 after the council filed suit against it, and a year later, two reports confirmed the disparity in the education of blacks and whites and recommended integration. The school board and the mayor nevertheless bowed to the vehement protests of the city's white population and voted against the implementation of a mandatory integration program (Kleppner 1985, 50–54).

The short-term failure of the school desegregation campaign was replicated in the later effort to desegregate Chicago neighborhoods. Hoping to revive the moribund civil rights movement and galvanize federal support for fair housing legislation, Martin Luther King Jr. and the Southern Christian Leadership Conference launched a local desegregation drive, highlighting racial discrimination in Chicago with all-night vigils, marches, and demonstrations. The threat of violence prompted Mayor Daley to agree to talks with the protesters, but the famed "Summit Agreement" was feeble. It had no deadlines and did not require real estate professionals to commit to fair housing practices, and when Daley won a fourth term in 1967 with more than four-fifths of the black vote, the administration felt free to ignore its commitment (Fairclough 1987). Not surprisingly, civil rights challenges regarding the construction and placement of public housing projects met with a similar outcome. In 1966, Dorothy Gautreaux, along with three other tenants, filed suit against the Chicago Housing Authority for discrimination in tenant assignment and site selection (Hirsch 1983,

265; Kleppner 1985, 47). The 1969 ruling in favor of the plaintiffs only revived, rather than ended, the conflict over residential segregation. Over the next five years, the city used a number of stalling tactics to prevent the city council from passing the site approval required by the 1969 ruling. When finally compelled to designate some areas for housing, the city just stopped building, so that "between 1969 and 1980 a total of 114 new subsidized apartments were built—an average of slightly more than 10 per year" (Hirsch 1983, 265).

The conflicts over desegregation were punctuated by a series of violent confrontations between the city's African American population and its police force. In April 1968, Chicago's black residents rioted after the assassination of Martin Luther King Jr., prompting Daley to issue his infamous "shoot to kill" statement, in which he ordered police to "shoot arsonists on sight . . . and to shoot to maim or cripple anyone looting any store" (Kleppner 1985, 8). During the same year, Daley's state's attorney Edward V. Hanrahan created a special gang unit to undermine the activities of the Black Panther party. In 1969 Hanrahan authorized a raid that led to the deaths of Black Panther leaders Fred Hampton and Mark Clark and wounded several others. While officials claimed to have been shooting in self-defense, subsequent investigations showed that "the police had apparently opened fire with little provocation and . . . misrepresented the physical evidence to whitewash their conduct" (Kleppner 1985, 76). This was only one of the more blatant and offensive instances of what was a sustained effort on the part of the Daley administration to contain Chicago's blacks, both physically and politically.

African Americans' first response to these rebukes was to decrease their electoral participation. Voting returns plummeted as early as 1963, and during the next two decades, electoral participation dropped so precipitously that almost two-thirds of the black voting-age population declined to vote in the mayoral election of 1975 (Kleppner 1985, 83). As a result, black wards were no longer providing a significant winning margin for the machine. In 1967, only three of the city's fourteen black wards were among the machine's top producers (Grimshaw 1992, 124–25). In absenting themselves from electoral contests, black voters were expressing their disapproval not just for powerful white machine leaders, but for black elected officials as well. Although elected and appointed officials continued to reap individualized benefits of status and influence, "the 'selective incentives' and 'insider privileges' that are extended to elites did not reach the masses" (Ferman 1996, 35). This withdrawal from electoral politics had a class dimension to it. The Second and Third Wards, where Douglas/Grand Boulevard was located, "did not turn against the machine so much as they turned away from politics" (Grimshaw 1992, 119). Middle-class voters also retreated from the machine. As a group, they had long been ambivalent or hostile toward machine politicians (Grimshaw 1992, 119; J. Wilson 1960, 66). During the last few years of Daley's tenure, voters from the more affluent black wards on the city's far South Side became the least likely to support the machine, and in 1975 and 1977 they provided "the organization's candidate the least support of all black wards in both mayoral primaries" (Preston 1979, 35). Yet these more affluent voters did more than withdraw from the machine; they also attacked it, running independent candidates in several elections. Despite their candidates' temporary staying power, three of these wards were able to elect three independent aldermen between 1963 and 1967 (Kleppner 1985, 86–90).

These electoral strategies, like the civil rights organizing that preceded them, were limited in their success. Not only did the mayor maintain his discriminatory practices in housing, education, and criminal justice, but as black margins diminished, he chose to shift his electoral base. Daley began to court white ethnic voters, and "rather than renegotiate its relationship to the [black] electorate, the machine fought back, substituting symbolic appeals for the decline in material resources . . . [becoming] the defender of white racial interests" (Ferman 1996, 33; Grimshaw 1992; Kleppner 1985, 74–78, 82; Preston 1979). Despite these setbacks, the challenges waged by black voters had significant implications for both the organization of racial politics and the future of neighborhood development. One consequence of these campaigns was that they encouraged Black Belt activists to use a protest framework to understand local conflicts (Ralph 1993; Gills 1991). As they formed alliances with local branches of national civil rights organizations, they began to define neighborhood issues as part

of the broader struggle for civil rights. They came to see the problems facing blacks as a function not just of segregation, but of a lack of community
control (Gills 1991). A second and related result was that these campaigns
disrupted the brokerage relationship endemic to the black submachine. As
many scholars have argued, support for the machine was dependent on its
ability to suppress issue-based politics, particularly in electoral contests. Yet
in raising the issue of discrimination and publicizing it through marches,
demonstrations, boycotts, and other direct-action techniques, black activists
broke the unspoken agreement between the machine and its beneficiaries.
As the Democratic Party withdrew what paltry resources it had thrown to
local black officials, it widened the breach between the machine and black
voters, leaving the latter searching for an alternative. That alternative was
provided by community-based organizations, the establishment of which
was the final and most significant consequence of these campaigns. Not
only were community groups central to the efforts of the Coordinating
Council of Community Organizations, they also laid the groundwork for
the future development of grassroots black political organizations that
operated at least somewhat independently of the machine (Ralph 1993, 227).
These organizations ultimately provided the institutional framework for
the development of a new community development elite.

The New Kids on the Block:
Black Civic Leadership, 1970–85

The community organizations that emerged in the 1960s were varied in
their origins, purpose, and methods. Some were block clubs and faith-based
organizations, which were reminiscent of Alinsky neighborhood organizations and devoted much of their energy to development (Gills 1991, 43).
Others were established under federal antipoverty legislation and emphasized advocacy and service delivery. While they were designed to promote
the political participation of the poor, they were kept on a tight leash by
the Daley administration, which controlled their membership and leadership (Greenstone and Peterson 1973). While these organizations were not
a source of strong opposition to the machine, they nonetheless served as "an
organizational infrastructure of trained organizers and leaders, especially

in poor and minority neighborhoods" (Clavel and Wiewel 1991, 25). The most well known of Chicago's first-wave community organizations were those like the Woodlawn Organization and the Kenwood–Oakland Community Organization, which focused on organizing and building the political capacity of neighborhood residents. They often found themselves in opposition to the city and financial institutions, as they emphasized "opening up access, shaping government policy and practice, or fighting for constituent representation on public boards and commissions" (Gills 1991, 43).

By the next decade, however, the protest and organizing orientation of these community groups was overshadowed by a focus on community economic development. As Rast (1999) argues, Chicago's neighborhood organizations began working "not so much in opposition to growth as in favor of an alternative set of economic development priorities to those being advanced by the city's traditional growth coalition of business, labor and government leaders" (85). They adopted instead what he refers to as a "local-producer strategy," which emphasized preserving and enhancing neighborhoods' abilities to sustain economic institutions. Community organizations in Douglas/Grand Boulevard reflected this broader trend. By the 1970s, first-wave community groups had been largely replaced by a band of community development corporations that emphasized "the technical details of development over community empowerment" (Stoecker 1997, 9; Gills 1991, 44) and provided information and financial aid to those seeking to invest in their homes and businesses. In 1976, for example, the Douglas Development Corporation was founded by a group of Douglas residents. A year later, a group of current and prospective residents formed the Christ Mediator Housing Group to aid residents in home purchase and improvement efforts (Young 1980). Around the same time, residents living in a section of Douglas formed the Gap Community Organization.[3] Neighborhood residents used these organizations to challenge or circumvent the institutional racism that prevented blacks from building wealth and had material consequences for their quality of life. For example, they worked to link private rehabbers with reputable contractors, as well as with loan and legal services (Young 1980). In addition, the staff of the Douglas Development

Corporation gave technical assistance to people trying to move into the neighborhood and rehab their homes.

To some degree, this change in strategy and focus reflected changing economic conditions. The decline in manufacturing employment that began in the 1950s caused Chicago to increasingly lose jobs to the nearby suburbs. These changes hit the city's blacks particularly hard: from 1963 to 1977, for example, factory employment in the near South Side neighborhoods dropped by 47 percent (Squires et al. 1987, 17, 29–30). The newly unemployed could not follow their jobs out of the city, nor were they prepared for the service jobs being created by glittering Loop revitalization. By 1980, Douglas was the better off of the two communities, with 42 percent of its population living below the poverty line and an unemployment rate of 11.3 percent. Grand Boulevard was in worse shape, with just over half of its residents living in poverty and nearly a quarter of them without jobs (Chicago Fact Book Consortium 1990). Such poor conditions encouraged community-based organizations to put more of their energy into economic development (Betancur, Bennett, and Wright 1991; Clavel and Wiewel 1991).

The turn to community development also reflected a new analytical framework that emphasized the neighborhood and its residents as the proper locus and generator of both economic development and political power. That framework emanated in part from black nationalist and black power frameworks emphasizing community control and economic independence (Gills 1991, 43). Another source was the broader neighborhood and economic development organizations with which Black Belt organizations began collaborating. They established links with one another through a series of citywide campaigns, including the fights against the Crosstown Expressway and the proposed 1992 Chicago World's Fair (Rast 1999; Reardon 1990; Ferman 1996, 73; Schlay and Giloth 1987). These ties were reinforced throughout the 1980s as black organizations worked in concert with economic development groups in the Jane Byrne and Harold Washington mayoral campaigns. Groups like the Chicago Area Rehab Network, the Chicago Association of Neighborhood Development Organizations, and the Community Workshop on Economic

Development protested urban renewal policies, redlining, insurance practices—virtually any financing and development strategies used by the city,
banks, and lenders to undermine neighborhoods (Gills 1991, 44; Fisher
1994, 13; Pogge 1992). Working in coalition with these organizations
allowed neighborhood groups to maintain their racial and community focus,
while simultaneously working with other groups on economic issues. In
doing so, they broadened their framework for analyzing the causes and solutions to neighborhood problems. Not only did they come "to perceive their
communities increasingly as sites for both consumption and production"
(Rast 1999, 90), but they saw such activity as a way to combat both contemporary racism and its legacies.

This second wave of community organizations formed the institutional base
for a black community-development elite that, like its predecessors, was
largely middle class. Despite their grassroots origins, these organizations
affirmed the traditional dominance of the middle class in politics and
pressed an agenda that reflected their concerns. The founding members of
the Gap Community Organization, for example, included a bank president,
the owner of a real estate company, the president of the South Side Planning Board, a mortgage banker, and the owner of an accounting firm (Green
1983). These organizations "were staff driven. Even among the few that
were board driven, the central character of their leadership was middle class
by function, orientation, accumulated experience, and training" (Gills
1991, 44). Moreover, they appealed to a black middle class that was experiencing both upward class mobility and the constraints of racial subordination. The 1964 Civil Rights Act, while most well known for outlawing
discrimination in public accommodations, had also helped to increase the
number of middle-class blacks by tracking employment discrimination in
private firms and bringing suits against noncompliant companies.[4] At the
same time, federal agencies modified their own hiring and employment practices, creating a boom in public employment, establishing the dominance of
government jobs among black workers, and establishing contract set-aside
programs that "helped to expand both the size and type of black firms by
giving black entrepreneurs a chance to compete for sizable contracts in a

protected setting" (S. Collins 1997, 22). These policies had minimal influence on working-class blacks, but they significantly expanded both the number of blacks employed in the professions and the types of positions available to them. Between 1960 and 1980, the proportion of black men working in professional, technical, and managerial jobs doubled, with more than half of the increase due to public social welfare programs (Brown and Erie 1981, 308; S. Collins 1997, 25). In Chicago, the percentage of jobs held by blacks increased from 18 to 27 percent from 1960 to 1970, and these trends were evident in the rising incomes of Douglas/Grand Boulevard's middle class (Brown and Erie 1981, 318). Throughout the 1970s, Douglas median family income rose more than a third, from $6,300 to $8,600. In the census tracts that contained newly built middle-class housing, that figure was even higher, ranging from $11,000 to $30,000. Yet these residents still wrangled with issues of racial inequality. Not only did they inherit the physical legacy of urban renewal and neighborhood neglect, but they continued to experience problems with redlining and discrimination by insurance firms, which prevented them from acquiring home and business loans. The experiences of Ernest Griffin, former owner of Griffin Funeral Home in Douglas, are representative. Griffin claimed that "thirty-three times he went to bankers looking for funds to build a new, more modern, funeral parlor on King Drive, but until that last time, the answer was always no the minute he mentioned his address" (Grossman 1985, 1A). In light of the historical and continuing experience of disinvestment, the neighborhood's middle class actively sought new strategies for securing the rewards of upward class mobility.

Even more important than the composition of community-based organizations were their underlying ideology and strategy. Like black elites from Douglas/Grand Boulevard's past, this leadership cadre defined race advancement in a way that reflected both their particular class position and their present political opportunity structure. Steven Gregory (1992; 1998) notes how middle-class residents of one New York neighborhood formed block associations that both privileged their interests as homeowners and defined those interests as a form of racial advancement. In a similar fashion, Douglas/Grand Boulevard community-based organizations addressed economic development issues that reflected their concerns as homeowners, yet they understood themselves as helping all the neighborhood's black residents by, in the words of organization member Delia Chester, "basically . . . help[ing] redevelop this community . . . bring[ing] the Douglas community back." Some of their projects were designed to be inhabited by lower-income renters. The Douglas Development Corporation, for example, built several residential buildings for seniors and Section 8 recipients, including the Corneal A. Davis and Paul Stewart apartments. But because of their focus on private residential rehabilitation and development, they were much less concerned with organizing and mobilizing residents. Instead, Douglas/Grand Boulevard community-development corporations sought individual and commercial investment in the area through historic preservation. While Mid-South would eventually gain the greatest citywide attention for its promotion of historic Bronzeville, the roots of this strategy lay in the plans of earlier organizations such as the Douglas Development Corporation and the Gap Community Organization, both of which emphasize the "rich history" of the area's black population (City of Chicago 1987a, 1987b; Douglas Development Corporation 1979). After discovering the existence of homes designed by Louis Sullivan and Frank Lloyd Wright, for example, Gap residents secured historic district designation for three north-south streets between Thirty-first and Thirty-fifth Streets. And in the six years between 1981 and 1987, Gap owners are estimated to have invested "over $4 million to purchase and rehabilitate the Gap's historic homes" (City of Chicago 1987b).

The strength of this development agenda was enhanced by the election of Harold Washington in 1983. The progressive, neighborhood-based orientation of the Washington administration constituted an impressive reorganization of the relationship between cities and neighborhoods. For the first time, blacks, Latinos, and women occupied key positions in the mayoral cabinet (Gills 1991). Washington also increased community organizations' access to the decision-making *process:* not only did he announce the institution of the Freedom of Information Act on his first day in office, but at the behest of community organizations with limited information-gathering capacity, he expanded the act to include the Affirmative

Information Policy, through which data was collected and made available to community organizations (Kretzmann 1991). Hearings on the city budget were made public, and "a panel of neighborhood organizations was formed to determine the distribution of Community Development Block Grants" (Grimshaw 1992, 188). These policies provided direct support for the development efforts of Douglas/Grand Boulevard's new community-development corporations. In 1986, when Mayor Washington finally wrangled control of the budgeting process from the recalcitrant city council, he was able to implement the financing strategies of the Chicago Works program, which resulted in $1 million in infrastructural improvements in the Second Ward (City of Chicago 1987a). Second Ward alderman Bobby Rush began working with preservation advocates in the mid-1980s to revamp the Thirty-fifth Street commercial strip along the southern end of the Gap and encourage the owners of the nearby Lake Meadows Shopping Center to invest $7 million to update the declining complex. He also helped them maintain and rehabilitate the buildings in the Black Metropolis, an eight-block area of land containing structures that formed the business district of the neighborhood in the early twentieth century. These actions provided both an economic anchor to the incumbent upgrading and a political anchor to the new civic leadership.

The historic preservation strategy adopted by these organizations appealed to young, professional blacks, who, like their counterparts in other cities, were reluctant to move to all-white areas so far away from their jobs in the central city (Grossman 1985; Washburn 1983; Washington 1977; Young 1980; Taylor 2002). These would-be residents were also attracted to the low cost of the Gap's aging structures, some of which were priced under $10,000 at the time. According to Wendy Brown, a development consultant, these residents appeared

> in the early eighties. . . . The first signs of it appeared in the Gap neighborhood, which is between Thirty-first and Thirty-fifth Streets and King Drive and Michigan Avenue, just east of IIT. And then you began seeing some evidence of that toward the late eighties and early nineties south near Washington Park around Provident Hospital.

As Ms. Brown's comments suggest, the changes in the Gap echoed similar but less systematic efforts at historic preservation that were taking place in other parts of the Douglas/Grand Boulevard neighborhood. For example, homeowners at the southeast corner of Grand Boulevard had begun restoring homes along King Drive, Vincennes Avenue, and Washington Park Court south of Thirty-fifth Street (Chicago Fact Book Consortium 1990; Mid-South Planning and Development Commission 1993; Center for Urban Economic Development 1980, 1993). The efforts of these groups formed the first isolated and infrequent efforts at incumbent upgrading that often presages wholesale gentrification. From 1980 to 1990, the median value of homes in Douglas skyrocketed from $25,000 to over $125,000 as a result of their rehabilitation efforts (Chicago Fact Book Consortium 1990). During the same time period, four of the historic homes in the Gap were selling for between $275,000 and $300,000 (City of Chicago 1987a; Douglas Development Corporation 1979; Stevens 1982). As the presence and efforts of the black middle class increased throughout the 1980s, so did the degree of income polarization in Douglas/Grand Boulevard. By 1990, the census tracts in which the Gap is located boasted a median family income ranging from $23,000 to $68,000, while in some nearby tracts, that figure remained as low as $7,400 (Chicago Fact Book Consortium 1990). The efforts taking place in the southern part of Douglas/Grand Boulevard were far less visible than those taking place in the Gap, but together they marked the beginnings of a new era of community development, one in which portions of the homeowning, middle-income population challenged racism through preservation-based community redevelopment.

Preserving Power:
Mid-South and "Restoring Bronzeville," 1987–93

Despite their achievements in incumbent upgrading, Douglas/Grand Boulevard community-development corporations nonetheless felt vulnerable and regarded their hold over community revitalization as insecure at best. One thing they feared was the southward movement of commercial and residential development, which carried the threat of political and physical displacement by whites. Wendy Brown claimed that "when Mayor Daley . . . decided to put in 'the New Downtown' at Central Station, then that's when black people started saying 'Oh my god, they're coming for our neighborhood.'" These concerns made sense given the aggressive development taking place in other areas of the city that had previously been considered too risky for investment. As places like the Cabrini Green public housing development and sections of the West Side caught the eye of both the city and the real estate industry, it did not seem so unlikely that developers could start to move in on their neighborhood (Bennett and Reed 1999).

Concerns about outside developers were magnified by residents' anxiety about the population in and around the neighborhood. In describing the communities surrounding the Illinois Institute of Technology, Jackson Landers, an employee of one area university, suggested that Douglas/Grand Boulevard actually contained within it four or five different communities. He explained that you could

> start with the university itself. IIT's campus is oftentimes described as a microcosm of the city. Perhaps even of the country, in that its racial, cultural and economic composition [has] international students, African American, Latino, Asian, etcetera. So we have a full range of ethnic, racial and economic groups you know, on the campus. To the *east* of us . . . we have the Gap area. Which is a primarily African American community. . . . [It has] a number of historic homes . . . in the area. There's [a] church designed by Louis Sullivan on Thirty-third and Indiana; there are I think, one of the few examples of Frank Lloyd Wright townhouses on Thirty-third and Calumet; there's another house designed by Louis Sullivan on Thirty-second and Calumet; there's just a wide array of old, beautiful stone mansions and mini-mansions in that four square block area. . . . [T]o the *south* is actually Grand Boulevard, which is one of the poorest communities in the country. That's Stateway Gardens, Robert Taylor housing complex. And that's primarily, if not exclusively, an African American community, probably about 80-some percent of the households are headed by women. I think the per capita income is about $1,200 per person per year. So you know, there's a very high youth population in the area that's under seventeen, so that's another reason why the per capita is so low.

Mr. Landers's description points to both the diversity within Douglas/ Grand Boulevard and the separation of its different components from one another. Not only is there an educated, nonblack population tied to the university, but the black population itself is divided by severe economic polarization. He augments this portrait of intraracial and intracommunity variation with a description of its even greater interracial complexity:

> To the *north* of us is another public housing development that's different in its construction and style. . . . Dearborn Homes is one of the older versions. They don't have the high-rises as tall as ten or sixteen [floors]. These are primarily eight- and nine-story buildings. . . . And then to the north, farther north [of] Dearborn is the primarily young white population of professionals that are moving to [places] like Dearborn Park or Central Station or a number of the older warehouse buildings that are now being converted to lofts. To the *west* of us is the Bridgeport community. Bridgeport has been primarily known as an Irish, though not currently so, working-class community. Home to many mayors. There have been significant racial tensions historically in that community between the working-class white ethnic populations and other groups that were either moving in or adjacent to. So it's a really—a diverse community economically, diverse racially, culturally.

With these words, Mr. Landers captures another important feature of the Douglas/Grand Boulevard neighborhood: it not only includes, *but is surrounded by*, sizeable and powerful nonblack populations and institutions, such as Michael Reese and Mercy Hospitals, the Illinois College of Optometry and De La Salle High School. Thus, while Douglas/Grand Boulevard's individual residents are primarily black, they are not the only significant members of the community. White institutional residents, while perhaps a numerical minority, were important, legitimate, and powerful neighbors who could not be ignored.

Community development corporations were particularly leery of the Illinois Institute of Technology because of its hand in the urban renewal that took place less than a generation before. The university painted itself as having been responsible for "revers[ing] the blight" that plagued the neighborhood in the 1950s and for taking "responsibility for rejuvenating its environment" (Long 1996). The community's eventual decline, it suggested, was due not to the university's actions, but to the spread of public housing. But urban renewal was a not-so-distant memory for some community members, many of whom remembered things differently. In addition to commercial property loss, residents remembered the role of white institutions in displacing blacks: on a tour of the community, one longtime resident pointed out that several apartment complexes were

> the result of black displacement. A lot of black people lived in Douglas. Maybe the area wasn't pretty, but. . . . Then New York Life Insurance Company and Michael Reese Hospital decided that they wanted the land. As a result, forty-five to fifty thousand people were displaced.

Despite all its efforts, the university had suffered from the incomplete investment in the neighborhood. By the late 1980s, the school's enrollment was declining and its faculty retention efforts were less than successful. In a well-publicized 1995 speech, President Lew Collens claimed that the university's location got "mixed reviews in the marketplace," explaining that "the perception of crime, the location amidst CHA high-rises . . . and the lack of an immediately adjacent university village with shops and entertainment, provide significant recruitment deterrents." The university realized that its continued growth and vitality depended on comprehensive reinvestment in the entire neighborhood. As one administrator explained it, the university

> got a grant from the McCormick–Tribune Foundation to . . . enhance the campus: do some work at the student residence halls, the athletic facilities, and general upkeep of the buildings, et cetera. And one of the anticipated outcomes of that grant . . . was to attract additional capital, capital investment to the area. We at IIT thought that . . . capital could be attracted a lot easier if there was a designated land use plan or plan from the area. Historically what had happened had been some corporate development, i.e., Lake Meadows Prairie Shores, South Commons; there had been some institutional

development—Michael Reese, Mercy, IIT; there had been . . . some building. But it wasn't really coordinated in the larger scheme of things. We thought that, in order to attract that money, we [should]—you know, probably . . . have a plan for the area.

Faced with the efforts of developers and the university's plans, Douglas/ Grand Boulevard community-development corporations felt that the most serious problem facing the neighborhood was that it "had no indigenous planning infrastructure. Consequently, the community was vulnerable to being defined from without, and it lacked an articulated vision and a constituency in back of that vision to resist disinvestment" (South Side Partnership 1999).

Hostility toward the university was reignited in 1989, when it sought to shut down the local public transportation station at Thirty-fifth and State Streets. The plan crystallized black residents' concerns over community control of neighborhood revitalization and set off a firestorm of protest. In recalling the meeting, one resident said

the community went up in arms about that. . . . It was havoc. They were talking about rerouting it [the Red Line] at the time. Rerouting it away from their campus so they could have the room to expand. That's what they wanted to see happen. And everybody in the community was like, "We do *not* want to see that happen. Because we depend on that for our work, our school." And they were like "Well ridership is down." Ridership will be down when you demolish a lot of the houses, right. And decentralize the neighborhood, ridership's going to go down. But those who are left [are] dependent on that El in order to get to and from work.

After sustained protest, Douglas/Grand Boulevard organizations decided to collaborate with the university, a decision that was prompted by several factors. First, the two shared a common concern about the lack of local economic development. While community groups opposed the university's plans to disrupt local "El" train service and suspected its motivations, the university's concerns reflected and overlapped with their own. At the same time, community-development corporations faced a shrinking pool of funds for their activities. Where previously they had relied on Urban Development Action Grant and Community Development Block Grant resources, federal funds like these had been shrinking since the end of the Jimmy Carter administration (R. Fisher 1994). The ending of this funding stream signaled an even more important change—a consensus that state and local authorities rather than federal agencies should be responsible for initiating and managing urban policy (Bennett 1999; Eisinger 1998). In an environment where urban change was increasingly financed and directed by nongovernment forces, it was even more important that the community residents be involved in formal decision-making processes. Their fear that "another relocation plan was in the offing and that they would have no significant voice in planning nor receive any tangible benefits as community residents" provided additional incentive for collaboration (Gills 2001, 32). The university made efforts to earn the trust of neighborhood residents by hiring long-time South Side resident and former Woodlawn organizer Leroy Kennedy as its vice president for community relations in 1989. While the position itself was not new, the university hoped the selection of Kennedy would help improve relations with the community. The move was not lost on area activists, one of whom cynically suggested that "for Leroy Kennedy, who comes out of . . . a really grassroots organizing position— I think his father was a grassroots organizer or something like that—for him to work at an institution like that, you know and people would say, 'Oh God, that's little Leroy Kennedy! He's our friend!' you know, and 'He's over there!'"

While the initial protests had resulted in significant resident participation, the original membership of the Mid-South Planning Group was small. As one of the founders put it, it was a "group of committed individuals who met . . . every Tuesday over at the King Center to discuss how they viewed the future of the community." Yet early participants soon expanded the membership base significantly. They initially attempted to secure funding for a planning group from the McCormick–Tribune Foundation, which was the original funder of the university's campus enhancement grant. The foundation declined, however, insisting that the group develop the plan with the participation of both city officials and community residents. At the funder's behest, the working group expanded its institutional partnership to include the nearby Mercy and Michael Reese Hospitals, De La Salle High School, the Illinois College of Optometry, and First National Bank. It also worked with the Chicago Department of Planning to write a second proposal and was awarded $271,000 in June 1990 (Mid-South Planning and Development Commission 1993). The planning group expanded the number of community members as well, which not only made it compliant with funding requirements, but also mobilized the community development corporation's political base. Thus, from 1991 to 1993, Mid-South employed an organizer and held community meetings designed to identify the problems faced by the residents. In addition to holding regular meetings, Mid-South held four planning charettes to publicize their activities, solicit input, and recruit volunteers. The Bee Building Charette, for example, was held in February 1993 to solicit ideas for the rehabilitation of the former home of the black newspaper the *Chicago Bee*, which was eventually turned into a branch of the Chicago Public Library. Similar meetings were held for the additional committees of the Mid-South Planning Group. At the height of the process, its regular residential membership included not only homeowners, but renters and public housing residents.

Mid-South used planning charettes not just to gauge public sentiment, but as a way to develop blacks' support for the neighborhood revitalization process. Charettes are public meetings held by neighborhood organizations in which attendees discuss and plan for the dispensation of a building or property. While land-use plans involve the long-term participation of a small, dedicated, and often expert group of community members, planning charettes are one-time events designed to attract and involve a larger and more diverse group of people. They generally include introductory speakers and presentations that set the priorities, framework, and background for the session, followed by an array of small group workshops in which participants are encouraged to brainstorm and generate ideas for the project. At the end of the workshop, participants reconvene and present their ideas to the group, and the organizing body solicits continued participation from those present.

Charettes build support for revitalization because they represent the openness of a decision-making process that has historically been closed to the average black resident. This openness is ritualized in the inclusion of community members, past and present, as introductory speakers. This field-note excerpt, for example, shows how the Overton Charette was opened by a young college student who presented a mini–history lesson on the building's founder, Anthony Overton. The director of Mid-South

> introduced her by saying that Chandra Bennet was a student at the University of Illinois at Urbana and that she was "hit with the spirit" to do some research so even though she's not on the agenda, "we'd like to hear what she had to say." Chandra explained that she was researching the portrayal of blacks in marketing at the turn of the century and that she "wasn't finding very flattering portrayals in the mainstream media so I went to the African-American newspapers." She went on to explain where and how Overton had started his cosmetics business in Kansas in 1903, and how he moved to the Chicago area.

Chandra not only builds support for revitalization by celebrating Overton's achievements; her appearance also asserts the community-based nature of the event. The decision to place her on the program was presented as spontaneous and based on genuine interest in her contribution. Moreover, Chandra's inclusion indicates how welcoming the neighborhood planning process was in general. She was a typical resident who stood shoulder-to-shoulder with community elites, and whose contribution to the process was valued as much as that of the well-paid keynote speaker. Thus, her inclusion represented the inclusion of all residents.

Using the information gathered from residents, and with the help of Wendell Campbell Associates, an African American architectural firm, the Mid-South Planning Group began in 1991 to develop a strategic planning document. The plan, "Restoring Bronzeville," was ultimately released in September 1993. Mid-South was only one of three organizations driving Bronzeville's restoration. The second was the Black Metropolis Convention and Tourism Council. Black Metropolis was established in the mid-1990s when Harold Lucas, previously an organizer for Mid-South, left the group to focus on the promotion of neighborhood tourism business development. Lucas and the Tourism Council were primarily focused on winning landmark status for the Black Metropolis historic district, securing funding for the development of one of its structures (the Supreme Life Building), and creating community development partnerships with neighborhood businesses. The third organization in the coalition was the Bronzeville Organizing Strategy Session, whose primary responsibility was to educate and organize residents in support of Mid-South activities. Sokoni Karanja, head of the Strategy Session, was a Gap community resident and the director of Centers for New Horizons, a social service and welfare agency in Grand Boulevard. In response to what Mid-South leaders perceived as elected officials' attempts to wrest control of the community development process from Mid-South, the Strategy Session coordinated or contributed to several development charettes, rallies, and public forums in the neighborhood. They also helped established the Bronzeville Organizer's Alliance, which coordinated the activities of community-based organizations and attempted to mobilize individual residents. Together, these organizations formed the core of the Bronzeville Coalition.

By promoting the area as a heritage tourism destination, the "Restoring Bronzeville" plan both echoed and expanded on plans from the 1970s and 1980s that emphasized the importance of historic preservation. These sites of tourism celebrate the history and culture of racial and ethnic groups through the preservation and restoration of historic structures, districts, and cultural practices. Bronzeville's proposed designation as a heritage tourism destination included two primary components. The first was the designation and development of the Black Metropolis Historic District, an eight-square-block area including a statue and eight buildings that once housed black businesses and social institutions. Plans for the area included a visitor information and technology center that would house online historical and genealogical archives, guided walking tours, and a historic house depicting the life of a "typical" nineteenth-century middle-class black family. The second component of the heritage destination was the development of a "blues district" on one or more of the area's commercial strips. Coalition members argued that using tourism as the driver for economic development would encourage small business development among the community's middle-income residents, which would in turn provide local employment for poorer residents. Such a strategy not only reflected the concerns of the neighborhood's more affluent residents, but it also acknowledged the needs of poorer community members. Most important, it emphasized the importance of maintaining the area's current racial composition.

Mid-South's Excellent Adventure

The "excellent relationship" shared by the university and the Coalition was in many ways a vast improvement over the accommodationist politics of the early and mid-twentieth century. Its very existence represented the reconfiguration of traditional brokerage relationships. Where conservative race advancement organizations like the NAACP and the Urban League were too weak to challenge the black submachine in the 1940s and 1950s, they were augmented (and ultimately strengthened) by community-based organizations of the civil rights period and after. These groups provided an avenue for expressing grievances and pressing demands, and in doing so, they defied black machine officials. They also formed part of the broad-based alliance of neighborhood development groups that in the 1960s and 1970s challenged pro-growth development, countering racial containment and disinvestment with a neighborhood-based approach. The collaboration between Mid-South and the university also reflected changes in the assumptions regarding urban development. The creation of a new black leadership cadre, its challenge to machine politicians, and its participation in broader electoral and development coalitions helped improve the lives of black residents in Douglas/Grand Boulevard and the rest of the Black Belt. Not only did it delegitimize the routine practice of racial discrimination, but it contributed to the redistribution of crucial development resources to black neighborhoods, especially during the Washington administration.

Yet participating in neighborhood planning also placed significant constraints on community organizations such as Mid-South. While partnerships with community elites provided them with strong allies and development resources, it shaped the way they could respond to these conflicts.

This strategy turned the organization's attention away from organizing and thereby diminished their willingness and ability to make demands on the city and control developers. One staff member told me that

> it'd be nice if we could get the plan adopted to the point where it . . . actually directs developers . . . to only build this kind of housing here, or to focus your commercial on this street, but the politics of the community don't allow for that to happen—not just the community, but the larger politics of the city.

While they tried to establish themselves as the organization to which residents and developers should submit their plans for approval, Mid-South had no such authority. Developers did publicize and explain their projects at Mid-South meetings and were often met with pointed questions about the design, timeline, funding, and employment base of the project. The organization nevertheless lacked both the power and the authority to block any particular plan; neither did they establish a formal mechanism for bestowing approval. That developers recognized this fact is illustrated by the comments of Aaron Vargas, an architect who told one Mid-South meeting that, in presenting plans for his upcoming project, he was "asking for your participation, not for your approval or denial." In that sense, Mid-South functioned as worse than a rubber stamp—it served as a *representation* or symbol of community approval, rather than an actual mechanism for it. It was a symbol that developers and elected officials could draw on as proof that they had informed the community or received community consent.

Because it was unable to demand that the city adopt the plan, Mid-South focused instead on its role as a community-building intermediary. In that capacity, said one staff member, the organization aimed to "identify the gaps in services, or, the needs that the community has, and work with other organizations to come up with solutions and then try to identify resources for that." It concentrated as well on economic development by purchasing and restoring buildings, and it provided technical assistance by offering entrepreneurial training and assistance to residents starting businesses or renovating projects. To the extent that it focused on these activities, Mid-South sustained, rather than rearranged, the traditional class bias of neighborhood leadership and development politics. Class concerns continued to shape the trajectory of neighborhood change as they had in the past, though they were expressed in different ways and in relationship to different issues.

If anything, the development of Black Belt development organizations may have heightened class distinctions in Douglas/Grand Boulevard by funneling most middle-income homeowners into neighborhood community-development corporations, while steering poor blacks into service and welfare programs.[5] At a minimum, this institutional transformation complemented the latest shift in the black class structure, highlighted by numerous scholars, in which black elites function to regulate and govern poor blacks. Likewise, Douglas/Grand Boulevard's black community groups functioned as mediators between the neighborhood's low-income residents and its institutional and city allies, particularly in their role as community representatives in public–private planning partnerships. In a graphic description of Mid-South's beginnings, Wendy Brown suggested that

> what ended up happening is IIT, for fear of really having a community uprising—you know them being right across from the projects, and in those days there was sniping from Stateway Gardens into the office building—and so they gave the money down to the city and said, "Why don't you take this money and create a planning district?" And that was actually the origins of Mid-South.

It is unclear whether university officials feared community violence, yet Ms. Brown's explanation of Mid-South's origins is useful because it captures one dimension of the role Mid-South played in the neighborhood planning process. As the organization formally recognized as the community representative, Mid-South acted as the "voice" of Douglas/Grand Boulevard residents. It also functioned as a mediating body, one whose presence helped to mollify irate residents and funnel their anger into less disruptive channels.

Community organizations such as Mid-South, the Bronzeville Organizing Strategy Session, and the Black Metropolis Convention and Tourism

Council claimed to represent resident preferences, and they undoubtedly did when compared to other neighborhood institutions, and possibly even city officials. Their membership was constituted in part by individual residents, and participation in their organizations was open and strongly encouraged. But Mid-South was squarely in the tradition of second-wave community-development organizations. The process of development at which the coalition was now the center, was, in fact, generated by the endeavors of the areas' most affluent residents. Moreover, the leadership of these organizations remained largely middle class and even with their resident constituency, the de facto definition of "community" tended toward the most affluent members of the population. It was the homeowning population in the neighborhood that took the lead in promoting racial heritage tourism and other cultural development strategies as the drivers of neighborhood redevelopment. As the next chapter will show, their doing so set the stage for the articulation of a racial identity based on nostalgia for the Jim Crow era.

CHAPTER 3

Back to the Future:
Marketing the Race for
Neighborhood Development

In May 1996, three years after members of his planning department helped create the "Restoring Bronzeville" land use plan, Chicago Mayor Richard M. Daley established another panel to make a second set of recommendations for the redevelopment of Douglas/Grand Boulevard (Bey 1996a). The so-called Blue Ribbon Committee was staffed by twenty business and community leaders and represented the Bronzeville Coalition's success in gaining the city's attention. Despite the apparent victory, the coalition was less than enthusiastic. One staff member at the Mid-South Planning and Development Commission described the move as the mayor's effort "to take credit for what is already happening . . . to take credit for what happened in Bronzeville." As participants in the planning and implementation process, neighborhood residents were authors and stewards of Douglas/Grand Boulevard's redevelopment, something they could not be as outsiders to the Blue Ribbon Committee. Only one of the committee's appointees was active in neighborhood organizations, a fact, Mid-South's executive director griped, that made "it likely the board will be controlled by City Hall" (Hill 1997, 4).

Not only did the committee's plan challenge Mid-South's position as author of neighborhood revitalization, it also contested the boundaries and meaning—the very existence—of the Bronzeville community itself. Contrary to the "Restoring Bronzeville" plan, the Blue Ribbon Committee report defined Bronzeville as a smaller area, one "generally bounded by 31st Street on the North, 39th Street on the South, the Dan Ryan Expressway on the West, and Cottage Grove on the East" (City of Chicago 1997). Randolph Jeffries—an original member of Mid-South and a participant in the Bronzeville Organizing Strategy Session—complained that some of the committee members

> don't even know where Bronzeville is. One of the members of the Blue Rib-
> bon Committee, I heard him say, 'I never even knew this *was* Bronzeville.'
> He said that twice to me! And then, some of them didn't even acknowledge
> that it was Bronzeville. [They say that] it's overrated. But regardless, you
> know. *This is what we've decided it is!*

Mr. Jeffries's comments point to a pattern that shaped the behavior of Bronzeville Coalition members even though they did not often articulate it: notions of community are constructed, subject to constant challenge, and in need of continual maintenance. Because of this fact, members of Mid-South "decided" what the community was, inscribed their notion of black community on both the physical and ideological environment, and—as Mr. Jeffries points out with exasperation—they had to defend these notions to both those who lived in the neighborhood and those outside of it.

This strategy—of making, marking, and marketing neighborhoods— reflects recent trends in urban economic development. Postwar economic changes have forced cities to rely on tourism and cultural development to regenerate deteriorating downtown areas (Boyer 1992; Judd and Collins 1979; Law 1992). These efforts, at both the city and the neighborhood levels, are "underwritten by an explicit marketing text, a strategy of 'place advertisement' which . . . defines a commodity laden with mythical content" (Mills 1993). As they compete for tourists, localities use these narratives to create an idealized vision of urban space, to distract visitors from the city's less appealing qualities, and to distinguish it from would-be competitors (Kearns and Philo 1993; Kotler, Haider and Rein 1993; Judd and Fainstein 1999; Holcomb 1999). Douglas/Grand Boulevard's transformation into Bronzeville is therefore not a random revision of community boundaries and meaning: it is a calculated use of place marketing in a context where such strategies are crucial to the economic survival of communities.

Place marketing has received a significant amount of scholarly attention. What is less frequently discussed is how remaking place depends on remaking race. Often the latter is achieved through the wholesale displacement of one population by another (Muñiz 1998). Other times it is accomplished through the public policing and degradation of populations that do not fit the image that place entrepreneurs are straining to achieve (Pérez 2002). The Bronzeville Coalition sought to avoid both these outcomes: instead they constructed a narrative about the neighborhood's past that they used as the basis for claims about its present and future. These claims focused on both the course of development and the nature of collective racial identity. Thus, they refashioned popular depictions of place by refashioning portrayals of its inhabitants.

Reimagining Place and Race

According to Gieryn (2000), place is constituted by three things: geographical location, material form, and social meaning. The geographic location of Bronzeville was fairly well established by the multiple development plans that identified Douglas/Grand Boulevard as the center of black Chicago in the early twentieth century (City of Chicago 1984, 1987a, 1987b; Douglas Development Corporation 1979; Center for Urban Economic Development 1986). Although they sometimes held competing definitions of Bronzeville's exact boundaries, the majority of plans focused on the areas around Thirty-fifth and Forty-seventh Streets, east of the Dan Ryan and west of Lake Michigan. They also echoed one another's assertions about the designation and location of historically significant buildings. In the early 1990s, when the Mid-South plan was published, the material form of Bronzeville consisted of the private residences, public housing units, and historically significant commercial buildings in the Black Metropolis. What remained most malleable at the time was the meaning attached to this neighborhood, and community developers deliberately adopted a place-marketing strategy that would allow them to reshape both place and race.

Marketing Place: Making Claims to Space

The place-marketing strategy that Bronzeville coalition members used derived directly from the "Restoring Bronzeville" plan's focus on heritage tourism destinations. These destination sites combine what have generally been regarded as two separate forms of tourism: heritage tourism, which is concerned with places, people, and practices deemed historically significant, and racial tourism, where "the prime attraction is the cultural exoticism of the local population and its artifacts" (Van den Berghe and Keyes 1984, 344). Both forms of tourism require the creation of a cultural product that consumers will find interesting and pleasing. Heritage scholars insist that while the terms *history* and *heritage* are often used interchangeably, the former is the remembered record of the past and the latter is "a contemporary commodity purposefully created to satisfy contemporary consumption" (Ashworth 1994, 16). The racial tourism product is similarly "modified according to [the] perception of what is attractive to the tourist" (Van den Berghe and Keyes 1984, 346) and has just recently become an important feature of the leisure- and tourism-oriented development strategies of U.S. cities (Dickinson 1996; Eskridge 1998). It was spurred, in part, by federal and corporate initiatives to increase the awareness of ethnic tourist districts and cultivate opportunities for minority-owned, tourism-related business (Doggett 1993). In particular, cities are focusing on the African American tourist, whose favorite travel activities include "visiting historical places and attending cultural events or festivals," and whose participation in these activities ranks far above that of other groups (Hayes 1997, 44). Residents and entrepreneurs in black neighborhoods, eager to revive their devastated neighborhoods, are understandably supportive of these efforts. Unlike development policies of the past, these efforts are predicated on the existence of minority populations and businesses. Moreover, promoters ensure that this endeavor "will not only increase income and create jobs for cultural minorities but also enrich cultural and community pride and values" (Doggett 1993, 8). As one trade journal enthusiastically exclaims, "Claiming Our Heritage Is a Booming Industry!" (Hayes 1997, 43).

These strategies exemplify an important distinction between selling and marketing. While the former involves convincing consumers to make purchases, the latter entails creating a product to fit the tastes of the consumer (Urry 1999). The Mid-South plan acknowledged that its goals hinged particularly on marketing, on both "changing the negative perception that many outsiders now have of the area . . . [and] the creation of both a new image and a new reality for the area" (Mid-South Planning and Development Commission 1993, 96). Residents themselves sometimes held these negative perceptions. On one bus tour of the neighborhood, our neighborhood guide suggested that "the fundamental question we have to ask ourselves is, who wouldn't want to live in a safe place that's this close to the heart of the city?" The older black woman sitting next to me muttered to herself, "Yeah, but what about that 'safe' part?" Not only did residents and outsiders see the area as unsafe, they also viewed it as a place where investment would be wasted (Feder 1994). According to one planning professional, developers had

> perceived it as being dangerous and being undevelopable because of the high concentrations of public housing. They witnessed the disinvestment, if you will, over the years, people moving out and abandoning their property and they felt that, you know, it's never gonna happen.

To counter that view, redevelopment supporters deliberately reconstructed the neighborhood's black history, tailoring it to the desires of potential consumers. Steven Anthony, a long-time community member and frequent neighborhood tour guide, told one of his audiences that

> there are many terms we could use [to describe the area]. "Black belt" refers to the whole area. "Black Metropolis" refers to the historic buildings. We use "Bronzeville" now because it's sale-able. We couldn't call it the Black Belt and sell it to anyone but me [a black man]. Bronzeville sounds nice and romantic.

While coalition members used these place images to try to accomplish economic goals, they also drew on them to achieve a number of political and cultural objectives. The reconstruction of history and culture on which they relied is just one form of imagined community used to legitimize institutions and values (Anderson 1983). The Bronzeville heritage was specifically used by coalition members to assert and legitimize African Americans' right to remain in the space designated for revitalization. As the previous chapter illustrated, neighborhood activists had long felt the need to assert that right, in part because of the particular history of the neighborhood. Yet their sense of urgency about this issue was triggered during the establishment of the Mid-South Planning Group. Portia Silk, an active member of multiple coalition organizations, described for me the moment when she realized the significance of the place-marketing metaphor:

> You know, probably one of my eye-opening days was when we were . . . getting ready to have, you know, the opinion leaders and the banks and the [developers], you know . . . talk about [a planning group] being formed. But the conversation is about the name of the community, [and] one of the names that apparently has been bantered around would be East Bridgeport. I'm going, "Oh my God!" No way. That, I knew, couldn't happen.

The significance of both the suggested name and Ms. Silk's reaction is apparent only when placed in the context of Chicago's political and racial history. Bridgeport is a mostly white neighborhood west of Douglas that has a long history of racial antagonism and organizing against black residents (Biles 1995). Although the neighborhood had recently seen an increase in the number of Asian American and Latino residents, blacks constituted less than 0.1 percent of the area's population in 1990. Even since then, Bridgeport has remained a site of significant racial violence (Main 2004). In 1997, the ward in which Bridgeport is located received the second highest number of hate crime reports in the city. It was also home to two of the three suspects in the infamous attack on Lenard Clark, a thirteen-year-old black boy who was beaten into a coma in a nearby park (Thomas and Marx 1997). The neighborhood was also the home of several of Chicago's mayors, including the Daleys, whose policies had undermined the economic health of the Douglas/Grand Boulevard community for decades (Hirsch 1983). The name itself signals hostility, violence, and racial privilege. The last thing it signified was black people. Ms. Silk continued on to explain how, in response to the suggested neighborhood designation, she began to emphasize African Americans' history and role in the neighborhood, and to direct the discussion back toward the black community:

> Ms. SILK: So now what they're asking is for me to come to the table and try to weave in the community perspective. . . . [I am] calling the campaign Restoring Bronzeville.
>
> INTERVIEWER: Why was that important?
>
> Ms. SILK: Because I'm doing this thing where they're looking for a name. . . . And this East Bridgeport has jumped on the table. And so I'm now taking it back through a strategy of "we need a campaign to involve people." Grady [Karl] knows what he's doing. He knows he's doing consensus building. But I'm doing [it] from a marketing PR perspective, I'm doing education and awareness of the area. . . . We want to acknowledge that it's Bronzeville, because it means that what once was can be again. . . . That's why we're restoring it, not building it, not creating it. We're talking about we want to educate people on the historical contribution, all these things. I'm showing them why it should be [Bronzeville].

Ms. Silk's comments demonstrate activists' awareness that place marketing plays both political and economic functions. She identifies a political process of "consensus building" that Mr. Karl is using to mobilize support for the redevelopment agenda, while she is simultaneously engaged in the process of selling the neighborhood to would-be investors and planning partners by promoting it as a site of black history. As her comments reveal, even the use of the word *restoration* is designed to emphasize the place of blacks in the area. It draws attention away from the history of the native and immigrant white populations that preceded black migrants and, by extension, promotes the idea that Bronzeville, rather than Bridgeport (blackness, rather than whiteness), is the proper referent for the emerging neighborhood.

At its simplest level, then, the concept of historic Bronzeville acts as a model for what the neighborhood could be: it is the centerpiece of a strategy of place advertisement designed to encourage investment in homes and businesses. But Bronzeville is more than just a marketing ploy for urban economic development: it is also a political tactic, a redefinition of the boundaries and content of community. The notion of the neighborhood as historically significant allows the residents of Douglas/Grand Boulevard to define themselves as integral to redevelopment. Portia's associate, Grady Karl, suggests that the notion of Bronzeville goes beyond justifying a black presence in the neighborhood. For him, Bronzeville

> carries with it the whole struggle of black people. . . . And it is a clear tool for us as African Americans, to claim a turf. To claim that turf and to redevelop that turf and to fight off those outside forces who would like to take that turf from us, who care nothing about our struggle, historically.

In this remark, Mr. Karl argues that coalition activists are justified in using heritage as a tool to preserve not just their place in, but their control over, the neighborhood. The Bronzeville designation not only names history a desirable commodity, but offers African American residents the opportunity to portray themselves as the natural legatees of that history, and therefore essential to the process of redevelopment. In short, place marketing matters in racial conflicts over urban space because at heart, claims *about* the neighborhood are claims *to* the neighborhood.

Marketing People: The Narrative of Race and Reform

Heritage place marketing not only has a number of political, cultural, and economic functions. It is also a key component in the creation of place identities, many of which present the past in such a way "that currently powerful political ideologies and groups can justify their dominance by an appeal to the continuity of the past and present" (Ashworth 1994, 14; Ashworth and Tunbridge 1990). In Eastern European countries, for example, the reconstruction and marketing of heritage in the context of socioeconomic transformation provides economic stability and support for the existing government (Hoffman and Musil 1999; Mitchneck 1998). Moreover, by reviving cultural practices, heritage tourism can "serve as [a mechanism] of collective mobilization," helping to bolster identities that act as a resource in claims against both the state and other racial groups (Nagel 1994, 163; Wood 1984).

Neighborhood leaders were acutely aware that achieving their economic and political goals would require them to transform prevailing ideas about people as well as place. Dempsey J. Travis, a well-known black real estate businessman, expressed this sentiment when he asked, "Who wants to look at a historic building on Martin Luther King Drive, marvel at it, and then get shot?" (Quintanilla 1994, 5). Travis's comment illustrates that Bronzeville, like other places, took its value as much from its residents as from its built environment. Places are considered dangerous not merely because of the buildings they contain. Equally important is the behavior—real and perceived—of the people who inhabit them. Likewise, the value of place is partially based on who one's potential neighbors are, a fact clearly illustrated by historical as well as contemporary housing choices (Seligman 2005; Massey and Denton 1993). Whites often avoid neighborhoods with black residents because of racist assumptions linking African Americans to crime, drugs, and lowered property values. Blacks also express a desire to live near people of the same race, not because of assumptions about whites, but because they feel safer and more comfortable in neighborhoods where they do not have to withstand racism or marginalization (Taylor 2002; Farley et al. 1994). Therefore, attempts to reconstruct a place are always fundamentally related to depictions of the people who live there.

Within this set of constraints, coalition activists have engaged in a strategic reimagining of racial community, reconstructing Douglas/Grand Boulevard as a neighborhood that reached its peak during the first wave of black migration from the rural South to northern and urban areas. Although Chicago's black residents were successful in establishing a wide array of economic, political, and social institutions to ease their adjustment to urban life, the strategies adopted by migration-era leaders were no match for the physical segregation, economic marginalization, and political exclusion that African Americans faced at the time. Yet in public descriptions of that history—including promotional materials, tours, development charettes, and public education meetings—redevelopment supporters emphasize blacks' accomplishments at the time, and claim that Bronzeville was marked by four principal characteristics.

First, they describe it as including an enormously successful middle class. Coalition members often refer to historic Bronzeville as the "economic capital of Black America" and are quick to recite the achievements of the early twentieth century's black elite. These sources are most likely to mention entrepreneurs like Joseph Jordan, Anthony Overton, and Jesse Binga, men who constructed the buildings and founded the businesses that make up the "Black Metropolis." In the local paper, the *South Street Journal*, Harold Lucas of the Black Metropolis Convention and Tourism Council argued that prior to the Depression, economic institutions in the neighborhood

> had become so powerful and prosperous that in 1925, the main business district on south State Street between 31st and 39th was known internationally a[s] the Black Wall Street of America. (1997, 3)

This portrayal highlights the financial success of black business owners, the miniscule percentage of the black population that was able to establish and sustain an economic enterprise in the early twentieth century.[1] Although promotional materials and events do not often make claims about the number of residents who fit into this category, the disproportionate amount of attention paid to this segment of the black population elevates their importance and gives the impression that affluent blacks were numerous, and their impact far-reaching. In the swell of enthusiasm, supporters implied or even stated outright that "black-owned and black-operated businesses were the norm, not the exception" (S. Davis 1996, 1).

In fact, redevelopment supporters often portray the successes of these men as successes for the race. During a planning charrette, journalist William Ingram explained the inspiration and pride he felt as a young man, knowing that blacks built and owned buildings in his neighborhood. He recalled going by

> the old Pythian Building and be[ing] so impressed that black people [in that era] had enough ambition to build a nine-story building. The Binga Bank,

that was the first skyscraper I ever saw—it was a skyscraper to me. . . . I went over to Thirty-fifth and South Parkway, I had never seen a black statue before. The Supreme Life Building, the Chicago Metropolitan Mutual Life Insurance Building—we don't realize the total psychological impact of this achievement, as meager as it is.

This comment illustrates how those who are reimagining Bronzeville's history often interpret individual entrepreneurship within the framework of racial uplift, the crucial assumption of which is that the actions of the few reflect well on the many (Gaines 1996; Drake and Cayton 1993). Building structures involves creating physical monuments to the potential and abilities of the entire race, in part because it disproves assumptions about group inferiority. Thus, these buildings are seen as achievements of which the entire community can be proud.

The emphasis on black entrepreneurship is related to a second claim about Bronzeville—that it was independent of white control. One common tendency among Bronzeville supporters is to refer to the area as "a city within a city." Coalition members often assert that during its golden age, the community was nearly self-sufficient because, as the "Restoring Bronzeville" plan argues, "the goods and services to support the black population were . . . supplied from within the community itself" (Mid-South Planning and Development Commission 1993, 19). According to some older residents, leaving the community was neither necessary, nor desirable. Steven Anthony, a proponent of redevelopment and a long-time resident, told one tour group that

> there was the foundation of the economic, political, and social system inside the larger community. It wasn't necessary to leave the community, other than to go to your job. . . . We didn't have to go downtown, we could stay in the neighborhood. We had everything we needed right here.

This perspective suggests not only that Bronzeville was independent from white control, but that it was economically self-sustaining, a racial separatist's dream.

Third, coalition members depict the financial and political independence of Bronzeville as being complemented by a tradition of cultural innovation. A Mid-South pamphlet applauds its citizens for having historically "developed their own cultural institutions and forms, built their own buildings, and founded and supported their own businesses." Neighborhood promotion materials often mention a long list of artists and musicians who lived and worked in the area. For example, the "Restoring Bronzeville" plan and other Mid-South literature repeatedly mention "such notables as Joe Louis, Scott Joplin, Jesse Owens, Redd Foxx and Dinah Washington" (Mid-South Planning and Development Commission 1993, 2).

The practice of cultural innovation is closely linked to entrepreneurship: music and dancing establishments are some of the most celebrated of Bronzeville's historic businesses. Neighborhood revitalization proponents claim that the entertainment venues that lined State Street prior to the expansion of the Illinois Institute of Technology created "a vital and thriving cultural scene and an eager audience for jazz, blues, gospel, literature and visual arts" (Chicago Historical Society n.d.). They also insist that Bronzeville did not just feature this music, but was its original source. On one community tour I participated in, our guide told us that blacks have made "three great cultural contributions to this world: jazz, the blues, and what's the third one? Gospel." While these artistic innovations are valued on their own terms, they have a particular economic significance in the redevelopment efforts. Steven Anthony complained that "now we have to go north for BBQ, for jazz. If you don't retain pride in your heritage, then people make you feel ashamed of it, so you reject it. And then they steal it from you and make you pay for the privilege of experiencing it!" Mr. Anthony emphasized the importance of maintaining black cultural traditions, not merely for the joy of experiencing them, but because these traditions are increasingly commodified in the contemporary marketplace.

Cultural innovation includes not just artistic product, but everyday interaction. In particular, coalition members portray Bronzeville residents as having displayed a high degree of social and political cohesion. This racial solidarity is the fourth characteristic that marks the Bronzeville heritage. Coalition members often look back on the segregation era as a time when neighborhood residents lived and worked together without class tensions. In a November 1997 *Chicago Sun-Times* article, Mid-South director Pat Dowell-Cerasoli insisted that "the beauty of Bronzeville in its heydey *[sic]* was that it was home to all people from different economic backgrounds who worked together and played together." This sense of unity is credited with causing, directly or indirectly, the great successes for which Bronzeville is famous. Harold Lucas, director of the Black Metropolis Convention and Tourism Council, suggested that living in close quarters fostered a deep racial unity, "a greater sense of cultur[al] awareness and self-sufficiency" (1997, 3). It was this racial unity, this capacity for class cooperation, that provided the foundation for the financial success of the community. This understanding of a community void of any serious or lasting class conflict is widely accepted and often repeated by residents in public forums. According to Byron Williams, a businessman who left the suburb of Naperville for Bronzeville in the early 1990s,

> there were millionaires, doctors, entertainers and athletes living with housemaids and railroad porters. Everyone lived together because there wasn't anyplace else in the city where they were welcomed. And the community thrived. The money was made in the community and stayed in the community. (S. Davis 1996, 12)

Two things are striking about this portrayal of segregation-era racial solidarity. The first is how neatly it echoes scholars' recent arguments that blacks displayed greater cohesion during the segregation era (W. Wilson 1996). The second is how these assertions, whether made by scholars or lay people, understand cross-class social cohesion as being limited to the sharing of common space. They do not specify kin networks, social ties, or resource exchanges that knitted together African Americans of different class categories. Instead, they emphasize their physical proximity and the benefits brought by an entrepreneurial middle class that lived in harmony with its lower-income counterpart. The common thread that runs through the whole of this vision is the idea that the residents of historic Bronzeville, particularly its middle-class residents, acted collectively and primarily on behalf of the group merely by living near blacks poorer than themselves.

This thread is embroidered by the final component of the vision of Bronzeville's golden era: the explanation of its fall from grace. This descent had two causes, according to coalition members. The first, less frequently mentioned but still relevant, is the urban redevelopment initiated by the South Side Planning Board. Although the board was a multimember partnership supported by the city and several nearby private institutions, the Illinois Institute of Technology is the entity most often associated with this effort. Despite its responsibility for much of the recent damage to the neighborhood, this external source of decline is mentioned much less often than the second: the physical and psychological abandonment of the neighborhood by the black middle class. A story told habitually and almost universally is that desegregation destroyed Bronzeville by allowing its more affluent residents to move away. Steven Anthony, along with many other residents, claims that

> up until 1970, the land and the buildings in this area was 80 percent owned and occupied by people of color. . . . Eighty percent of this area was occupied by the residents. . . . Many of them were older people whose children moved out to the suburbs. . . . They said it wasn't good enough for them.

It is important to note that this explanation includes not just a description of black residential mobility, but a judgment about the motivations of those who moved. Mr. Anthony portrays the decision to leave as a selfish and snobbish abandonment of the community, rather than as an expression of a long-denied freedom of choice.

Although it is not always explicitly expressed, this judgment has specifically racial connotations. Randolph Jeffries claimed that

> there has been a tendency on our part to think that white is better and so we're always running—I mean the reason that this community got so stripped in the first place, is that we always thought that something was better outside here. . . . In '54, when they said "y'all free!" boy, we just, I mean we lit

outta here and buying up these crummy houses the white folks were selling, we bought churches, and all that kinda stuff. And left all these fine buildings down here to crumble. And that's—that's how they felt.

Mr. Jeffries's comment goes beyond Mr. Anthony's, suggesting not only that blacks who left the neighborhood were elitist, but that they were color-struck, wanting so much to imitate whites that they were blind to the richness of resources available to them in their own neighborhood.

This last element of the Bronzeville heritage is particularly important because it elevates the portrayal of the neighborhood's past from a mere description of the past to a full-fledged narrative—a depiction of a series of events that performs additional ideological functions (Polletta 1998). Taken together, the claims about neighborhood heritage tell a coherent story about the neighborhood's past and its transformation. This tale—which might be entitled "The Rise and Fall of Bronzeville"—is a local expression of the Jim Crow nostalgia that marks black politics at the national level. It expresses that nostalgia by celebrating early twentieth-century black culture, locating that culture in the black middle class, lamenting its loss, and fervently wishing for its return. Moreover, it confirms the notion that the collectivist orientation of previous generations was crucial to their success.

This narrative of achievement and decline helps sell the neighborhood by imbuing its residents with heroism and historical significance. It explains how Douglas/Grand Boulevard came to be such a "dangerous place" in a way that accepts dominant interpretations about the effects of concentrated poverty while simultaneously rejecting ideas of black cultural inferiority. Moreover, this narrative replaces the "Urban Jungle" metaphor, which frames poor and minority communities as wild and unmanageable, while portraying gentrifying families and individuals as a necessary civilizing influence (Smith 1992). Where the revitalization of low-income neighborhoods was once dependent on the removal of these less powerful populations, new visions of heritage can "become the foundation for new strategies of urban accumulation" (Mele 1996, 13). As entertainment and culture industries rely increasingly on images of racial difference and urban culture, the populations that supply those images are included, rather than excluded, from those economies. By the same token, racial tourism offers the opportunity for marginalized populations to remain in their communities, to cultivate community pride, and to participate in the benefits of economic regeneration.

Realizing Race and Place

The Blue Ribbon Committee failed to recognize this tale in part because the definition of space and race is not a naturally occurring process. Place must be actively and continually designated, named, and marked in ways that invest it with particular meaning. The restoration and preservation of the eight buildings in the Black Metropolis is one way to accomplish that task, along with the construction and rehabilitation of homes. But acquiring and renovating buildings is a long, expensive endeavor, at which Mid-South and other coalition members have been only marginally successful and over which they have only partial control. Another way that neighborhood organizations can more easily remake notions of space and race is by rhetorically and physically declaring the neighborhood's heritage.

Storytelling: Creating Community Folklore

Social movement theorists, among others, have illustrated that social actors construct their identities in the process of political struggle. While the literature initially emphasized the functioning of this process with identities that were not race-based, it eventually recognized its importance even with racial identities that are mistakenly thought of as "natural" or embedded in law (Robnett 1997). One way identity construction takes place is through framing, the assignment of meaning to social events in ways that guide and promote action and mobilize support (Snow et al. 1986; Goffman 1974). Not only do frames identify grievances, they also assign blame and suggest appropriate solutions, strategies, and targets of action. In doing so, they help "make clear the 'identities' of the contenders, distinguishing 'us' from 'them'" (Polletta and Jasper 2001, 291). A second way identity is constructed is through narrative—the telling and retelling of stories. While frames "represent identities as developed through discursive processes of analogy and difference," narratives describe the individual's place in an evolving process and "in telling the story of our becoming—as an individual, a nation, a people—we establish who we are" (Polletta 1998, 140). One way that coalition members invest space with meaning is through the constant retelling of the Bronzeville narrative. When asked about residents' awareness of Bronzeville lore, one Mid-South volunteer asserted that "there's so much rich history here, in terms of famous people who started here, or grew up here, or were born here, that that information is just common—common knowledge." The mere existence of the history, she suggests, explains why people know and remember it. But as another informant suggested, this history might be best understood as a kind of community "folklore," which is conveyed through acts of formal and informal storytelling.

The folklore around Bronzeville is supported by one academic source in particular: St. Clair Drake and Horace Cayton's *Black Metropolis* is quoted and referenced constantly as providing proof of the emerging vision of the neighborhood. Most people I encountered were familiar at least with the existence of the book, and many people referred me to it when I told them about my project. The following fieldnote describes a conversation I had with a Mid-South volunteer when I first began attending meetings in the neighborhood. One resident

> suggested to me that I read *Black Metropolis*. "I can't remember the names of the authors," she said, "but it's this book, *Black Metropolis*, it's a history of this whole area, it tells all about the migration and everything. I haven't quite gotten through all of it" she said and we commiserated about how thick it is. She also told me that she knew a number of high school students who were familiar with the book and that they were "amazed to know that this is their community, this is what they come from."

Black Metropolis is well known and often cited among community residents, and residents active in the Bronzeville Coalition draw directly from the text to contextualize their understanding of the neighborhood's current conditions.

Grady Karl, the founder of a community organization, credits the book with not just validating this vision, but initiating it. He explains that he

> got involved in Black Metropolis by reading a book *Black Metropolis* and contacted the author who was the last of the living of two people who wrote the book. Horace Cayton and Sinclair Drake wrote the book. Now fortunately I was able to communicate with Sinclair Drake shortly before his death . . . and he challenged me, matter of fact I have the letter that's from him, directly, saying, "This is a great idea to take the history, that's why we wrote the book, we were hoping that the next generation would pick this up and continue to carry it out."

Mr. Karl not only cites Drake and Cayton as a data source for the heritage of Bronzeville, he also proffers the comments of the author himself as further support for the redevelopment agenda. This move is echoed by Portia Silk, who was criticized for romanticizing the name Bronzeville. When older residents claimed the name was not as glamorous and flattering as contemporary developers are suggesting, her response was to tell her challengers that the neighborhood

> absolutely was called Bronzeville, too. If you read the book *Black Metropolis* it's referred [to] there. If you look at, what John Johnson is talking about in his books, whatever. But also, even from a cultural perspective, that's why Gwendolyn Brooks has written a poem called "A Street in Bronzeville." . . . So you know, sort of the Bronzeville name is . . . talking about the cultural heritage!

Ms. Silk points to *Black Metropolis* and other academic sources as proof that her perception of community is not just admirable, but authentic. Her reliance on these sources does not indicate an unthinking revision of history. Ms. Silk herself continues on to admit that "you know everything gets revised. It gets to the point where you erase, tear down everything, you got no memory! And then nobody can tell you were anything!" Instead, political actors realize, to varying degrees, their role in reconstructing history;

but this realization exists alongside their contention that their particular reconstruction is the correct one.

Another set of "sources" that coalition members rely on in their construction of neighborhood folklore are the older residents in the neighborhood, some of whom have actually lived this history and provide testimonies of what life was like back in "their day." When asked if people know the history of the neighborhood, resident Wendy Brown claimed that

> the older people definitely do. They did know the history of that neighborhood. When they built the projects, I presume they built it like that because most of our institutions were there on State Street. Then here comes this school and takes the institutions out. Then all you have left is the projects. . . . They remember that. They remember that.

In short, history is alive for some members of the community. Newspaper and magazine articles delight in the reminiscences of older neighborhood residents. In public meetings as well, older members of the community are celebrated for their stories and experiences—pointed out in meetings, given time to talk, and rewarded with warm applause at the close of their comments.[2]

These tales are the source of the younger generation's knowledge about the past. They learn about Bronzeville's "golden era" through "people's parents or family relatives relating the days when they used to live in the neighborhood." Louie Ogden, a twenty-three-year-old community organization member who lived in the neighborhood all his life, told me that

> when I was younger, my mother used to take me up and down King Drive, and there was actually a . . . it was a story with every building, you know how people do oral histories or whatever? She was like, well this is the Marx brothers' house, and this is where they stayed you know. Or my dad used to say Louis Armstrong was here on Thirty-fifth. . . . My mother grew up with Dinah Washington's little sister.

Mr. Ogden points out how in Bronzeville, history is site specific, linked to particular buildings that serve as reminders and expressions of the past.

Community members who are new to the neighborhood are also edu-cated by their older relatives. One social-service organization director who was well informed about Bronzeville had not moved to the South Side until the early 1970s. When asked how he learned about neighborhood history, he told me that his

> father-in-law was a musician. So he used to tell me about all of the clubs that used to be here. And he told me about Nat King Cole and all the musicians that used to be around here. He was a side man for most of them. And so he, he would talk about [it]. So I knew that the area had a lot of deep, rich history.

Knowledgeable peers may also be a source of information. Many infor-mants credited Grady Karl in particular for being the "visionary" behind the Bronzeville heritage and the push for heritage tourism. Mr. Jeffries explained to me in an interview that

> Grady Karl, who has been here all his life, is one of the persons who helped me understand this place because he was the organizer and sort of, a com-munity politician, everything. And he was the one who first introduced me to preserving all of this . . . the Binga Bank Building, the Overton Building, the building where they just put the library, all of that. The armory. He introduced me to all of that. First time I met him, in '78 was at a meeting over at IIT, we were trying, focusing on preserving buildings. So that came out of that, and then my—a lot of conversations with Mr. Steven Anthony, he's like the community historian. And so between the two of them I really gained a sense of—and my father-in-law—a sense of what this community used to be like.

This admission illustrates how learning this part of the neighborhood's history and folklore was clearly and deliberately linked to the neighbor-hood's long-term historic preservation agenda.

Community folklore is also conveyed through more formal storytell-ing processes, such as the "Neighborhoods: Keepers of Culture" project, an exhibit that detailed the history of four Chicago neighborhoods, including

Douglas/Grand Boulevard. In the early 1990s, the Chicago Historical Society began collaborating with several neighborhood organizations to gather and organize information for the exhibit. In it, ten neighborhood teenagers collected more than twenty videotaped oral histories from older members of Douglas/Grand Boulevard, which were then incorporated into the final exhibit. Much the same function is served by community tours. In 1995, Mid-South began holding an annual house tour to showcase residents' recently renovated homes. The Black Metropolis Convention and Tourism Council also holds tours on request, and a neighborhood tour is even included in the organizers' training class, held by the Lugenia Burns Hope Center. These tours mimic the process of informal storytelling, in that they often rely on the experiences of longtime community residents. Mid-South's 1997 Annual House Tour, for example, was led by Steven Anthony, an eighty-year-old historian who has lived in the community all his life. Not only did he point out the new housing, but along the way, Mr. Anthony drew on his personal experience and extensive historical knowledge to paint a portrait of the traditions of the neighborhood, mentioning spots with which he was personally familiar along the tour, including schools, clubs, and the famous people who used to hang out in them. Tours like this elevate the practice of storytelling to more than personal recollection. The tour guides, museum staff, and researchers who repeat the story of Bronzeville are understood to have and communicate an "expert" knowledge. These sources of knowledge help validate the identity and agenda contained in the plan and assert its vision of neighborhood identity. Unlike personal testimonies, whose accuracy and validity are easily challenged, they contain an air of authenticity and authority. Therefore, their transmission of community folklore also creates new "official" sources of information.

Branding the Neighborhood

The use of narrative is complemented by the more concrete process of *branding*, in which organizations create and display cultural symbols that assert the identity of the neighborhood. The branding process not only marks the area as a historical site, it also creates objects for tourist consumption. Branding in Bronzeville occurs largely through the display of visual arts in the neighborhood's public areas. For example, one of the stops on the city's elevated train system was renamed the "Bronzeville-IIT" stop when it was renovated. It displays two murals, one with the word *Bronzeville* painted in bronze, the second containing portraits of musical artists such as Nat King Cole and Dinah Washington, artists who are commonly referred to as having frequented the neighborhood in its golden era.

The location of these works in the public transportation station highlights their function as markers that identify the neighborhood, and suggests their potential as indicators (for future tourists) that this is indeed a historic area. The Bee Building, one of the structures in the Black Metropolis historic district, holds a painting that performs a similar function. Renovated in the early 1990s as a branch of the Chicago Public Library, the Bee Building stands across the street from the former site of the Stateway Gardens public housing project. Above its entrance hangs a mural that depicts the view one might have had in the early twentieth century, standing across the street, looking at the Bee Building and the ones surrounding it. In contrast to the abandoned buildings, empty lots, and deserted streets that marked Stateway in the 1990s, this painting portrays a thriving thoroughfare, full of businesses and residences, peopled by a variety of well-dressed men and women going about the business of the day. These are just two of the pieces of artwork in museums, parks, businesses, and streets that mark the neighborhood as Bronzeville. Both of these paintings are located in areas that are deteriorating, and each provides a reminder of what the community used to be in its supposed golden era, thereby confirming the specific vision of community contained in the "Restoring Bronzeville" plan.

Another important site for brands is the hoped-for commercial center of revitalized Bronzeville. In 1994, Mid-South began collaborating with the city to design an art project that recognized the intersection at Thirty-fifth and King Drive as the official "gateway" to the Bronzeville neighborhood. Based on its proximity to the neighborhood, the Gateway planning group asked for money from the Metropolitan Pier and Exposition Authority, the administrators of the city's convention center. This instance of branding illustrates the connection between marking space and acquiring resources. One participant explained that the planning process helped coalition members realize that

> we needed to be able to bring people from two big generators: White Sox Park and McCormick Place. And if we could focus them all in at Thirty-fifth and King where there could be a visitor's center, we could send them out into the community to spend money. So, the King Drive Gateway was really thought of as a way of drawing people into the neighborhood, where that, once they arrived there, there would be things for them to do and spend their money while they were happened to be up the street at the convention, or going to a ballgame. . . . So they thought well, if we could create some sort of a gateway into the neighborhood and use the statue [and put] a plaza around it or maybe an arch of some sort, so that people know that they were officially entering this neighborhood, then you know, that will help our cause.

The artwork includes several components. The first is the *Walk of Fame*, which extends ten blocks from Twenty-fifth to Thirty-fifth Streets along King Drive. At both its beginning and end, the walk is adorned with Recognition Panels that promotional materials describe as serving "as a symbolic gateway to King Drive and a unifying element of the Gateway Project" (City of Chicago 1996, 9).

In between, the *Walk* celebrates significant historical and contemporary figures from the neighborhood with ninety-one bronze plaques embedded the entire ten blocks on the sidewalk. And for those who choose to take the whole tour but need the occasional resting place, twenty-three sculptural benches have been placed in plazas and at bus stops along the way. The head of the *Walk*, at Twenty-sixth Place and King Drive, is marked by the *Great Northern Migration Monument*, a fifteen-foot sculpture the artist describes as depicting

> a man wearing a suit made of shoe soles . . . rising from a mound of soles. The soles, worn and full of holes, symbolize the often difficult journey from the South to the North. The figure carries a valise bound shut with rope.

> Though the case appears to be bursting with its contents, upon closer inspection it is empty . . . except for the creative spirit and culture brought from the South.

At the farthest point south, the *Historic Bronzeville Street Map* at Thirty-fifth and King Drive holds a seven-foot bronze map of the Bronzeville neighborhood that includes relief impressions of thoroughfares and buildings, as well as "artifacts culled from Bronzeville's heyday—the mastheads of its newspapers, examples of its musical legacy, advertisements from successful businesses, poems and excerpts from renowned authors, and other souvenirs of 'Negro Progress'" (City of Chicago 1996).

These pieces of work mark the space with not just a generic racial designation, but with the specific, place-based notion of blackness expressed by neighborhood developers. By strategically placing representations of Bronzeville history and culture along a major thoroughfare, the Gateway pieces mark the neighborhood as a black neighborhood and reiterate the vision of community heritage in the "Restoring Bronzeville" redevelopment plan. The impression made and called to mind by these works of art is not Dempsey Travis's random drive-by shooter, but a community where middle-class blacks live side-by-side and in harmony with their less affluent counterparts; where blacks have set down roots and established a history of valuable, viable cultural and economic institutions that benefit the city; where being a good neighbor means being emotionally and financially invested in their community and united across class lines; and where blacks are self-sufficient and in control of their future.

Coalition members also work to involve residents in the manufacture and exhibition of community cultural symbols, a strategy that is directed primarily toward children and young adults and that helps to inculcate personal identification with the markers of local racialized identity (Almada 1997). Throughout the planning and implementation process, community organizations have collaborated on several projects that invite, and sometimes pay, black students to create the art scattered throughout the neighborhood. The murals at the Thirty-fifth Street el station, for example, were painted and tiled by students from area schools, Phillips High and Mayo

Elementary (Bey 1996b). The South Shore Cultural Center commissioned and displayed the drawings of six area high-school students in an exhibit entitled "Young Artists View Today's Bronzeville" (Glanton 1997). High-school students have even been involved in designing architectural plans for the restoration of landmark buildings, including the new Bronzeville Military Academy. The students themselves suggest that the art projects help them to understand and take an interest in the community. The *Chicago Tribune* reported that sixteen-year-old Loretta Taylor, whose work was shown at the South Shore exhibit, said she had passed the Overton Building many times, "but it wasn't until she decided to sketch it that she fully understood what it had meant to the community" (Glanton 1997, 3).

One of the most highly publicized instances of this strategy took place in spring 1996, when the *Chicago Sun-Times* announced a contest for the essay and illustration that best showed the importance of preserving Bronzeville. Area high-school students were invited to submit hand-drawn illustrations featuring one of the eight buildings or essays explaining "why preservation of Bronzeville's landmark buildings is important to all of Chicago" (Black 1996, 3). The *Sun-Times* initially offered the winners a one hundred dollar gift certificate for books or music, but as the entry deadline grew near, South Side residents and organizations added more prizes, including U.S. savings bonds, cash, a copy of Drake and Cayton's *Black Metropolis*, and a day as the guest editor of the neighborhood weekly, the *South Street Journal* (Chapman 1996, 6). Thus a publicity and public education campaign that originally sought to capture the attention of teens and their families grew to become a broad-based community event as individuals and businesses contributed to the winnings.

The comments of Angela Stevenson, the first-place winner of the essay contest, echo the sentiment that the heritage of the neighborhood shaped her understanding of self. As part of her argument for why the buildings should be preserved, Ms. Stevenson argued that they tell her who she is and that

> renovating the Bronzeville landmarks would help to create a more positive image of African Americans. When some think of African Americans they

> think of poverty, pain and projects. Preserving these historic sites would help to put an end to this stereotype. Tearing down these buildings condemns and deprives African Americans of their history. Seeing these buildings helps me to see who I am, where I came from and how the way was once paved for me. Black Chicago life in the 1930s and 1940s should be preserved so that it can be relived. (Stevenson 1996, 31)

With these words, Ms. Stevenson suggests that these buildings, and the history they contain, represent the people that make use of them. For her, these representations not only undermine the negative perceptions that others hold of the neighborhood, but also counter negative self-perceptions that African Americans may have internalized.

The comments of these young people illustrate an important pattern: claims about the neighborhood's history often form the basis for claims about contemporary collective identity. This is apparent in the following fieldnote excerpt, which describes a member of the Bronzeville Organizer's Alliance in conversation with a community volunteer who

> mentioned that she had to go down to Sixty-third to get toys for the kids to sign up for Christmas toy programs. Nina Ellis told her that they did that at Forty-third Street and "you don't have to go down to Sixty-third to get your toys, we take care of our own. . . . That's the spirit of Bronzeville . . . we used to take care of our own and we can do that now . . . we had so many toys, I was on the street trying to find kids to give the toys away to!"

In this exchange, Ms. Ellis explicitly makes a link between what used to be and what is; between the "spirit" of Bronzeville and the behavior of its contemporary residents. Most significant, Ms. Ellis manages to evoke or embody nearly every feature of the Bronzeville identity with her comments. Her reference to the self-sustainability of the community refers not only to its independence from whites, but its independence from other black neighborhoods. She makes this point by distinguishing between Forty-third and Sixty-third Streets, implying, as does the "Restoring Bronzeville" plan, that the Douglas/Grand Boulevard neighborhood is separate from the area to the south. Her assurances about the abundance of toys available through the local program suggest the presence of a class of residents economically secure enough to make almost too many donations to the poor. Their generosity is proof positive of the neighborhood's intraracial solidarity and, together with her management of the program, it serves as one example of the social organization among blacks. As a paid staff member, Ms. Ellis is perhaps more conscious of linking the historical and contemporary identity of the neighborhood. Yet residents of various levels of activism also make this association when discussing the neighborhood's history. One speaker at a charette made the same point when he argued that preserving buildings in the area was important because "we need a sense of history, we need a sense of self-definition."

As the Gateway project shows, the branding of space can take material form, manifesting itself in physical markers that display and assert the presence of a particular population. The presentation of cultural forms may also be more symbolic, taking place through the establishment and repetition of cultural practices. These acts are a form of invented tradition, which Eric Hobsbawm defines as

> a set of practices, normally governed by overtly or tacitly accepted rules and of a ritual symbolic nature, which seek to inculcate certain values and norms of behavior by repetition, which automatically implies continuity with the past. In fact, where possible, they normally attempt to establish continuity with a suitable historic past. (Hobsbawm and Ranger 1983, 2)

The annual Blues Fest, held each year by Mid-South's Economic Development Committee, is an instance of invented tradition, in that it aims to reestablish the custom of public music performance that is a part of the Bronzeville heritage.[3] This event, which hosts local and national musicians and is timed to occur the day before the city's well-known Blues Festival, rarely makes money for the organization. Instead, the festival is a project designed to encourage the norm of community involvement by establishing social and organizational ties among the residents of Douglas/Grand Boulevard.

For example, Mid-South organized the 1998 Blues Fest in collaboration with the Muddy Waters Blues District Business Association, a group of area businesses on or near Forty-third Street. During and after this process, Mid-South staff and committee members expressed their desire to act not as the body that directed the Blues Fest, but as its "facilitator," the resource that would enable the business association to eventually take over the organization of the festival. Mid-South was also directly involved in helping the business association establish its nonprofit status. The purpose of collaborating with business owners was to increase their independence and build their capacity for working together as a commerce association. "Cause you know," one staff member explained to me,

> with all the things going on on Forty-third Street, now is the time to do those things. . . . We are trying to do something where the economic development committee, the business association and the block club can work together, because Forty-third is a precarious strip. . . . We want to work on different projects and the business association can work with the economic development committee and work to sustain [themselves].

The viability of Forty-third Street businesses was particularly threatened by a development plan that aimed to rezone a section of the street from business to residential, eliminating small businesses located in the area. Within this context, the Blues Fest was both a cultural event and a tool for organizing business owners in accordance with the "Restoring Bronzeville" plan.

The Blues Fest also functioned as a mechanism for appealing to larger audiences. One advertisement for the event alerted community members that

> over the years, this event has become a popular and well attended community celebration of the Blues. We want to attract blues lovers from all over Chicago back to Forty-third Street. . . . AS WE AS A COMMUNITY STRUGGLE TO HOLD ON TO OUR HISTORIC BUILDINGS AND PROPERTIES WE MUST NOT FORGET OUR CULTURE AND HERITAGE. This is an opportunity to bring the whole family out to experience and nurture our blues tradition.

This flyer explicitly makes the link between the tradition of the blues and the tradition of community struggle to control the neighborhood. Thus, planning or participating in the event and celebrating the blues is defined as one way that residents and businesses can make political involvement part of the racial heritage and legacy of the neighborhood.

History Lessons

Scholars have noted that neighborhood-based social interactions can be important for political behavior because they help create a strong sense of group identification—that is, they increase the sense of attachment to and salience of particular group identities (Gay 2004; Huckfeldt 1986). Branding and narrative construction are important, therefore, in part because they reinforce the racial identity of the neighborhood for both residents and outsiders. These behaviors are also important because they help create a strong sense of group *identity*—that is, they establish and reproduce a clear understanding of the characteristics and values that make one a member of the group (Fearon 1999).

It is useful then, to consider what the Bronzeville Coalition does *not* say about the neighborhood history, for that reveals as much as what they do say. It does not mean segregation. When segregation is mentioned at all, it is usually for its "unintended positive side effect" of fostering racial unity (Lucas 1997, 3). Some residents even suggest that racial discrimination was inconsequential in the lives of Bronzeville residents of old. "We went downtown," claimed one longtime resident. "Sometimes we weren't welcome, but since this was Chicago, it didn't matter." Neither does Bronzeville mean overcrowding and the inability to find a decent place to live. Rather, the observer's eye is steered toward the wide boulevards and majestic stone edifices lining King Drive, whose style and form can no longer be duplicated. Bronzeville does not call to mind poorly paid, dangerous jobs, exclusion from unions, or domestic service. Nor does it conjure up images of black realtors and businessmen who sought to profit from the captive market created by residential segregation. Instead, we hear about the noble entrepreneurs and politicians who inhabited the area, contributing to race advancement through their professional activities. The less alluring features are all part of Bronzeville's history, but they are not the images being drawn upon and deployed in the process of neighborhood development.

There are many alternate stories that could be told about Bronzeville, all of which could retain the positive spin desired by neighborhood residents, the empirical complexity preferred by academics, and the commodity appeal required by place entrepreneurs. Bronzeville was a place where African Americans went to escape the political suppression of the South and where they made their first significant foray into electoral politics. The migration era marked the large-scale entrance of black men into industrial work, which, although it subjected them to poor working conditions, provided blacks with increased pay. Bronzeville was also the home to one of the strongest branches of the Brotherhood of Sleeping Car Porters, which, partly because of the ties it established with other black organizations, was responsible for defeating the notoriously powerful and abusive Pullman Company. Although particular to Chicago, these conditions reflect what was happening in cities across the Midwest and Northeast at the beginning of the twentieth century, and they reflect the heroism inherent in the efforts of ordinary men and women to make a life for themselves in the context of racial, economic, and gender subordination. They also illustrate the costs involved in developing economic and political strength through coalitions that bridged differences. Yet none of this forms a significant part of the story being told in Douglas/Grand Boulevard. The point is not that the contemporary understandings of Bronzeville are inaccurate, or that redevelopment advocates are somehow being false or deceptive. Rather, the point is that "the terms they appl[y] to their traditional past and to the institutions and practices they [see] as emergent from that traditional past [are] a function of their preoccupations of the present" (R. Smith 1991, 180–81).

One of the principal preoccupations of the Bronzeville Coalition was controlling the image and imagery of the neighborhood, so that they might maintain the racial composition of the neighborhood. In that sense, the narrative that coalition members have wrought has worked its magic, marketing blackness in ways that have sparked the interest of city officials, generated private investment, and slowly changed the reputation of the neighborhood and its residents. Yet as the next chapter illustrates, that preoccupation was just one of many that existed in the neighborhood. Even as neighborhood activists labored to transform Douglas/Grand Boulevard's history into the Bronzeville heritage, they faced opposition not only to their vision of the neighborhood's past, but to their plans for its future.

CHAPTER 4

Ties and Chitlins: Political Legitimacy and Racial Authentication

> Oscar DePriest is a race man. I have never definitely
> found out what they mean by race men, but that is
> what counts. If you can get that characterization you
> are sure of getting the Negro support.
>
> —Neighborhood resident in Harold F. Gosnell,
> *Negro Politicians: The Rise of Negro Politics in Chicago*

In fewer than ten years, the Bronzeville heritage product has gained support both in and outside the neighborhood. Despite the city's refusal to formally adopt the land use plan, city administrators, mainstream and independent news media, developers, and real estate agencies all know the area as Bronzeville. Perhaps most telling are recent versions of tourism and real estate maps that have merged Douglas and Grand Boulevard, expanded them, and renamed them in accordance with the Mid-South Plan. The dominance of the Bronzeville vision goes beyond name recognition: the meaning of the community has changed as well to coincide with that offered by Bronzeville Coalition members. Once infamous among policy wonks as one of the poorest communities in the nation, the Douglas/Grand Boulevard neighborhood is now publicly recognized as a "south side gem" and hailed as an area with a "golden past" (S. Davis 1996). The area is widely recognized as the developing (and developable) community in the mid-south area, and, as a result of the influx of affluent residents, one community real estate agent asserted that the area has "gone from people thinking this is just another ghetto to being considered prime property" (Severinsen 1995, 5A; Rodkin, Whitaker, and Wilk 2004).

Nevertheless, this reconstruction of Bronzeville's history remains a contested issue. In describing her negotiations with neighborhood organizations, Nell Rochester, a Metropolitan Pier and Exposition Authority representative, asserted that

> we've gone back and forth, back and forth, back and forth about "what are the limits of Bronzeville?" . . . There are some people who don't even want it called Bronzeville. . . . I've been at meetings where they just had to table that discussion because they couldn't get past the name. And people got so caught up in the fact that [an organization] was referring to the area as Bronzeville—they'd say, "It's not Bronzeville. It's not Bronzeville!"

Objections to the name *Bronzeville* are based in at least two different complaints. Some residents object that the designation is historically inaccurate. Portia Silk describes how one resident reacted after he first heard the area referred to as Bronzeville:

> At the end of that show he comes over and says, "Portia, you guys have just marketed this whole Bronzeville thing. And you've glamorized it. Nobody— and I grew up in this area—nobody walked around and called this community Bronzeville. We just didn't. And if somebody said that you were from Bronzeville, you wanted to fight them. 'Cause they basically were saying 'You from Bronzeville, you from whatever, shanty-town.' We always got a name, whatever. . . . And what you all have done, what *you've* done, you've marketed this into something glamorous. And it's just not."

The resident objected not to the marketing of the neighborhood per se, but to the ways that this marketing ploy distorted and ignored his personal experience and that of others in the neighborhood. In objecting to the "glamorization" of what was once a slum, he echoes the concerns of scholars who object to the homogenizing and falsifying effects of urban tourism strategies (Sorkin 1992).

Other residents object less to historical inaccuracy and more to the racialization of the area. This objection makes sense for residents of the Gap, whose surrounding area contains a university, a hospital, a private high school and two large apartment complexes, all of which serve or are managed by a racially integrated population. One participant in early meetings between Douglas/Grand Boulevard residents and a McCormick Place representative explained that some residents felt the name was inappropriate because the area was "multicultural":

> To call it Bronzeville ties it only into one cultural [group], which is black Americans. . . . It is majority [black]—but still. They don't want that to be the identity of it. And these are blacks who are saying this.

Similarly, another early participant in Mid-South described how some residents reacted to her referring to the neighborhood as Bronzeville: "These women say, we are not bronze, black anything, we're a diverse community and we don't want to be called that. And it's our community, too!"

While they might appear at first glance to be superficial and inconsequential, these disputes over place names are quite meaningful. They are the symbolic dimension of substantive struggles over the course of neighborhood development; as such, they reflect a number of competing personal and organizational agendas. Some of the clamoring for a less racialized name, for example, stems from a desire for an integrated neighborhood. Delia Chester told me she is

> hoping to see this area come back to be diverse. And when I say that I mean, that we do have black, white, Spanish, Chinese, all of us, some of us, all living together; and that anybody's welcome on my street; that it will become a street that's also frequented by students [from] IIT, De La Salle, students at the hospitals, you know; that we become more of a busy community, upscaled, so to speak. . . . I think it has to if it wants to survive. I think just like we don't want nonblacks, white or whomever preventing us from moving up, we shouldn't do it either. It doesn't help. . . . I think because this community has a black base, it doesn't mean that we can't have some diversity. And I don't know if the name, whatever we end up calling it, how big a key is it going to play to someone wanting to come here.

Ms. Chester expresses interest in a racially diverse neighborhood, as do many of her neighbors. But her comments also reveal another, less explicit concern: that an all-black neighborhood may not be affluent enough to sustain itself financially.[1] She wants the neighborhood to be economically diverse, containing the businesses and amenities that will entice nearby non-black populations to spend money in the neighborhood. She cares less about its resonance with personal history and more about the impact it may have on neighborhood revitalization.

As these comments illustrate, intraracial conflicts over the course of neighborhood development were often couched in the language of authenticity. Although coalition activists presented "Restoring Bronzeville" as the direct expression of resident preference, the planning process leading up to it nevertheless drew sharp lines between middle-income and lower-income residents, and increased tensions between community leaders and black elected officials. In the preceding remarks, the dispute over the racial composition of the neighborhood was played out through debates over the "real" name of the community. In a similar fashion, power struggles between local leaders were often expressed in debates over who was a "true" member of the community. These debates over authenticity shed light on how constructed identities matter for politics—that is, how participants use them to negotiate and manage conflict. Both black politics and neighborhood development analyses often operate "as though there [were] a monolithic community," downplaying the divisions that exist *within* urban black communities (Bratt 1997, 24). As a result, these literatures sometimes overlook the strategies African Americans use to justify competing perspectives and behavior. In Douglas/Grand Boulevard, coalition members drew upon the notion of collectivism contained in the depiction of Bronzeville heritage and adopted that notion both to assert their own legitimacy and to challenge the legitimacy of their opponents.

Authenticity and Representation

The notion of authenticity is easily recognizable in common pop culture references to "Oreos" and "bananas."[2] These food metaphors are used to describe the hidden nature of racial and ethnic minorities, suggesting that individuals who have the phenotypic characteristics that lead them to be placed in a particular racial category may, at heart, lack the culture, emotions, or attitudes that would make them true members of that group. Standards of authenticity posit more than a unique or particular experience as a result of racial designation. As Favor argues, "The difference between 'uniqueness,' that which distinguishes, and 'authenticity,' that which privileges distinct features, lies herein: authenticity derives from uniqueness, but it also fixes that uniqueness to a limited range of possibilities" (1999, 5). In other words, standards of authenticity assert that only one particular experience or expression of blackness qualifies as the "true" or "correct" one. These commonsense understandings of racial authenticity treat race as a natural category that reflects something inherent to the group. Social scientists' treatments of racial authenticity, by contrast, have criticized its essentialism and highlighted its shifting and ultimately insubstantial nature. Sociologist David Grazian, for example, has defined authenticity as "the ability . . . to conform to an idealized representation of reality: that is, to a set of expectations regarding how such a thing ought to look, sound, and feel" (2003, 10–11). Black racial authenticity, then, can be understood as the ability to reflect and conform to expectations regarding what constitutes "true" blackness.

Markers of racial authenticity are neither random, nor stagnant. Rather, they are constructed within and in response to particular ideological, economic, and political contexts. As these contexts change, so do the specific referents for black authenticity—yet many observers define blackness as fundamentally rooted in poverty and suffering. Harlem Renaissance writers, for example, frequently defined blackness in terms of geography and class (Favor 1999). Their vision of authenticity emerged in response to black urbanization and proletarianization and was part of a self-conscious effort to distinguish the "Old" Negro from the "New" Negro. Similarly, recent attempts to correct the racial bias of Western thought and culture have spurred numerous black scholars to assert the existence of black literary and intellectual traditions based in "folk" or everyday traditions of speech and music (Baker 1980, 1984; Gates 1989; Collins 1990, 2000). Intellectuals' interpretations of blackness mirror lay understandings that locate authenticity in behavior, dress, and class (Jackson 2001). Governments, too, are involved in the construction of racial authenticity. As post–World War II political economic shifts have caused urban areas to use tourism as an economic engine, municipal governments have taken pains to rework their place images, presenting them as the site for a host of racially specific consumer experiences (Grazian 2003; Mele 2000).

While scholars routinely condemn essentialism, black political actors frequently deploy authenticity in political struggles. They attempt to legitimize themselves by insisting that they as individuals or their agendas reflect the essential nature of the community. Equally important is how individuals and groups attack one another for failing to conform to or reproduce what they consider to be essential racial features or characteristics. This strategy is fundamentally a criticism about the *representativeness* of the individual or group. The charge is that the individual is so outside the experience of the larger group that he or she is unable to stand for the group and its preferences. Such was the language used, for example, to express opposition to the nomination of Clarence Thomas to the Supreme Court (Morrison 1992). These framing strategies matter, because political actors' claims about their own or others' racial authenticity fundamentally shift the terms of political debate by introducing a different standard of political representativeness. Representation is traditionally defined as descriptive or substantive: the former occurs when the spokesperson reflects the characteristics of the constituency, and the latter occurs when the spokesperson can substitute for someone else because they share the same interests and policy positions (Swain 1995). While these traditional definitions of representativeness measure the extent to which an individual reflects the character or opinions of some majority of the aggregate, authenticity measures the extent to which the individual reflects and reproduces the "essential nature" of this community.

While political scientists have traditionally understood representation as an act, Fenno suggests that it is best understood as "a never-ending process, whereby the politician works at building and maintaining supportive connections with some proportion of his or her constituents" (2003, 5–6). Similarly, I argue that racial *authentication* may be thought of as a process of claiming and establishing one's adherence to expectations of blackness. Racial categorization and identification do not translate automatically into adherence to certain values or positions. As a result, black political actors repeatedly authenticate themselves, using acts and utterances to assert and adjust themselves to notions of what it means to be a real member of the black community. In Douglas/Grand Boulevard, coalition members expressed interracial tension in the conventional language of displacement, yet they adopted the language of authenticity in intraracial conflicts, asserting their legitimacy and challenging that of their opponents by declaring their belonging in both the racial and spatial community.

The Outsiders: Interracial Conflict and the Language of Community Belonging

Racial tensions were significant for the residents and organizations of Douglas/Grand Boulevard—not in spite of, but because of their cooperation with white elites. Neighborhood residents of every income level expressed substantial concern over the possibility that neighborhood development would result in their displacement. At meetings, rallies, and in casual conversations, community residents agonized over the probability of a white "invasion." Ken Lacey, a resident and business owner in Bronzeville, expressed the views of many when he told me that

> I'm hearing the thing that's going on is . . . the whites coming from the suburbs into the city, and they look at [the neighborhood] and you're walking distance from downtown, McCormick Place [the city's convention center], everything else and they're saying "Well hey, you know, maybe this isn't that bad after all and we want it back!"

Like many residents, Mr. Lacey perceives whites to be deliberate and purposeful in their attempt to "recover" Douglas/Grand Boulevard from the black residents who live there. In this sense, he expresses both resident concerns and scholarly arguments that gentrification is an expression of a "revanchist" desire among racial and economic elites who seek to take back the city from marginalized populations (N. Smith 1996). Many in the area saw the construction of expensive housing as a strategy used by whites to remove blacks from the neighborhood. At a meeting designed to educate residents about tax increment financing (TIF) strategies, one resident charged that "people are going to be taxed out and out-priced in this neighborhood. We can't afford housing at $180,000. It seems like you're pricing people out. You've seen what happened on Lake Park—people can't afford these places!" The audience clapped loudly after he finished speaking.

The strength and import of this feeling is exemplified in responses to my inquiries about renting an apartment in the area. I was told twice during phone conversations with building owners that I didn't "sound like" the type of person who would be comfortable in the neighborhood. "Do you *know* where this neighborhood is?" one woman doubtfully inquired. Finally, she asked me directly if I was African American. After I assured her that I was and told her about my research project on the area, she replied with relief, "I just want to keep it in the neighborhood, you know. There are so many white people moving in here."

A related concern expressed by both residents and coalition activists was the lack of adequate job opportunities, particularly for the area's young black men. The dearth of jobs, some coalition members argued, would make it impossible for poor blacks to stay in the neighborhood once development did begin. As a result, one of the questions most likely to be posed to a developer or an architect making a presentation at a Mid-South meeting was whether his or her project would provide jobs for area residents. The following fieldnote excerpt describes an exchange between a developer and a resident at a general Mid-South meeting:

> Kevin Howard, a resident of the neighborhood and owner of the South Side Development Corporation, gave a presentation to Mid-South on his commercial development project on Forty-third and King Drive. He was asked a number of questions about the opening date of the project, parking accommodations, and his willingness to work with Mid-South. Then an older woman asked him "Are you going to have some jobs for us?" Mr. Howard replied that he already had his team "in place." Incredulously, the woman asked, "Are you saying you're not going to have any jobs for people in the community?!" Mr. Howard replied, "I'm saying I already have my team in place. I may have some jobs, but I don't know that."

These concerns were addressed in the "Restoring Bronzeville" plan in two ways. First, the plan explicitly articulated the importance of maintaining the "indigenous" residents. Second, it called for material outcomes that would help those residents stay in the neighborhood. The plan emphasized, for example, that the area should be developed into a mixed-income residential area. Instead of advocating demolition and reconstruction, it promoted the rehabilitation of existing structures and construction on vacant lots. In addition, "Restoring Bronzeville" emphasized the importance of providing jobs for the current residents through the tourism industry.

Coalition members were as concerned about political displacement as they were about physical displacement. Collaboration may have provided opportunities for intraracial understanding and cooperation, but it also put black community leaders in contact with the very institutions toward which they felt hostile. Particularly as the Bronzeville Coalition tried to implement the agenda of the "Restoring Bronzeville" plan, its leaders came to worry that white elites would take over the process of redevelopment in a way that would hasten the displacement of the neighborhood's black residents. Coalition members were particularly concerned that "this development process is controlled by city hall, and people who have no accountability." One community organization director and founding member of Mid-South claimed that

> now everybody takes credit for it, but it was really a group of very thoughtful people putting a lot of this stuff together and making it happen. . . . 'Cause when they first started talking about "keep your eyes on the South Side," they laughed at us.

"They," that is, white city and development elites, stopped laughing when Bronzeville's revitalization caught on, and they soon began participating in both its residential and commercial development.

Community members were particularly sensitive to Chicago mayor Richard Daley's response to redevelopment efforts, and what they considered to be their ideas and hard work. They were threatened by what they understood as the Daley administration's attempts to "take credit" and "take control" of the restoration of Bronzeville. The development plan released by his Blue Ribbon Committee, for example, not only redefined the borders of Bronzeville as encompassing a smaller area, but also made no statements about the importance of retaining the present population. This stance led to extended discussions among the members of Mid-South about whether the mayor was positioning himself as a "stakeholder" in the process or its "controller." It was particularly important, said one participant, that they "make sure that the city supports our project, and that we are not overwhelmed by them." The actions of the mayor, the interest of white development companies, and the presence of white residents all combined to reinforce Mid-South members' understanding and fear of traditional interracial gentrification.

Coalition activists used a rhetoric of community belonging to describe the behavior of white stakeholders, portraying them as outsiders who were trespassing in the community in an attempt to control it. For example, coalition leaders tended to frame whites as the primary displacing force in the neighborhood, glossing over blacks' role in launching and promoting neighborhood change. Wendy Brown, a community developer involved in multiple coalition organizations, did just that when she explained that residents' great fear was that "once the white folks find out that this is really a gem, you know, in terms of its proximity to the Loop and everything else, and they'll want the property and they'll buy it out then." This portrayal of development conflates both racial and spatial community: that is, while coalition members often speak in terms of "the community" or "the neighborhood," the geographic unit is understood as inherently black.

Coalition leaders used whites' status as outsiders to justify the demand for state and private resources. For instance, concern over jobs and economic development took the form of claims against white contracting and development firms doing business in the area. In the mid-1990s, the McCormick Place convention center, which lies just north of the neighborhood, began expanding its facilities. Darla, a development staff member at the Metropolitan Pier and Exposition Authority, explained that

> when everybody saw the plans for our new south building—I mean we relocated King Drive. So we made a major impact to the west side of Lake Shore

Drive. And so the community said, "You're now stepping out into our community. We want you to identify with us as well as we identify with you." And the King Drive improvement project was part of that.

The Metropolitan Pier and Exposition Authority donated $10 million for infrastructural improvements to King Drive, funding street resurfacing, curbing, and street lights. It also included a public art program that marked Thirty-fifth and King Drive as the "gateway" to Bronzeville. Yet the project was widely criticized by both elected officials and community organizations for failing to employ enough blacks. For example, U.S. Representative Bobby Rush, a long-time supporter of historic preservation in Douglas/Grand Boulevard, argued that he was "tired of walking around and seeing public works jobs take place and seeing idle African American males standing around and watching the work. . . . [T]here were no jobs for people here in the neighborhood" (Bey 1996c, 18; Garrett 1996). They made additional claims upon the city when Thirty-fifth and State Street was picked as the site for the new police headquarters building. In response, Mid-South collaborated with two other community organizations to monitor the affirmative action policies of the development company. They ran workshops to facilitate Minority/Women Business Enterprise certification and they developed two databases: one listing local firms interested in contract work and another listing individuals willing to do construction work.

The coalition expected preference not only in individual employment practices, but in lending and financing practices for neighborhood projects. Jonathan Isaacs, a First National Bank employee who gave a presentation on the bank's community lending program at a monthly meeting, saw evidence of this in his exchange with two residents:

Zeke Stevens, a former chair of Mid-South, asked, "What kinds of specialized programs do you have for this area?" When Mr. Isaacs didn't really answer the question, Mr. Stevens continued, his voice getting louder and sounding angrier, "No, I guess I wasn't clear enough in my question. What I'd like to know is how can your bank help indigenous people in this community? I understand that you can make the loan for five million dollars, but what about the person who needs a five-hundred-dollar loan, or five thousand dollars?" Again, Mr. Isaacs refused to answer the question, and instead insisted that "what is more important is that there is an honest assessment given to you." A few moments later, a local businessman and developer told Mr. Isaacs that "in order for this bank to be successful in this neighborhood, you need to have some guidelines that are specific to this area. In Lincoln Park, in the '70s, they had the 235 program, which is the reason for their success. You need to take that idea back [for this community]."

Both Mr. Stevens and the local businessman insisted that the bank was obligated to help community members, programmatically and financially.

The Insiders:
Intraracial Conflict and the Standard of Racial Collectivism

The terms within which Bronzeville Coalition members discussed redevelopment emphasized that the "Restoring Bronzeville" plan represented the shared interests of Douglas/Grand Boulevard residents. Yet the same process that encouraged neighborhood residents to identify issues of universal relevance also highlighted differences within the black population itself. Thus, interracial conflict was not the only one that animated and drove the process of neighborhood change. Another set of struggles that community activists had to contend with was the one that existed between blacks of different economic means—particularly homeowners and public housing residents, who held extreme opposite relationships to property and income. In addition, development activists found themselves locked in a power struggle with the area's aldermen, who were threatened by the coalition's challenge to their authority to manage and control neighborhood revitalization.

The class divisions that faced Douglas/Grand Boulevard development advocates are clearly related by Rachel Dean, an architect who participated in the planning process. She described the neighborhood's residents as a

very dichotomous population in terms of *need.* You've got very, very low income people on the one hand, who have a large need for social services that are not being provided and other types of neighborhood amenities that were not provided as a result of them being there. And then you had people who had stayed over the years, elderly people. And then you have some young people who are beginning to move back, because of the housing stock itself, and the quality of the buildings.

Ms. Dean's description reflects the variation in income and housing ownership in the neighborhood. Yet it also emphasizes the way that economic differences translated into diverse sets of preferences about and responses to development. Similarly, when asked about the participation of the neighborhood's poorer residents, Olivia Ethan, the director of one coalition organization, explained that

> there are a lot of people who know what's being done, but are fearful of it, and have opted, instead of participating in it, or to help direct it, not to participate in it at all. And then there are some who basically are so wrapped up in survival issues that if there's not an immediate gratification, or an immediate change in their circumstances, the length of time that it takes to impact institutions, systems, in order to realize a better community, you know, it's difficult for people to get involved with that, or support that. I would say most people in the community, if you walked up to them and you said "Bronzeville," would know what that means. Most people would know that the community's undergoing tremendous change, and a lot of people fear it.

Tensions between low-income and more affluent residents surfaced within the Mid-South Planning Group's housing committee, though they were rarely mentioned explicitly during the implementation process. Randolph Jeffries said that while planning for the land-use document, the housing committee endured significant tension. He said there was

> a faction that represented public housing. And there was a faction that had represented the urban pioneers, who came down and purchased a lot of their greystone homes and had invested, you know, a considerable amount of

money into maintaining them and they felt threatened by all the public housing people and the public housing people felt threatened by these people.

When faced with the issue of mixed-income housing, some homeowners vehemently resisted the prospect of having former public housing residents as neighbors. Mr. Jeffries explained that homeowners

> were jumping all over [saying], "We don't want those people living next door to us! Hell no!" you know. Oh yeah. Saying, "Not in my backyard. We don't want those poor people over here, they're going to be breaking into our houses! Our, you know, sweat and tears going into fixing these houses, these people are gonna break in and steal everything."

Low-income residents felt as fearful and hostile toward middle- and upper-income black residents as they did toward white outsiders and neighborhood institutions. At one meeting on Bronzeville, held outside the confines of the neighborhood, one woman commented that she was "a low-income person." She said she had a son, she was a good mother, and she was a good person, but that "the high-income people don't want us in the neighborhood. How can we tell them that the low-income people are good people too?"

Mid-South members suggest that low-income residents not only felt the hostility of their middle-income neighbors, but they felt threatened and alarmed by the changes taking place in the neighborhood. Louie Ogden suggested that

> you don't see a change in the people who I know sometimes, you know . . . I don't see it. I see it's like they have no control over this. You know, not the young people who are involved in universities you know, making they little money now. 'Course they see a change cause they're going to these universities and they wanna live in the new Harlem Renaissance. You know what I'm saying? They think this is like *something* or whatever, so they wanna come back and kick it. You know, but I don't see a change in people who haven't gone to those schools, 'cause they feel like they have no control over this. You see 200,000 dollar housing going up, and you ain't got a . . . you

know, you working at Mickey D's . . . you know there's no possible way in your mind, that you can live there in my opinion. So.

As Mr. Ogden points out, poorer residents had little influence over the revitalization process taking place in the neighborhood, and moreover, they understood how that process excluded them and threatened their ability to stay in the neighborhood.

Mid-South and its "Restoring Bronzeville" land use plan also created tension between Bronzeville Coalition leaders and supporters, on the one hand, and local black elected officials on the other. The sources of this conflict were many: first, the emerging notion of racial community articulated by the organization constituted a symbolic threat to the concept of community that undergirds ward loyalties. The boundaries of Bronzeville included two community areas (Douglas/Grand Boulevard) and portions of three separate wards (the Second, Third, and Fourth). It therefore crossed and superseded traditional political boundaries and suggested an alternative conception of political community around which to organize. Second, Mid-South's activities threatened to undermine the electoral base of local aldermen. It constituted a potential disruption to constituent loyalty to the Democratic ward organization by presenting residents with another option for becoming involved in politics (Ferman 1996; Gills 1991; Kleppner 1985). Mid-South was a source of information about what was taking place in the neighborhood; they advocated a more open development process and encouraged residents to participate in it; and they built a network of supportive organizations by helping to create block clubs, business associations, and innumerable other community organizations. Moreover, Mid-South's attempt to increase the number of middle-class residents threatened the electoral base of Second, Third, and Fourth Ward aldermen, whose voter bases came from public housing (Burnham 1994). One Mid-South meeting attendee wondered why "elected officials are so quiet [when it comes to neighborhood change] because when these areas get gentrified they're not going to be reelected."

Finally, Mid-South challenged, both directly and indirectly, aldermanic control of the redevelopment process. This threat was significant, as control over land parcels and decisions about redevelopment projects are some of the few sources of political patronage left to Chicago aldermen. In an effort to assert their control over redevelopment, Mid-South supporters repeatedly referred to the organization as

> the policy-making body for the Second, Third, and Fourth Ward. That's a positioning situation that is not being supported by elected officials, but as the organization grows, and it gets support, it's been able to more and more take on these kinds of responsibilities.

Not only did Bronzeville Coalition leaders attempt to direct and carry out development themselves, they also insisted that the aldermen's involvement in redevelopment projects was inappropriate, if not corrupt. One community director insisted that Second Ward alderman

> Dorothy Tillman has said publicly after receiving state and federal dollars that she's not going to work with the local merchants' association to do her Lou Rawls and African village concept on Forty-seventh and King Drive. Said it point blank. . . . [w]hen in fact, [she] shouldn't be doing development at all. And secondly, if you are doing development, you certainly gotta partner with the Forty-Seventh Street Merchant Association so that they can know what you're doing in this project and how it relates to them in terms of business and increasing their tax base. Elementary. But she has said she's not going to do that.

The strength of the challenge brought by Bronzeville Coalition organizations was partially a result of the collaborative process in which Mid-South and other organizations were engaged. By referring to the "bottom-up," "inclusive" process of community planning, Mid-South and the rest of the Bronzeville Coalition made a strong argument that they better represented the needs and wishes of the community. In addition, collaborative planning helped them establish and strengthen their alliances to powerful neighborhood institutions such as the Illinois Institute of Technology.

The danger posed by the Bronzeville Coalition was also exacerbated by the immediate political context. In fall 1993, President Clinton announced the establishment of the Empowerment Zone program, which aimed to use comprehensive, collaborative, "bottom-up" planning to provide jobs to residents of economically distressed communities. Because Mid-South had just finished a plan that reflected Empowerment Zone goals, they were well poised to participate in the drafting of Chicago's submission. When Chicago was awarded an Empowerment Zone grant, the city was accused of mishandling the money and steering it away from community organizations. But the award nonetheless gave Mid-South the potential to drift even further from the control of the Democratic machine. In response, neighborhood aldermen began placing holds on property in the community. The *Chicago Reporter* reported that by January 1994, Aldermen Haithcock (Second), Tillman (Third), and Preckwinkle (Fourth) were "responsible for 72.8 percent of all the aldermanic holds in the city. But their wards account[ed] for less than 20 percent of city owned land" (Quintanilla 1994, 5). While the aldermen claimed to be using this device to secure land for community groups and keep it away from undesirable developers, community organization leaders did not see it that way. Louie Ogden, a Mid-South member, insisted that the aldermanic holds were

> a deliberate thing. It's a deliberate thing. Because if you control most of the land in the neighborhood, you control that neighborhood. . . . On the South Side, in a certain period of time, it's a lot of buildings that get demolished and you create holes in the community. So the city owns this land, or they get control of this property, and then they can distribute it how they want to. . . . It becomes, it becomes like "Alright, you my boy, I'm going to give you a piece of land. You know."

Randolph Jeffries expressed the sentiments of many community leaders when he insisted that "as far as the politicians are concerned, I don't think they help much. I mean, they don't join things. They oppose things."

These kinds of intraracial divisions are not unique to this neighborhood or this time period. A large body of scholarship details how black communities have been highly stratified throughout history and have expressed class and gender divisions in exclusive social relationships (Drake and Cayton 1993; DuBois 1899; Foner 1990; Frazier 1957; Gatewood 1988; Meier 1962). These divisions shaped blacks' perceptions of and responses to their political world, often making themselves apparent in disagreements over tactics, rather than in the issues themselves. Dawson finds that even in the post–civil rights era, "class divisions play a critical role in shaping the debate on black political strategy" (1994, 121). Scholars suggest that limited political choices and the dominant fact of political disfranchisement in black political life have made these differences easy to ignore and difficult to capture (Dawson 1994; Pinderhughes 1987).

Intraracial divisions are further obscured by the recent shift in urban black politics from community organizing to neighborhood planning. Even as scholars and practitioners lament the disappearance of the racial solidarity that supposedly marked the civil rights era, this change masks and mutes intraracial conflict by conflating openness and representativeness. That is, neighborhood planning proponents often assume that access to decision-making processes necessarily leads to influence. Grady Karl hints at the flaw in this logic in his comments about the outcome of the plan. In his mind, it

> did an adequate job of at least trying to address and being inclusive in terms of its writing. But in terms of its involvement, local ownership of the plan, I think it was inadequate. . . . And that's because we didn't have enough in-depth organizing and enough views of those people who were in these sectors that we talked about earlier who were not included in the process. . . . Most people would say that they support what's in the plan. I think it was written with that level of compassion and consideration for those people who weren't at the table. . . . But, as far as the . . . you know, having ownership, or including my thoughts and my ideas, as a public housing resident . . . not true. . . . Ownership is that I can see my thought. I can see my time I spent in these committees in that statement. In that document. Or I can see my name on the list of people at the back of the document. That's ownership.

Mr. Karl suggests that despite good faith efforts to acknowledge, consider, and include a diverse set of needs, Mid-South's failure to maintain a varied membership base prevented them from truly being the representative organization they wished to be, a failure that reflects the conflict that arises when community-development strategies funnel resources away from organizing (Weir 1999; Stoecker 1997; Ferman 1996).

For the Race: Collectivism as Authenticity

While participants in the redevelopment process portrayed interracial tensions as conflicts between racial insiders and outsiders, they expressed *intra*racial schisms as conflicts between authentic versus inauthentic community members. Definitions of authenticity presupposed blackness: that is, the question was not whether one was black, but what kind of black person one was. Racial authenticity, then, depended on a number of criteria. One unsurprising indicator of racial authenticity was neighborhood residence. The following fieldnote excerpt describes one way that coalition members assigned meaning to the behavior of those who lived outside the boundaries of the two community areas:

> Nina is irritated because David Gunther didn't show up, and this is the second time this has happened. His company is a major developer in the area, and she feels they need to come to these meetings. Someone asks who his alderman is, as if to suggest that we might complain to her, to which Nina very pointedly remarks, "he doesn't *live* here." She asks the group to approve her motion to write a letter to Mr. Gunther, complaining about his having missed two meetings, and asks if she can attach a copy of the names of the people who attended both this meeting and the previous one that he missed. The entire group agrees.

Nina's reaction to the developer's absence makes deliberate reference to the fact that he does not live in the community. She mentions this in part to explain why it is impossible to pressure the errant developer through his alderman; yet the tone and inflection of her voice suggest that his non-resident status is in and of itself a cause for condemnation.

The significance of residence becomes even more clear in the following response of Mid-South members to a black representative of the

Communal Bank. After giving a presentation about the services and instruments available through the bank, Jonathan Isaacs sparked this response from meeting attendee Justin Kirk, who was frustrated with Isaacs's vague and noncommittal responses to the group's questions:

> We know why you're coming into this neighborhood, you're coming into this neighborhood to make money. You're not here because you want to do community reinvestment, you're here because this is an up-and-coming neighborhood! So we're not new to this, you're the new guy on the block, we've *been* here! Why don't you just tell us what kinds of things you can do for this community. I'm a businessman, I know you're here to make money!

In his remarks, Mr. Kirk uses residence to portray Mr. Isaacs and the Communal Bank as outsiders. He defines them as interlopers partly because they have come to the area from another community. Though he does not say so, the history of community lending and redlining in the neighborhood indicates that this other community is both racial and spatial—that is, the financial institution is owned and operated by whites in other parts of the city. Their entrance into the neighborhood thus has a dual significance. Yet this example is also intriguing because it illustrates that outsider status is not just a matter of where one lives. Equally important is tenure, or the amount of time that an individual or institution has been located in the neighborhood. As Mr. Kirk points out, the bank had only recently developed an interest in the neighborhood, which made it suspect. Likewise, Mr. Kirk uses tenure to position himself as a well-informed, trusted insider who is part of a broader "we" that has a long association with the community. He even goes so far as to mention their similarities (he, like Mr. Isaacs, is a businessman), so as to further demonstrate the significance of his long-time connection to Douglas/Grand Boulevard.

The importance of tenure is particularly evident in coalition members' descriptions of new residents. Many coalition members described newcomers as affluent individuals who did not come to the area until the phase of incumbent upgrading in the 1980s. For example, when mentioning the rise in property values, business owner Ken Lacey argued that those who could afford these homes at their new prices were "not the constituency that's been down there . . . so you know it isn't those people that were living there that's buying all this. It's outsiders that are speculating." This behavior does not just make them a different kind of community member. Redevelopment supporters suggest that these newcomers are "urban pioneers" who are not *really* a part of the Bronzeville community. For example, Wendy Brown, who grew up in the neighborhood, defined these residents as

> people that are not indigenous to the neighborhood, that move in and set up a settlement. Like they might set up two, three houses of people that they know. And then they don't really buy from the community businesses or [get] involved in other community stuff, they just come on in, live there, kind of hold on to their property and wait for the property values to turn.

According to Ms. Brown, what distinguishes the newer residents is that they consider their presence in the community and their purchase of buildings as a financial transaction. They value their property for its financial value, the way it enhances their personal status, rather than for its historical and cultural significance. This example is particularly useful because it illustrates how notions of racial authenticity are sometimes linked to notions of racial sincerity. Jackson argues that "sincerity is the attribute most often called upon to make sense of public debates and controversies," even when accusations of inauthenticity are the ultimate goal (2005, 12).

While race, residence, and tenure are important determinants of authenticity, each served primarily as shorthand for another criteria: collectivism, or commitment to the broader community.[3] Nina's comment about David Gunther, for example, is not merely a criticism that he lives outside the neighborhood; rather, his living outside the neighborhood is offered as an explanation for his greater crime of failing to meet his commitment to the community. He is suspect largely because of the ways he might exploit the residents and the changes in the neighborhood. Similarly, David Kirk criticizes Communal Bank representative Jonathan Isaacs not only for being "the new guy on the block," but also for entering the community for his and his institution's gain, rather than for "community" reinvestment. This emphasis on communal behavior echoes the claims made in the Bronzeville heritage narrative: just as intraracial cooperation supposedly marked the social interactions of migration-era blacks, so also should it mark such interactions in the contemporary period.

The primacy of collectivism is clear in coalition members' comparison of new and long-time residents. On the one hand, they tend to portray long-time residents as poor, long-suffering cultural custodians. Louie Ogden, for example, described older residents as

> the keepers, you know, the people who are here are the keepers of the culture, you know what I'm saying? Like the keepers of—the holders of all this history. . . . And the people who come back, they know about the history, but if it wasn't for the folks who were here, they couldn't have come back. . . . These folks who kept these homes and stuff, they could have left, too, sold their homes . . . doing all this kind of stuff, but we'll be here. You know what I'm saying, you got some old folks who been here since, I mean, shit, the '30s or something . . . if you didn't have them to interview, the Etta Moten Barnetts, the—you know, different folks, you know, you wouldn't have it. . . . They—folks who were here—they maintained.

Like other redevelopment advocates, Ogden portrays long-time community members as having preserved and been devoted to the community, even when it was in desperate condition. Moreover, he depicts their decision to stay in the neighborhood as an expression of community commitment, rather than a reflection of financial ability. Because they "maintained," they have kept alive the neighborhood history that redevelopment advocates are now trying to unearth and preserve, and upon which, they suspect, "urban pioneers" are trying to capitalize. Perhaps most interesting is what this class-based distinction between long-time and recent residents reveals about the function and working of standards of authenticity. Coalition members did not use claims to authentic blackness to demonize or delegitimize the poor. Quite the opposite: they used the standards of authenticity to align themselves with the poor, and thereby, the rest of the race. In this sense, long-time members—unlike newcomers—are both *in* the community and *of* the community.

On the other hand, newer residents are depicted in contradiction to older residents in far less positive terms. As Wendy Brown's previous comments show, coalition members may portray newcomers as a threat to the neighborhood. Mr. Ogden echoes this distinction when he claims that

> for a long time middle-class black folks left this neighborhood. I mean they were scared to live in the neighborhood. And now they're coming back. And now they're you know, calling it Bronzeville, calling it home. They've been down here for five years and we've made our home and . . . and that's cool, cause they're supposed to come back and you know, open arms, we're all black, right? But the thing is though, don't forget the people who've been here for thirty and forty and fifty years who, you know, who don't have the money to fix up their homes.

With this comment, Mr. Ogden expresses several widely held assumptions about the character of newer residents, their difference from long-time residents, and the relationship between the two. First, he locates their decision to leave in their fear, and portrays them as having abandoned both the space and the race. In addition, he uses a language of return to describe the new residents, which intimates that the residents who left are the same as those who are entering the neighborhood in the contemporary period. This assumption bolsters Mr. Ogden's assertion that newer residents owe their allegiance to long-time residents. He suggests that the sacrifice of these cultural custodians obligates the former to help preserve and protect the latter in the face of the threats posed by development.

Mr. Ogden's statements reveal much about the logic used to define community membership. His interpretation extracts blacks' choices about residential mobility away from the history of racism that contained them and the political economic shifts that made mobility possible. Instead, it uses psychological explanations to place middle- and lower-income residents in particular roles and relationships to one another, casting the former as the savior of the neighborhood and the latter as its cultural custodian. Sometimes this argument about resident responsibility is made with no direct reference to racial identity. At other times, Mid-South members see gentrification and entrepreneurship as a specific obligation of the black middle class. As Grady Karl explained,

> The black middle class, [returning] from its corporate isolation and having done the integration thing, are now saying I need to get back to blackness, 'cause I'm still being discriminated against. I went out, I found out that I ain't got no more liberation than my money'll get me, and I still don't have a sense of community. So I'm going back. Now, when you get back, are you going to turn on your brother, or are you going to try to use your resources to help empower him? And that's the issue.

Mr. Karl, like many Mid-South members, uses the language of return to discuss the physical and financial presence of the black middle class in Douglas/Grand Boulevard. He understands them as returning not just to the physical community of the neighborhood, but to their essential racial being, to blackness. Ultimately, comments like these illustrate the fact that redevelopment participants did more than value collectivism; they used it as a criteria for understanding authentic racial and spatial membership. Nostalgic visions of Bronzeville, which portray black elites as operating almost constantly on behalf of the race, provide the principles upon which coalition members asserted and challenged *personal* legitimacy. As the next section illustrates, these criteria were also used to frame the behavior of political opponents.

Establishing and Challenging Racial Authenticity

The use of this nostalgia-based standard of legitimacy is significant because it encourages residents to repeatedly racially authenticate themselves—that is, to publicly assert both their membership in and commitment to the community. One way they do so is by making frequent reference to where they live. In community and business meetings, residents often preface their comments to the group by announcing, "I am a resident," and then continue on to state their grievance, concern, or opinion. In addition to, or in lieu of, claiming Douglas/Grand Boulevard as their residential community, individuals may claim it as their work or volunteer community, as well.

Sometimes they extend the physical boundaries of black community to include themselves. That is, if individuals do not live or work in what has been defined as the Bronzeville area, they may assert their membership in the larger community of the city's blacks by mentioning that they live or work "on the South Side." Another way residents publicly establish their authenticity is to remind the audience of their experience with African American cultural forms. Franklin, an architect involved in several Mid-South projects, used this strategy at a planning meeting about the Overton Building:

> Franklin said that he had recently given a presentation where "one of the brothers from [a black organization] came up to me and said you're just a Negro with a tie" as well as some other accusations about his lack of commitment to blacks. In response, he said he told them that "I may be a Negro with a tie, but I also had to eat chitlins."

In telling this story, Franklin uses the unusual strategy of heading off a possible challenge to his racial authenticity by telling the audience of one he has already encountered. His response is particularly effective because it involves the assertion of two markers of racial authenticity: not only is he verifiably black (as demonstrated by his consumption of traditional African American food), but he has also endured the kind of poverty that required him to consume that kind of food in the first place.

Franklin's example indicates a related strategy for asserting racial authenticity: asserting a disadvantage that is associated with or emanates from racial status. This particular tactic was a favorite of one Bronzeville proponent in particular, who frequently mentioned the fact that he had lived in public housing as a child. As he told me in an interview, he came

> from the masses of black folks. Raised on ADC, came through Ida B. Wells, lived through Woodlawn, survived Woodlawn, came into Hyde Park and got a multicultural vision of life. I think that enabled me to do some of the things that I'm doing now. But I always feel victimized collectively, as a black man, over what has happened to us in this city. And have done everything

in my power since I was an adult, to try to address those issues and to try to address them forthrightly.

In one sense, statements like this call on the residence and tenure of the individual to establish authenticity: the Ida B. Wells housing project is well within the boundaries of Bronzeville, and the speaker's long history with the neighborhood specifically—and the South Side generally—is well established by his references to childhood and beyond. Even more important, however, is this speaker's assertion that his experiences as a public housing resident shaped his political consciousness and, according to him, connect him to the collective struggle of all African Americans.

In this sense, this speaker's remarks also make reference to another way black stakeholders maintained their authenticity: by pointing to behavioral "proof" of their own collectivism and commitment to the race. For example, architects, contractors, and developers who presented their projects at Mid-South meetings were well aware of the importance that members attached to their minority employment and hiring record. Without fail, they included information about the number of minorities on their staff. One architectural company representative's presentation to the Mid-South membership, for example, put information about the racial makeup of his firm second only to his assertion of experience. "I've been working for fourteen years, in the South Loop," he said. "I've also done projects on part of the South Side. I have fifteen people on my staff. Ninety-one percent are minorities, and 58 percent are female. I am 100 percent African American owned and staffed." At another meeting, where Mid-South members heard proposals to develop a historic landmark they had acquired, one architect explicitly suggested that his commitment to the community was the distinguishing feature on which he should be judged and chosen for a project. He and his competitors all had the same qualifications, he asserted: "We all went to school for five years; we all had three-year apprenticeships; we all took a thirty-six-hour exam . . . why should you choose me? Because of my commitment to myself, my family, my clients, and my community." He had demonstrated that commitment, he claimed, by being a former resident who had returned to do projects in the area.

In addition to defending themselves as authentic, black activists challenged the authenticity of those who advocated projects to which they were opposed. In March 1998, for example, Second Ward alderman Madeline Haithcock held a community forum to discuss the possibility of establishing a tax increment financing (TIF) district in the Douglas/Grand Boulevard neighborhood. When called on to speak, a well-known activist asserted that he wanted to "speak to the people who own the city, and the people who own the city are the taxpayers. This TIF is a sham." As he continued to express his opposition to the TIF, he accused the aldermen of not representing their districts and called them "handkerchief-head Negro leaders" who needed to be voted out. This attack referenced a fairly generic understanding of blackness.[4] Yet Bronzeville coalition members also frame individuals and organizations that do not conform to or agree with their agenda as lacking authenticity because they do not share in the collective experience and heritage afforded by a long tenure in the neighborhood. This strategy is apparent in an exchange that took place the following month, between Fourth Ward alderman Toni Preckwinkle and two members of the Bronzeville Coalition. The alderman appeared at a Mid-South meeting to make a presentation about the establishment of a different TIF district along Forty-seventh Street. Before she even began her presentation, she was challenged by several members of the coalition. The first was Grady Karl, who interrupted the alderman to ask, "What is the quid pro quo for the community in terms of the things we want to do? In other words, how will this affect the revitalization of Forty-third, where the policy-making body of this community has said there should be a blues district, and where the [Third Ward] alderman, Dorothy Tillman, wants it to be residential, not commercial?"

Mr. Karl's question was intended not to question Alderman Preckwinkle directly about *her* project, but to raise the issue of aldermanic control over neighborhood redevelopment generally, by mentioning the behavior of her fellow alderman and provoking her to take a stance on it. After a very long pause, Alderman Preckwinkle responded that

> my hope is that Forty-third will be a residential street. In the old days, when we rode on trolley cars and people did their shopping in the neighborhood,

having a commercial strip was appropriate. It's not anymore. On the South Side, commercial strips are suffering. We started working on this idea [of decommercialization] in the mid-80s, when I worked . . . under Harold Washington's administration . . . [and] we [concentrated] on nodes and not on saving every commercial strip, given its disarray. Candidly, I hope that Forty-third will be residential, and there are some existing businesses that we will help to move to Cottage Grove, at Forty-seventh and Cottage.

The alderman's response was strategic in its attempt to legitimize her work by linking it to Chicago's first black mayor, Harold Washington. Yet Mr. Karl is unimpressed and challenges the alderman again about development plans, asking her, "What about the business at Forty-seventh and King, where you have all four corners owned by African Americans. . . . Why would you make that totally residential when you know that the people are moving in who will be looking for the small businesses and the mom-and-pop stores? . . . Why are you working against the long-range plans of Mid-South, who is working to revitalize the area?" Twice more Alderman Preckwinkle tries to demure, insisting that Mr. Karl discuss his objections with Alderman Tillman, in whose ward the disputed territory and action are located. Impatient with Preckwinkle's repeated dodging, community organizer Bette Orlando interrupts the exchange with this comment:

Excuse me. . . . As a native Chicagoan, I want to say how important Forty-third Street is to me. I am the little girl who walked up and down Forty-third when the blues was there, when black people were happy. [She describes several repesentative scenarios.] I am here to say that [due to the Empowerment Zone], it is job-creation time. We have been abused, misused [several other mistreatments] all this time. I was here. You weren't here, Preckwinkle. You don't have the sensibility to the area that we do. I am concerned to make the blues [an important part of the development]. That was when black people were happy. You got here late, Preckwinkle. You were not here. So you don't remember when black people were happy and gay.

Ms. Orlando's comment is a deliberate attack on Alderman Preckwinkle, one based on the assumption that an understanding of and experience with the neighborhood's past is what confers the authority and knowledge necessary for good judgment and public policy making. Ms. Orlando asserts that the legitimacy of her remarks is based on the longevity of her residence, in both the neighborhood and the city, as well as her ill treatment at the hands of the powerful. She then argues that these experiences have given her an understanding of community needs and desires that the alderman, as an uninformed newcomer, cannot have. In her view, Alderman Preckwinkle lacks not just a personal history with the community, but an appreciation of residents' personal history, making her unqualified to advocate policies in opposition to Mid-South's.

These strategies of authentication were particularly important in two ways: first, they were a crucial part of conferring and denying legitimacy in public, small-group interactions. Mentioning ties to the neighborhood, for example, served as more than a method of introduction; it established the validity of the speakers' concern for and interest in the area and therefore their right to speak. One participant in a meeting of local businessmen made this clear when he introduced himself by saying that he had his "first teaching job at [a school] which is now Holy Angels. So I'm wedded to the community." In this instance, the speaker made an explicit argument that the length of time he had spent in the community was proof of his commitment to the area and the people in it. While he made this statement by way of introduction and in the absence of any direct challenge, development stakeholders also used references to residence and tenure to deliberately defend themselves against attack. The following fieldnote excerpt describes how developer Irving Clarke and his associate used their history in the neighborhood to handle hostility in a Mid-South meeting:

> Irving Clarke got up to speak and Grady Karl called out from the audience "Here we go again!" Mr. Clarke just ignored him without showing any irritation. Then he said, "I've been working in this community for a long time. Some of you know my work. I'm here to present the development concept for [a new set of homes]" and then he introduced his team of people. When one of his team members started speaking, Bette Orlando interrupted by standing up and asking, "Where did you come from?" Clarke's associate

said he was "born right here in the community, at Forty-fourth and Ellis." Ms. Orlando sat back down and muttered in a low voice to the woman sitting next to her, "But are you *gonna* be here? Where will you be in the next ten years?"

This exchange illustrates both the reach and the limits of this rhetorical strategy. Both Mr. Clarke and his associate made calculated references to their long experience with the neighborhood and were able to defuse public challenges from hostile Mid-South members.

Yet, Ms. Orlando's response demonstrates that claims to authenticity do not form an unbreachable barrier of protection for those who use them. Rather, they are a strategy for avoiding and deflecting *public* attacks that can be and are easily disputed in private. Ms. Orlando's private challenge to Mr. Clarke's associate mirrors Louie Ogden's response to a set of thinly veiled accusations, made publicly during a community meeting, that he and other staff members were abusing their positions:

> At the end of the meeting, Louie came up to me. He is usually so mellow, and I have never seen him more pissed. He was angry because Grady Karl had brought up the issue of money. He said, "You wanna talk about money? He's an organizer! He knows I don't make any money! I'm trying to work, I'm in school; there are times I can't get bus fare to come to work! What the fuck does he know?! He says he came out of Ida B. Wells, so what? So did I! I still got people from there, too!

Mr. Ogden's anger stems as much from the public nature of the statements as from their inaccuracy. Yet as his response indicates, the same assertions that establish one's own insider status may also be used against others, and he rejects the validity of the reference to class, while simultaneously asserting it on his own behalf.

In addition to establishing public legitimacy, the language of authenticity is significant because it has the capacity to set the terms of small-group debate and establish the arguments and issues to which participants must respond. Consider, for example, the response of one group to the coalition's push for historic district status in 1996. As part of the attempt to save the Black Metropolis's buildings from demolition, the Bronzeville Coalition began advocating for landmark designation. Initially, the group that owned two of the buildings supported the move and even planned to outfit one of them with a black military museum. A year later, however, the group opposed the landmark designation. A rainstorm had caused the roof to collapse in one of the buildings, and their insurance company was refusing to cover the damage. Landmark designation would have required them to repair the building without altering it, and deprived them of the less expensive option of demolishing it. Ms. Chester, one of the owners, explained to me that their objection was that the building was

> not owned by a corporation or a nonprofit organization, it is private property. There are some problems with that . . . unless the person that wants to landmark my property, or the city, or whomever, is going to give me funds to maintain this property.

In short, the owners objected to the financial burden that would be thrust upon them were landmark status to be granted. Yet they discussed their predicament not just as a financial issue, but also as a difference in the personal meaning of and experience with the building.

> Everybody is looking at the building as the old *Defender Building* because . . . it's where Robert S. Abbott started writing. And it is important to our black history. But I'm also saying, wait a minute. What about Congressman Dawson? I'm attached to him. I'm not—neither one of them is higher or lower than the other. But I'm saying this is the Dawson Professional Building because it's named after Congressman Dawson, because he bought it from [former *Defender* publisher John] Sengestacke. . . . As long as I have known it, from the time he bought it in the '60s, it's been the Second Ward headquarters owned by Congressman Dawson . . . so we inherited it. So my husband has a relationship that goes back with the congressman, I have one that goes back with the congressman, and we also have a relationship with the entire family. So we have a history there that's kind of like he was our mentor, so it's important to us.

What is significant about Ms. Chester's comments are the way she adjusts herself to expectations and standards around collectivism and the importance of history. She directly challenges the dominant interpretation of the building's historical value. In its stead she offers an alternative understanding of its significance, based on her own personal history, and uses this history to gain sympathy and support for her position. By raising the issue of Congressman Dawson, a respected community figure (and indeed a prominent part of Bronzeville history), she suggests that the Bronzeville Coalition's notion of heritage may be usurping identities that are equally meaningful for long-time community members. Thus, she challenges the Bronzeville Coalition agenda by questioning their notion of community heritage; while being careful not to prioritize her own interpretation of the property, she emphasizes that hers is equally valid.

In a context where identity is an important part of the political conversation, authenticating oneself and challenging the racial authenticity of others is an important strategy. Coalition members use this language to vie for personal legitimacy, defining authenticity as the degree of collectivism as illustrated by residence, tenure, poverty, and many other behaviors. These efforts help establish their right to frame and participate in public funds. As the next chapter demonstrates, these efforts are also central to establishing the legitimacy of their policies and programs.

CHAPTER 5

We're All in This Mess Together: Identity and the Framing of Racial Agendas

The group of Second Ward residents gathered in Hartzell Memorial Church on March 20, 1997, was no doubt both a pleasure and a disappointment to Madeline Haithcock, the alderman who had convened the meeting: a pleasure because turnout was decent (around 120 people), which gave her an opportunity to take credit for the redevelopment efforts taking place in Bronzeville. The lineup of speakers included the expected array of planning department staff, as well as a bevy of developers, representatives from the Illinois Institute of Technology, and, of course, the Mid-South Planning and Development Commission. The disappointment might have come because despite the pointedly upbeat attitude of the presenters, the residents who attended the meeting were anxious about the lack of affordable housing being constructed in the area and afraid that they would be pushed out of the neighborhood. In their questions and comments, they emphasized that they had been in the community their entire lives, long before the "newcomers." What was going to happen to public housing? How could they get loans for relocation or renovation? In what world, they wondered aloud, were $200,000 homes considered affordable housing?

Even more significant than the concerns that emerged among residents was the strategy neighborhood leaders used to try to address them. At the end of the meeting, Alderman Haithcock responded to her constituents' worries about affordable housing by praising the efforts of the African American–owned development company heading the project. "It's only eight homes," she exclaimed, "but at least we got somebody black [to build them]!" With her comment, the alderman suggested that the project had a significance that extended beyond its immediate impact. In reminding her constituents that the developer was African American, she implied that his individual achievement provided a benefit that competed with, if not outweighed, residents' concerns about the project's material impact.

This tactic is a common one in Douglas/Grand Boulevard and black communities across the country. Faced with intraracial divisions and the competing preferences they generate, African American leaders attempt to frame their agendas in ways that "[initiate] feelings of linked fate and the perception of advancing the interests of the entire black community" (Cohen 1999, 11). In other words, they link their agendas to the African American population and suggest that their strategies are relevant for all blacks. Alderman Haithcock's comment illustrates one common way black leaders do this: particularly when it is clear that the material benefits of one strategy are likely to favor one portion of the black population over another, black elites make reference to shared racial identity in order to urge residents to set aside their concrete concerns and instead consider the symbolic victory their strategy will bring. Thus the alderman makes an explicit assertion that Douglas/Grand Boulevard residents share a generic blackness, and in doing so, she implicitly asserts that this shared racial identity results in a shared symbolic outcome.

Another way political leaders link racial agendas and racial identities is by framing the former as the natural expression of the latter. That is, they assert that their agendas reflect the most fundamental elements of African American identity. Coalition leaders and supporters frequently adopted this strategy in Douglas/Grand Boulevard, particularly when discussing neighborhood demolition. This issue touched the lives of all residents in some way, yet the nature and degree of its impact varied across class. While the neighborhood faced the possible destruction of historic buildings that would form part of the Black Metropolis tourism destination, it also faced the demolition of public housing in the area, which constituted the only affordable housing option for many of the neighborhood's residents. Mid-South focused its attention on the threat that demolition held for historic buildings and promoted historic preservation and black gentrification as solutions to that threat. More important, the organization and its allies drew heavily on the Bronzeville identity, arguing that their strategy embodied its tradition of collectivism and middle-class leadership and also safeguarded those traditions by preserving the buildings that represented them. This tactic ultimately prioritized property value enhancement over the provision of affordable housing. Yet coalition leaders justified these priorities and asserted their universal benefit by highlighting their consistency with, and degree to which they expressed, the Bronzeville identity.

Rethinking Racial Group Interests

The attempt to identify a universal racial benefit is one response to an issue that concerns many contemporary observers of black politics. With the removal of legal segregation and the recent class polarization of the black population, analysts have raised new questions about the relationship between racial identity and political preferences. Some question the relationship between elected officials and black constituents and the extent to which the former are willing and able to represent the interests of the latter (Swain 1995; Whitby 1997). Others wonder whether blacks will maintain the uniformity in opinion and voting patterns that they exhibited prior to the civil rights era (Dawson 1994; Tate 1994). This latter concern has manifested itself primarily in the popular and scholarly debate over whether race or class has more impact on black political behavior, and it is clearly a concern for leaders in Douglas/Grand Boulevard. In both cases, observers are concerned with understanding how racial identity is related to political preferences. Yet the consideration of this question has been hampered by our reliance on the notion of racial group interests, which *assumes* that certain preferences are racial, rather than explaining the process through which they are racialized.

While widely used in political science literature, the racial group interests concept is marked by considerable ambiguity.[1] No works of which I am aware adequately establish what phenomenon is captured by the concept. Thus, despite its centrality in the research, it is unclear exactly what the concept represents and what it is meant to measure. Are racial group interests those preferences that blacks share in common, regardless of their source or differential impact? For example, if two African American men support affirmative action in college admissions and only one of them is likely to benefit from it, does that make it a racial group interest? In other words, is the emphasis on the word *group?* Or should the focus be on the *racial* part of racial group interests? These questions are particularly important given the fact that the concept itself was developed in an attempt to understand the implications of multiple group identities.

One way to determine the implicit definition of racial group interests is to examine how scholars operationalize it—that is, what variables they use to indicate its existence. The term is frequently operationalized as the policies and positions toward which blacks display significant homogeneity, such as partisanship or political orientation (Dawson 1994; Swain 1995). Since the 1940s, for example, blacks have voted overwhelmingly for the Democratic Party, and scholars frequently define the seating of Democratic candidates as being in the interest of African Americans as a group. This definition of racial group interests, while seemingly straightforward, ultimately raises more questions than it answers. What is the racial group interest in instances where the black population is evenly divided? How many people must hold certain interests before they can become those of the group? If not everyone agrees with them, are they not group interests? Or are the dissenters not sufficiently racial?

These questions illustrate the fact that quantitative definitions of racial group interests presume a particular relationship between group membership and support for a certain outcome. That is, although racial group interests are operationalized in a way that focuses on the *number or proportion* of blacks who hold an opinion, the assumption behind this measurement is that when a majority of group members hold an opinion, it reflects preferences that derive specifically from the condition of racial designation. Because the majority of blacks support the Democratic Party, for example, scholars assume that their doing so reflects their concern for advancing the social and economic interests of the race. This assumption becomes even more clear when considering how those who do *not* adhere to what is defined as the racial group interest are characterized. Using this definition of racial group interests, black conservatives would be described as responding to something other than racial status. Racial group interests, then, are implicitly defined as those that blacks hold because of their racially subordinate status.[2]

This conceptualization of group interests is limited in two important ways. First, it assumes that preferences themselves are racial. That is, the very idea of racial group interests itself—not merely the operationalization of the concept—is based on the assumption that certain preferences and positions (e.g., Democratic partisanship) derive naturally from race, while others (e.g., Republican partisanship) derive from some other status category—that the interest itself is somehow racial. Second, the concept of group interests assumes that preferences are *only* racial. In other words, it assumes that those preferences deriving from one's racial status are not influenced by other social status categories, such as gender, class, or sexuality. Yet feminist scholars have detailed the ways that multiple social statuses intersect to shape the experience and interpretation of race, and therefore interests (King 1989; Robnett 1997; P. Collins 1989). Moreover, empirical research has clearly indicated that identities and consciousness are more accurately captured by interactive measures (Dillingham 1981; Gilliam and Whitby 1989; Simien 2004, 2005).

Ultimately, these two problems are rooted in the fact that the concept of racial group interests assumes, rather than illustrates, the link between racial group status and the development of preferences. This is particularly apparent when we consider a second way that racial group interests have been operationalized—as the policies and programs pursued and promoted by black political organizations, such as antidiscrimination policies, affirmative action, or social welfare services (Dawson 1994; Gay 1994; Tate 1994; Swain 1995). Using public agendas as an indicator of racial group interests assumes that the interests articulated by certain groups are an unmediated expression of aggregate individual preference. Yet organizational agendas are the end result of a bargaining and negotiation process. Even the integrationist agenda of the civil rights movement—generally considered unproblematic as an expression of racial group interests—was a contested one, and its dominance reflected the political and financial strength of its proponents (Valocchi 1996). The idea of racial group interests does not take into account the distinction between the preferences held by blacks and the framing and expression of those preferences by organized groups. While it might be expedient empirically, conceptually it creates more confusion—are we measuring group members' interests? And if so, which group—the racial group or the political group? Racial group interests, that is, preferences that are intrinsic to one's racial designation, do not exist. Even in the unlikely event that blacks were unanimous in their support for a particular position, referring to that *position* as racial would make little sense and reveal very little about the relationship between racial status and preference formation. When scholars refer to certain preferences as inherent to blacks or any other group, we inadvertently do the same thing that political leaders do—we racialize interests, framing and representing narrow factional preferences as both inherent to and beneficial for the entire group.

To best understand the link between racial status and political preferences, we must examine the internal logics and arguments that leaders and organizations use to unite the two. To do so, it is helpful to use terms that distinguish between the outcomes that political actors desire, the mechanism through which those desires are publicly interpreted, and the impact of those outcomes on various members of a group. I use the term *preferences* where others use the term *interests,* that is, to indicate what individuals seek and understand to be in their benefit. The term *preferences* avoids the quagmires associated with the word *interest* (the debates over subjective versus objective interests, as well as the current association of interests with identity) by focusing on what people want, as opposed to what is good for them. It also captures the relative nature of political choices, the fact that sometimes choices are made in relation to other, less desirable ones. For example, an individual who generally opposes gender-conscious policies might prefer affirmative action policies in city contracting if the alternative outcome—a decrease in the number of women admitted—is disagreeable to them. I purposefully omit a racial modifier in this term in order to emphasize the fact that, although people's particular preferences are related to their group status, the preference itself has no racial content.

The sense that one's preferences are related to one's group membership is best captured by the term *group consciousness*, which scholars define as both a sense of group membership and "a political awareness or ideology regarding the group's relative position in society along with a commitment to collective action aimed at realizing the group's interest" (Miller et al. 1981, 495; Morris 2001). This definition is useful because it highlights distinctions that are muddied by recent definitions of racial identity: it clearly differentiates between identity (the characteristics by which an individual is defined as a member of a group), identification (the degree of attachment to the group), and consciousness (the interpretation of group status). It also allows for considerations of the strength of consciousness (it may be high or low), as well as its content (it might be nationalist or integrationist).[3] Whatever its manifestation, political consciousness is related to, but distinct from, the preference for a particular outcome.

The designation of certain goals as representing the fulfillment of preferences is not a direct result of group status, nor is it a natural or necessary expression of racial identification. Rather, African American elites attempt to define particular preferences as what Cohen refers to as *consensus issues*, those that are "representative of the condition of an entire community and thus worthy of a group response" (1999, 11). In doing so, black elites do two important things: first, they identify its *racial dividend*, which I define as the set of benefits and disadvantages that individuals receive or endure from a program or policy as a result of their racial categorization.[4] This notion is similar to the idea of racial privilege, the unearned advantage that attaches to skin color (McIntosh 1988; Lipsitz 1998; Brown et al. 2003), yet it highlights the fact that not all outcomes are positive, and that individuals experience "both privilege and penalty" as a result of their membership in and identification with social hierarchies (P. Collins 1989). Because consensus issues represent the subordination faced by the entire racial group, the racial dividend is necessarily concrete for some parts of the black population and symbolic for others. The second important result of elite framings of consensus issues is the designation of what might be called a *consensus agenda*, a set of goals, policies, or strategies whose realization they claim would adequately address the consensus issue, and thus achieve advancement for the entire racial group. This agenda is often asserted by formal, organized groups to verify the claim that they address a broad-based set of preferences and reflect a wide range of groups. While it is often presented as reflecting unified agreement in public, the consensus may be highly debated in private and is likely to be the result of coalition building and negotiation between and within groups.

The construction of racial identity is important to the framing of both consensus issues and their associated agendas. African American elites assert that consensus issues reflect or embody some aspect of black identity, and exhortations to support a certain agenda often rely on explicit and implicit claims that they preserve that characteristic. This strategy is apparent in the debates and discussions about demolition that took place in Douglas/Grand Boulevard from the mid to late 1990s. During this time, two sets of events increased the community's sensitivity to the issue of demolition combining to highlight the ways that class differences shape blacks' quality of life. Mid-South devoted its attention and resources to the form of demolition that threatened more affluent residents and advocated a strategy that would best address their concerns. Yet the organization nevertheless framed both the issue and the proposed strategy as providing resolution for all neighborhood residents.

Danger Zones:
Demolition and the Construction of Consensus Issues

The first set of events to increase sensitivity was the gradual discovery that a number of buildings in the proposed Black Metropolis historic district were in danger of being demolished: one by the city and two others by indemnity corporations that had purchased back taxes on the abandoned buildings. The Wabash Street YMCA, the "undisputed birthplace of Black History Month," came under threat of demolition in 1994 (Miller 1996). It had been purchased by the St. Thomas Episcopal Church for one dollar in 1981 and was scheduled for rehabilitation as a low-income apartment building, to be completed by 1998. The rehabilitation, sponsored by three religious organizations, was supported by Mayor Daley, a fact that made the threatened demolition in November 1994 all the more galling.

In addition, the Douglas Development Corporation was in danger of losing the Eighth Regiment Armory, also a part of the Black Metropolis Historic District. In March 1996, its back taxes were purchased by the National Indemnity Corporation, which threatened to demolish it. Finally, members of the Bronzeville Coalition faced multiple threats to their ownership and maintenance of other Black Metropolis sites. The Supreme Life Building, owned by the Black Metropolis Convention and Tourism Council, was threatened with receivership. In addition, Mid-South's attempt to purchase the Overton Building was being blocked by its absentee owner. In the midst of these struggles, neighborhood community groups became aware of the city's use of an accelerated demolition program, a noncourt procedure through which buildings are demolished within one to two months after the issue of a warning citation. In combination, these activities put community-development corporations and residents in a state of high alert.

The second issue that increased residents' concern about demolition was the Chicago Housing Authority's announcement of the impending demolition of several public housing complexes in Douglas/Grand Boulevard. In response to federal policies mandating the renovation or demolition of inadequate public housing, the authority established a "Plan for Transformation," which sought to demolish most of the public housing in the area and replace it with a mix of market rate, affordable, and low-income housing (Chicago Housing Authority 2005). The "Plan for Transformation" occupied a peculiar place in the plans for Bronzeville's revitalization and highlighted the conflicts between low-income residents and more affluent homeowners. On the one hand, the housing authority's plan to demolish Stateway Gardens, Robert Taylor Homes, and Madden Park/Ida B. Wells Homes was a direct threat to the immediate survival of public housing residents. Although the housing authority pledged to construct adequate replacement housing, residents had good reason to suspect their commitment.[5] On the other hand, "Restoring Bronzeville," like the Chicago Housing Authority's "Plan for Transformation," advocated the development of mixed-income housing; as such it was in complete accordance with the broader agenda of the city. Thus Mid-South's stance toward demolition reflected the difficult contradictions inherent in redevelopment strategies that claim to protect the interests of all African Americans through mixed-income development.

The issue of demolition is particularly instructive, for two reasons. First, it neatly illustrates how class status colors blacks' experience of their racial status. Low-income renters and public-housing residents, along with more affluent homeowners and business owners, were all vulnerable to the demolition taking place, though for the former group, demolition threatened their survival, while for the latter group, demolition threatened their quality of life. Second, this issue reveals the extent to which the middle-class framing of issues prevailed, even though the issue held great potential for both consensus and conflict. Coalition leaders could have easily framed demolition as a threat to affordable housing, and in fact, individual Mid-South members sometimes pushed that position. Yet the coalition's primary framing of the demolition problem and its programmatic focus emphasized the threat demolition posed to historic buildings that were crucial to preservationists and tourism developers.

The portrayal of demolition as a consensus issue relied on the notion that the threatened buildings represented the shared heritage of the neighborhood. For example, one Mid-South member described area buildings as "a part of the fabric of this community . . . part of the history of this area and we need to preserve them" (Hill 1997, 3). For supporters of Mid-South, history is not just contained in these threatened buildings: it *is* these threatened buildings. The commentary that accompanies neighborhood tours illustrates how buildings represent the role that Douglas/Grand Boulevard played in significant historical events. Recall, for example, Mr. Anthony's comments about Quinn Chapel:

> the Quinn Chapel [on Twenty-fourth and State Street] is one of the most famous of urban developments. It was named after an AME bishop who was an abolitionist. It is one of the oldest religious buildings built and constructed by blacks, and it was a station on the Underground Railroad. If my grandparents, for example, had escaped from slavery, and run north to Chicago, this is a place they might have come.

So Mr. Anthony identifies this building as significant partly because it stands as a physical marker of an important event or era in racial and national history. In that sense, Quinn Chapel is like most of the buildings in the Black Metropolis Historic District, which are likewise linked to moments of widely recognized historical importance: the Eighth Regiment Armory, for example, was built in 1914 to house a World War I black infantry unit, and the Overton Building was the site of the first black insurance company.

Many other structures are understood as historically significant, even though they may not require or be eligible for landmark status because they, too, represent the Bronzeville heritage. This fieldnote excerpt considers the same guide's commentary on the building that housed a popular black newspaper:

> As we approach Twenty-fourth and Michigan, the guide says, "This is the Defender Building. The new one. The old one is at Thirty-fourth and Indiana. This building housed the most influential newspaper in America. . . . At one time, they had a subscription of 300,000. But for every one subscription, there were two to three people who read the paper. That's almost a million readers. And the *Defender* had a lot of extra information that you didn't get in the mainstream newspaper. A lot of extra information, lots of gossip." Someone on the bus asks him if the newspaper is for sale and he replies, "The whole thing. The whole thing is leaving. And I hope some blacks get together and try to buy it. 'Cause you know, when I look at the obituaries—I look at the obituaries a lot now—according to the white newspapers, you didn't die. But the *Defender* listed it."

The guide notes the new building, as well the old, on his tour. Its significance lies not in its representation of a particular architectural style, nor is this a building like the Overton—impressive as a marker of black financial success. Instead, the Defender Building is meaningful because it represents the value of collectivism that coalition activists understand as reflective of Bronzeville's culture.

Because they understand the buildings as the embodiment of racial heritage, coalition members also defined demolition as a threat to black culture. When describing the problems facing the community, Grady Karl asserted that the residents of Douglas/Grand Boulevard are "at war! And we're fighting for our culture and our history!" Helena Nichols, a woman in her eighties, expressed a similar sentiment about an already demolished building during a building charette in November 1997. She said,

> I was very upset about the demolition that's been going on in this community. . . . I almost cried when they tore down the Binga Building. And I was heartsick [over] the Regal Theater. . . . The Pythian was where we always used to go and have dances because there was no place else to go. If we keep tearing everything down, there'll be nothing left for our children's children.

Residents see not only the history of the community, but their personal history as being threatened by demolition. One resident, reporting on the city's demolition program to Mid-South membership, prefaced his presentation by explaining the effect it was having on his own life: "I'm saddened that I can't take my grandkids to see where I lived. It's my life. My history is here and it's being destroyed." Particularly for residents who have lived in the community for a long time, demolition constitutes the destruction of individual and family history.

Understanding physical structures this way is hardly unique to blacks or to inhabitants of this neighborhood. While land and property are the physical entities being considered, the value of place is "defined through social relationships, not through nature, autonomous markets, or spatial geometry" (Logan and Molotch 1987, 45). For the Bronzeville Coalition, historic buildings are not just pieces of individually owned property, but symbols of community spirit and expressions of racial achievement. But not all buildings are seen this way, and the difference in how various buildings are interpreted illustrates the preferences and concerns of coalition activists. Yet this framing of the buildings as representative of culture, rather than, say the human right to housing, relied heavily upon the Bronzeville identity and prioritized some buildings over others. It did not, for example, depict public housing complexes as emblems of historical black culture or achievement. Such a depiction would only make sense outside the "Restoring Bronzeville" narrative.

For example, neighborhood public housing projects were richly celebrated when they first opened. Moreover, residents established a host of networks and organizations, both formal and informal, to maintain their social, economic, and political well-being in the face of the financial and physical neglect of their buildings (Venkatesh 2000). Yet discussion of public housing projects such as Stateway Gardens and Robert Taylor Homes was meager, and what did take place was generally negative. Madeleine Evans, a young volunteer with the Bronzeville Coalition, expressed the views of many when she said of their impending demolition, "They say they're only going to tear down a few, but [I think] they're starting at Fifty-first and just working their way up. . . . I personally, I'm not for these houses . . . they look like cages . . . they look like prisons with those bars up . . . and if they can find housing for the residents I think it would be a good thing." Ms. Evans's comments are a perfect illustration of the ambivalence or benign neglect of the coalition. She claims she wants to see the projects demolished so residents' quality of life improves, but she says little about how to address the issue of replacement housing. Similarly, Mid-South wanted residents with a mix of incomes, but as an organization it did not make the creation of affordable housing or the preservation of public housing a priority issue. This was the case despite attempts by citywide organizations such as the Coalition to Protect Public Housing to building alliances and working relationships with Mid-South.

Cultural Preservation as Racial Agenda

Not surprisingly, coalition members portrayed historic preservation as a consensus agenda item, one whose material and symbolic benefits would represent progress for the entire neighborhood. Specifically, they depicted saving buildings from demolition as not just a strategy to save physical structures, but a way to affirm and maintain racial heritage and culture. When Bronzeville Coalition supporters have protested the wrecking ball or engaged in public discussions about how historic buildings should be rehabilitated, they have often referred to these processes as being about something more than mere brick-and-mortar projects. One participant in the Overton Planning Charette, for example, commented that because the loss of buildings represents the loss of history, saving and rehabilitating them "is about the reclaiming of lost space." In other words, saving physical structures is a strategy for claiming what rightfully belongs to the black community. Coalition members and leaders also regard historic preservation as an important tactic for maintaining more ephemeral elements of culture. On a tour of the community, our guide explained to us that he was

> honored to give the tour and be a part of the community. He said that it was very important for people to take care of the buildings and keep them from becoming demolished because "when you destroy a community physically, you destroy people's memories. Then their children and their grandchildren can't know what the history was. What if they had torn down the pyramids? There is no way I could describe them to you."

In short, the problem with demolition is not merely that it takes land and property out of the hands of today's black children, but that it will deprive them of knowledge of their racial history. As a result, rehabilitating threatened structures creates a sort of structural archive that maintains the physical representations of racial memory. In this sense, the tour guide echoed the sentiments of former resident William Ingram, who said that "when I look at the building, you're not just involved in the reconstruction of the building, but the reconstruction of ideas."

Bronzeville supporters also frame the rehabilitation of threatened buildings as a fundamentally community-oriented activity. Avery Williams, an architect involved with the Overton Building restoration, told the participants at one event that

> this building is more than a building. This project goes to the soul of what [Bronzeville] is all about. It gives me a chance to extend myself to the group and to apply a different kind of commitment. My purpose is to maximize the investment of people in the community. . . . There are educational, social, and community needs that the building can accommodate.

Mr. Williams understood restoring buildings as not just a job, but as a way for all participants to reestablish their bond with the black community.

This interpretation of historic preservation and rehabilitation is part of a broader claim that gentrification by blacks has collective symbolic benefits. As defined in academic literature, gentrification is the process through which "poor and working-class neighborhoods in the inner city are refurbished via an influx of private capital and middle-class homebuyers and renters" (N. Smith 1996, 32). By arguing for the development of mixed-income housing and promoting the "return" of black middle-class residents, Bronzeville Coalition members promoted black gentrification as the strategy that would best address the problem of saving culture and preventing racial displacement. They framed middle-income residents' personal and financial investment in the community as a communal act whose benefits would raise the status of all blacks. Grady Karl, a redevelopment proponent, expressed this widely held opinion in an interview when he described to me the appropriate role of the black middle class. He said that

> housing directs everything. So, first of all, you've got to come in and anchor the housing by the black middle class buying these homes . . . two and three hundred thousand dollar houses, that's gonna stabilize the community. . . . Stabilize the community means to be able to create a tax base first of all, and you do that by creating new businesses that [the] state taxes. You have people being employed, pay taxes, you create a tax base. That tax base supports the redevelopment of the community.

Mr. Karl emphasizes that black gentrification should take the form of residential investment, that is, the purchase of homes that will "stabilize" the neighborhood. With this comment he expresses the fairly conventional assessment that increasing the number of homeowners in a neighborhood establishes a population that will bring disposable and taxable income into a community. This strategy emphasizes a standard benefit that accrues from individual investment.

Yet Mr. Karl also argues that black investment strategies should have a broader purpose, one reminiscent of the collectivist orientation of the reimagined Bronzeville. He maintains that it is also the responsibility of the black middle class to

> come in and buy land, to create development groups. To create investment clubs, investment organizations; to attract new businesses to take care of their needs, in terms of their lifestyle; to establish new businesses to provide these services to the community; to work as part of a team effort to revitalize the commercial business strips.

In this comment, Mr. Karl defines commercial investment as also being a part of the obligation of black gentrifiers. In one sense he sees this establishment of businesses as a self-interested act responsive to the particular needs of the individual. Because residents lack services such as dry-cleaning establishments, banks, and grocery stores, community leaders expect that affluent blacks will establish these businesses to supply themselves with these amenities. Yet at the same time, this vision of investment is a vision of collective self-help in which residents will work in teams pooling resources to meet their needs. According to him, African Americans should take responsibility for more than their personal financial well-being; they should also work to increase investment among other residents.

Coalition members also view gentrification as having an important impact on the use value of the neighborhood. *Use value* refers to the worth or meaning of places that comes from the way individuals spend time in them (Logan and Molotch 1987). Neighborhoods are sites that give individuals a sense of membership and community. Coalition members see this sense of belonging and pride as yet another way that black investment improves the neighborhood for all its residents. This sentiment is also expressed about contemporary entrepreneurs and businesses. After giving me an interview, long-time resident and business owner Mr. Franklin took me on a tour of his business establishment, pointing out pictures of the founder and showing me additional rooms that could be rented for receptions. He concluded by telling me that "when people ask me, 'what do you give back?' I say what I give back is a facility where they can hold their meetings, a business they can be proud of." According to Mr. Franklin, he has improved the community not only with his initial investment in commercial ventures, but by his continued ownership of the business. With this statement he makes a classic racial uplift argument that his individual accomplishment is in fact a communal accomplishment because of the sense of pride it engenders in community members, who may or may not ever be able to afford his services.

While coalition members see black entrepreneurship as enhancing African Americans' self-perception, they also see it as having the capacity to shape the way outsiders see African Americans. Consider, for example, a remark made by Delia Chester, a developer and business owner in the neighborhood. She suggested that it is not just the *existence* of area businesses that matters, but the fact that these businesses are catering to the "better" classes. She told me that they

> didn't come in and take the project as it was and open the business back up and the same kind of thing. We looked to upscale our neighborhood; to upscale this commercial project and make it stand out to say "This is us. This is who we are. We want upper-class commercial businesses in here."

Who they are—and who they tell other people they are—is a well-to-do group of African Americans who have the desire and capacity to revitalize their community. By "reflecting credit on the race," economic investment bolsters the image and self-image of the neighborhood's African American population.

Framing narrow preferences as consensus issues depends on the assertion that the culture embodied in the neighborhood buildings belongs to all blacks living in the neighborhood. Thus coalition activists drew explicitly and heavily on the Bronzeville identity when describing and interpreting conflicts. One woman who was active in the planning process explained to me that

> one of the things that remained consistent through [the planning] process was everyone's belief that this area had been so significant in the history of the city's development historically, because all of these people used to live

here, famous black people from across the board, surgeons, opera singers, musicians, writers—it was almost like a little Harlem Renaissance. And if we could just tap that one aspect, enthusiastically, then people could rally around that and get excited about redeveloping the area.

To garner community support for "Restoring Bronzeville," redevelopment supporters draw heavily on the notion that residents share a common racial heritage that is expressed in the buildings. They believe that "the key thing that we have in common is culture, culture is a commonality and a community asset; it is a part of the Restoring Bronzeville plan, it is part of the attempt to develop Bronzeville as a heritage tourism destination." Thus, they rely on that commonality in their attempts to garner support for the agenda contained in "Restoring Bronzeville."

The idea that Bronzeville represents a universal heritage is repeatedly articulated in the stories that residents tell about the history of Douglas/Grand Boulevard. What is important about this strategy is not that nostalgia is used to justify historic preservation in itself: indeed, without a vision of the past, there would be nothing to preserve. What matters is how visions of the past are used to assert the universal applicability of the historic preservation strategy, how they are drawn upon to bolster the assertion that historic preservation constitutes a racial agenda with positive dividends for all residents, regardless of class status.

On the rare occasion that the issue of intraracial class differences is raised, Bronzeville Coalition leaders draw on the invented tradition of racial unity to minimize the existence and impact of those differences. Redevelopment supporters are quick to remind residents that these tensions were not a part of the spirit of unity that pervaded historic Bronzeville, and admonish that

we had to learn to be friends back then. . . . We're all in this mess together. We have to learn how to identify ourselves with our friends. In unity is strength. We used to know that, and we will know it again.

Thus, they point to the past as proof that racial unity is both possible and necessary for success. Development supporters may sometimes acknowledge the existence of class conflict, but even then, the Bronzeville heritage is offered as a palliative. This fieldnote excerpt describes organizer Sandra Marcus's response when the issue of class differences was raised at a meeting for residents of Lake Meadows, a middle-income apartment complex at the northern end of Bronzeville:

> A middle-aged man in the audience says that "there are a lot of different incomes in this community. What are the bonds that you think will hold us together?" Ms. Marcus responds that "there have always been class divisions in the community, but in the past we've been able to overcome those divisions. During the civil rights movement we were united against a common enemy. So we think that we can focus on common community values. Whether you're in public housing or you have a $200,000 house. We all want a good education for our children. We all want clean, safe neighborhoods."

To address the participant's concerns about community discord, the organizer mentioned innocuous and vaguely defined issue positions with which everyone—Douglas/Grand Boulevard residents or not—can agree. But she also referred to the racial tradition of unifying around a single agenda, suggesting that contemporary residents should do the same. Most interesting, however, was her reference to "a common enemy," the recognition of which is the spur for putting aside intraracial differences and uniting around a single agenda. Her reply represents the tendency, common among revitalization proponents, to use the invented tradition of Bronzeville to guide the values and behaviors of residents. What is most important about Ms. Marcus's response is not her assertion that blacks share some common concerns. Douglas/Grand Boulevard residents are indeed widely interested in jobs and housing, whatever their economic circumstances. And as mentioned before, most fear displacement by whites. Rather, the problem lies in how referring to these commonalities enables revitalization proponents to sidestep the issue of competing preferences of renters, public housing residents, and owners of high-priced housing. Nor did she ever articulate what agenda might be pursued or what compromises might be reached to address those competing preferences. Instead, she presupposes that commonalities themselves will naturally overwhelm conflicts, or at least minimize them.

This illustrates the extent to which the racialization of preferences assumes that shared culture translates into a shared racial dividend. Even when they do not depict class differences as subordinate to racial bonds, coalition members may suggest that the needs of Douglas/Grand Boulevard residents are at least compatible. Portia Silk provided an example of this during a business council meeting in which she described the Douglas/Grand Boulevard population in market terms. In her presentation to business council members, she gave suggestions regarding the strategic vision of the council. Ms. Silk suggested that the arrival of middle-class home-owners was leading to the development of a new market in Bronzeville, one she referred to as a "New Working Family Community." This group, she asserted, consisted of two primary parts: the first was what she referred to as the "Indigenous Families," who would be increasingly working as a re-sult of the welfare-to-work program. The second group she referred to as "Urban Pioneers," those middle-class families who were new to the area. When trying to assess their market potential, she suggested that the "need for goods" would change for the Indigenous Families, whose recent employ-ment would provide them with disposable income. They would soon want the same goods and services as the Urban Pioneers, who want to maintain their lifestyle. In this depiction, Ms. Silk assumes the increasing ability of poor families to find work, to find child care that meets their work sched-ules, to earn a living wage—all circumstances that are necessary for unem-ployed and working-poor families to do their share in the new community. More important, however, she suggests that gentrification will bring to pub-lic housing residents, retired people, underemployed adults, unemployed teens, middle-class professionals, and low-wage service workers an equally paced improvement in their present circumstances that, like a rising tide, will lift all boats.

While it is true that black residents shared the threat of displacement, the source, nature, and extent of that threat varied by class. Homeowners, for example, faced the fear that their property taxes would rise beyond their ability to pay. Older homeowners living on a fixed income were particularly susceptible to this threat. Similarly, renters were afraid that they would be unable to afford rising rents. Public housing residents, on the other hand, had as much to fear from the shifts in national and municipal social welfare policy as they did from the potential influx of individual white gentrifiers. Despite promises to the contrary, the Chicago Housing Authority has failed to replace demolished neighborhood housing with an adequate amount of affordable units, and the use of housing vouchers has not addressed residents' concerns about maintaining the social networks that are crucial to their economic survival (Bennett, Smith and Wright 2006; Fischer 2004; Longini 2000). We can see the difference in potential dividend when we consider this distinction between economic and racial gentrification. Ms. Dean characterized homeowners as unconcerned

> about economic [gentrification]. That would be great! That would enhance their personal property, but I think there's a feeling that "hey, we saw the value in this neighborhood first, we moved here, we sunk our dollars here, we worked to try to make it great, we don't wanna get pushed out."

This distinction—between racial gentrification and economic gentrification—highlights the different dividend that accrued to more financially secure residents to support revitalization, even though poorer blacks were more likely to suffer its ill effects. As one Mid-South member announced in a meeting, "We don't mind gentrification; we want to minimize displacement." While the former is generally understood as encompassing the latter, the two were not necessarily the same in his mind. Gentrification referred to efforts to "upscale" the neighborhood and increase the number of middle-class residents. Displacement was an undesirable but preventable by-product of this effort. Poorer residents, on the other hand, saw the situation differently: according to one public housing organizer, "There are two separate populations in Bronzeville. One group is trying to buy up all the big, pretty houses. They want to restore the area. . . . But the people on State Street are saying where are we going to go [after demolition]?" This comment captures both the depth of the schism and the nature of the different racial dividend.

You're History: The Limits of Constructed Community

In March 2004, *Chicago* magazine published a cover story entitled "The New South Side: A Special Report on the Remarkable Boom That's Transforming a Historic Slice of the City" (Rodkin, Whitaker and Wilk 2004). Bronzeville took center stage in the piece, with the photos depicting the public art and award-winning architectural projects that now dot the neighborhood. In their description of Bronzeville, the authors attempt to minimize the history of racial segregation and public and private disinvestment that has plagued Douglas/Grand Boulevard since World War I. While they admit the area has been prey to "decades of white flight, poverty, and gangs," they quickly assure the reader that this kind of unpleasantness is a thing of the past. According to them, the demolition of the Stateway Gardens and Robert Taylor public housing units created a "wide open space" on which to build mixed-income housing units. And what some call the Black Belt, they call a "remarkable belt of home construction and rehab that stretches from Buckingham Fountain . . . to Sixty-third Street" (74). Readers concerned about the lingering impact of the area's infamous past might consider the prediction of city planning official Arnold Randall, who insists that in twenty to thirty years, "these communities will be such nice places to live that all the negative things in the past will be forgotten . . . people won't realize where we've come from" (75).

The elision of history this article strains to achieve—the attempt to erase "where we've come from"—is remarkable because it contrasts so sharply with the nostalgia upon which the neighborhood's revitalization had until very recently been based. During the late 1980s and early 1990s, journalistic, academic, and everyday accounts of Douglas/Grand Boulevard emphasized its historic significance as a crucible of black cultural, economic, and political accomplishment. The neighborhood revitalization strategies adopted by community organizations in Douglas/Grand Boulevard expressed such a nostalgia, for they reimagined the Jim Crow era in both ideological and concrete ways. Residents, elected officials, and pundits expressed a remarkably consistent recollection of and longing for the way Douglas/Grand Boulevard had existed in the past. Many residents and community leaders saw the excavation and preservation of that history as the neighborhood's saving grace: a safeguard against the displacement that a different kind of revitalization—one uninformed by historical memory—might bring. In their recollections and retellings of history, residents portray the early twentieth century as a golden era in the organization and operation of black community. Yet nearly twenty years later, the neighborhood's history was secondary to its status as one of "the area's hottest neighborhoods." The past, as city planner Arnold Randall suggested, was a pesky detail that the public would just as soon forget.

The shift in the kind of story being told about Douglas/Grand Boulevard's history reflects both the risks and rewards that come from relying on nostalgic visions of racial community in the revitalization of black neighborhoods. The reward of nostalgia is that it serves as an alternative to the urban frontier rhetoric that traditionally accompanies processes of neighborhood change (N. Smith 1996). This framework portrays whites as pioneers forging a new path through savage, uncharted territory, and it depicts minorities as ill-mannered, unmanageable populations, justifying and even requiring—their removal for the achievement of the fabled "highest and best use of land." Racial nostalgia, by contrast, portrays the black population as an unending source of cultural, political, and economic accomplishment, and it *requires* the presence of blacks for cultural preservation. By evoking visions of a historically linked racial community, coalition members provide a justification for their continued presence and control. Yet the rhetoric of nostalgia can serve the same purpose as that of the urban frontier: justifying the displacement of the neighborhood's poorest blacks by shrouding the process of gentrification in the mantle of cultural preservation.

Nostalgia and Identity
in the Twenty-first Century

Relying on experience, myth, history, and nostalgia, African Americans create particular notions of racial identity, specific notions of what it means to be black. These visions are linked to specific times and places, and as this book has shown, they are often cobbled together as blacks determine and articulate their political goals. This constructedness does not imply that race is insignificant: despite academic clamoring for its end, race remains important in the political life of African Americans, continuing to structure our access to and involvement in dominant political and economic institutions.

Moreover, the construction of racial identity plays a central role in political elites' efforts to define certain preferences as appropriate for group support. In reframing the neighborhood as the crucible of black economic, political, and social achievement, community leaders have reinvented the residents who lived there, painting them as the natural successors of this auspicious past. These images of both the place and the people who inhabit it have increased the neighborhood's attractiveness to potential residential and commercial investors; they have bolstered black residents' claims to neighborhood space by defining it as fundamentally African American; and they have served as the basis for contemporary activists' understanding of what binds them together, what they share and owe one another as members of a black community. Thus, the meaning of racial identity has had important political consequences, providing black elites with a language, history, and moral argument that guides and frames behavior. This is particularly important given the limited resources available to black neighborhood organizations. As I have tried to illustrate throughout this book, contemporary neighborhood elites are responding to a legacy of racial discrimination and uneven development, and thus their behavior is embedded in a structure of racism that has limits and continues to limit their access to centers of decision making. Within this context, localized understandings of what defines blackness emerged as a crucial component of neighborhood planning in Douglas/Grand Boulevard.

Yet as is often the case, Mid-South's development focus limited its ability and willingness to organize and make demands on behalf of the neighborhood's poorer residents. Moreover, activists in this Chicago neighborhood drew on these notions of blackness in ways that reproduced the privileges and disadvantages of class. They advocated a revitalization process whose rhetoric and strategy were symbolically inclusive, but privileged the more affluent members of the neighborhood, both ideologically and materially. The historical narrative upon which contemporary claims to community are based obscures the existence and contributions of average black citizens, attributes racial accomplishments to the miniscule black middle class, and implicitly assigns blame for neighborhood decline to the black poor. Ultimately, Bronzeville Coalition members have drawn on these lopsided narratives to argue for historic preservation and middle-class investment strategies that sidelined the issues of affordable housing and largely benefited the more affluent members of the neighborhood, all the while representing these policies as ones that would advance a universally beneficial agenda.

These outcomes illustrate important principles about the relationship between race, class, and politics. Traditional political science theories argue that the degree to which race shapes black political behavior depends on its salience—the importance attributed to it *over and above* other status categories. Although more recent work argues for the interactive affects of race and, for example, class, these works also assert that the effect of race lies in the strength with which it is felt. The case of Douglas/Grand Boulevard expands on those arguments by illustrating that the impact of race lies also in the *meaning* with which it is imbued. These meanings are not a natural expression of racial status that lie dormant until triggered by the emergence of interracial conflict. Rather, they are constructed through and in response to political conflicts, and thus reflect the power dynamics of the particular community within which they arise. They are also constituted by other status categories in ways that make ranking their relative significance impossible and, in fact, unhelpful. This work suggests, then, that questions about the relative significance of race and class in the post–civil rights era are headed in the wrong direction; what is more illuminating and useful is an assessment of the processes through which each is constituted.

In addition, these findings suggest how important it is for political scientists who study race to expand beyond our own discipline and draw on the rich methods and traditions of inquiry that mark the other social sciences. The survey work that dominates the research on black politics provides a much needed explanation of what African Americans think about race, particularly in comparison to whites. Yet this work does not tell us much about *how* African Americans think about race—that is, what assumptions and arguments they use to think through and justify those opinions. Nor does it tell us much about the processes through which individuals come to develop those perceptions. Most troubling is its reliance on reified notions of race and racial identity, which cannot incorporate the recent conceptual advances of other disciplines. If we do not become more open to the use of qualitative and interpretive methods, I fear our contributions to the study of race and its relationship to power will fall even farther behind those of the other social sciences.

The case of Douglas/Grand Boulevard also offers some important insight into the character of black politics in the twenty-first century. First, it accounts for the growing popularity of Jim Crow nostalgia in urban areas over the past twenty years. Nostalgia is not just something that people feel randomly; it is a sentiment and perspective linked to neighborhood development and identity construction. The popularity of these ideas thus reflects the political opportunities presented by shifting urban economies.

These bouts of homesickness for a golden era in black history are not restricted to the current period, and Jim Crow nostalgia in particular was articulated at least as early as the 1980s in Douglas/Grand Boulevard. Yet, as this book shows, these sentiments grew in both importance and popularity as they became married to concrete economic development strategies. In this sense, nostalgia functions as a racial project in that it argues for investments from both individuals and institutions, based on the interpretation of segregation-era blacks as models of social organization and achievement. As both cities and neighborhoods turn increasingly to culture and tourism-based development, we can expect these ideas to gain greater adherence with a wider audience.

In addition, Jim Crow nostalgia is an important thermometer, an indicator not of what happened in the past, nor of what should happen in the future, but of what the present means to Douglas/Grand Boulevard residents and blacks across the nation. Nostalgia for the segregation era articulates a broader uncertainty about, and dissatisfaction with, the fruits of the civil rights movement. It celebrates the image of insular black communities in segregated spaces during a time when racial boundaries were less frequently crossed in work and social life. It therefore functions as an implicit criticism of civil rights strategies and integrationism and expresses a conservative racial separatism that emphasizes self-help and racial uplift rather than demands on the state. More recent articulations of this disappointment surfaced in response to the fiftieth anniversary of the *Brown vs. Board of Education* decision outlawing segregation in the public schools. In addition to sparking a flood of celebrations of *Brown*, the date prompted a series of retrospectives and ruminations about the advisability of desegregation (Ogletree 2004; Bell 2004; Cashin 2004). These discussions reflect the limitations of the political, economic, and social incorporation that the civil rights movement generated—specifically its inability to address structural forms of racism. They also reflect the degree of black discontent over these limitations, and the growing sense among some African Americans that the best way to address these inadequacies is through the establishment of greater social control by the black middle class.

It would be a mistake to interpret this line of thinking as indicative of growing class interests in black communities. As the first two chapters here indicate, both the preferences of black elites and the opportunities to pursue them have historically been shaped by class. The behavior of the Bronzeville Coalition in the 1980s and 1990s mirrors that of the black elite in both the migration and the post–World War II eras—not in substance, but in character. Each elite pursued its own interests and then interpreted that pursuit as beneficial for the rest of the black population. Moreover, each of Douglas/Grand Boulevard's leadership cadres has been embedded in, and thus constrained by, a particular racial hierarchy, expressed within a particular urban political economy. Attentiveness to these contextual features therefore yields a different characterization of contemporary black politics, one that acknowledges the classed nature of black middle-class agendas, but finds its source in the unwieldy combination of opportunity and constraint conferred by this group's position in class and race hierarchies. The case of Douglas/Grand Boulevard highlights three strategies that middle-class blacks are using to manage this bind.

The first of these strategies is the commodification of blackness, by which I mean the offering up of histories and habits that are understood as African American for purchase and sale. The development of heritage tourism in Chicago, New York, and Philadelphia is an important instance of this pattern, and suggestive of the ways that such strategies are linked to processes of urban change. Yet such strategies are not practiced only in relation to cities, as illustrated by the entrepreneurial efforts of Fredrika Newton, wife of former Black Panther Huey Newton and one of the founders of the Huey Newton Foundation. She hopes to convert the phrase "Burn Baby Burn"—once a slogan representing racial militancy—into a trademark tagline to promote a hot sauce. Cofounder David Hilliard suggests that they're

> just trying to be creative with our radical marketing, using our history as a marketing resource. . . . For those people who criticize and say that we sold out, this is actually capitalism with a conscience, if there's any such thing, because we intend to use some of the proceeds to support some of those ideas that we stood for at the heyday of our movement. (del Barco 2005)

The commodification of blackness requires a certain degree of sanitization and obfuscation, which troubles scholars to no end. More important, however, than whether we find this tactic personally palatable is the political purpose for which the strategy is adopted. African American elites claim to barter in blackness as a way to honor all members of their specific racial community. This claim diverts attention away from the ways that their efforts benefit—or worse, harm—specific portions of the group and instead lends a veneer of collectivism and representativeness to their behavior.

A second pattern that marks the post–civil rights political scene is what I call the appropriation of racial injury. This refers to the practice of claiming a greater racial disadvantage than one actually has experienced through asserting an explicit or implicit association with those who have suffered it to a great degree. Through reference to harms endured by an undifferentiated "we," black elites specify racial disadvantage, designate which individuals and groups are injured parties, and most important, place themselves within that category along with others. An obvious instance of this is when middle-class homeowners express a concern that "we" will be gentrified out of the neighborhood as a result of the demolition of public housing. On the one hand, this strategy is a standard framing technique that builds black solidarity by identifying the sides in a conflict. It has some validity given that the black middle class has inherited the cumulative effects of racism that affect life chances, health, wealth, and mobility. Yet this strategy moves beyond a simple framing technique to become an exploitative claim of "injury by association" when middle-class blacks assert first, that there is a universal racial disadvantage whose manifestations are undifferentiated across class lines, and second, that this universal disadvantage leads unerringly to a universal racial agenda, one whose benefits are also undifferentiated across class.

The first two trends raise questions about elite accountability and encourage black elites to adopt a third strategy—the performance of authenticity. As I indicate in chapter 4, this involves not just determining what constitutes the behavior of "real" black people, but also using racial authenticity as the measure of political representativeness. The disappointed hope of many is that using authenticity as a standard of judgment will help wayward blacks—whatever their class status—to "remember where they came from" and adopt the behavior the accuser deems appropriate. Yet as Douglas/Grand Boulevard's civic elite has demonstrated, defendants in racial inauthenticity trials are adept at proving their innocence, a fact that highlights the ineffectiveness of the charge. In mentioning these three trends, I do not wish to argue that these behaviors are new or in some way particular to the contemporary period. I merely suggest that in combination, they form an important set of behaviors that both heighten contemporary class tensions and are used to manage them. To a great degree, scholars and activists have argued that these tensions result from the growing strength of class identity among the black middle class. I have tried to argue in this book that the primary challenge for both practitioners and students of black politics is understanding these tensions within the context of post–civil rights incorporation, which has modified both black elites' historical role as political brokers, and the tools they rely on to act in that capacity.

Attentiveness to these tools highlights the importance of broadening our discussion of contemporary black politics away from concerns over middle-class racial authenticity. Some fear that middle-class blacks will "forget where they came from"; still others hope that references to authenticity will jog their memory, provoking more affluent blacks to champion the interests of poor African Americans *even when doing so would conflict with their own preferences*. This analysis illustrates the futility of trying to shame affluent African Americans into a more progressive stance. Regardless of the racial commitments of the black civic elite, black urban neighborhoods are still plagued by a legacy of racial discrimination and financial disinvestment. They are experiencing these conditions in an era when neoliberal responses are growing in popularity, so that urban planners and public officials are relying increasingly on market solutions to address issues of racialized urban inequality. This trend has manifested itself in concrete ways that further decrease urban black residents' quality of life. The gutting of social welfare programs has ripped out the social safety net at the same time the push for gentrification has razed the supply of public and affordable housing. Moreover, black political responses have softened in the post–civil rights era—particularly in urban areas, where the focus on economic development has diverted activists' attention away from organizing. The focus on the racial commitments of black middle-class actors distracts us from the more pressing question, which is whether racial identity is a useful mobilizing principle for low-income residents of black neighborhoods trying to spark the economic development that their communities so desperately need.

To consider this question, I turn, one final time, to neighborhood resident and Mid-South member Louie Ogden, one of the few informants who repeatedly expressed concern for low-income residents. When I ask him to tell me what he likes best about his neighborhood, he plops into his seat back with a slight shake of the head and says

> Mmmm. Man. Everything. You know what I'm saying? . . . You hear stories about Thirty-fifth and about, you know, different kinds of people. Criminals, you know, good folks. I mean I just—I love black people, you know what I'm saying? So, you know, when you love black people, it's like, you take the good and the bad. You know what I'm saying? And I'm not, you know, one of those folks who says "hey those people in public housing . . . " you know. Whatever. Cause I lived in public housing and I know it's good people over there, you know. And I know it's bad people over there. And I take both. I don't have to hang out with the bad but I still—they got a story, you know what I'm saying?

I find Louie's comments particularly compelling because they express a sense of affection for racial identity that, although unguarded, is not unreflective. His "love" for black people is easily lost in activists' angling for spoils and positioning, and in academic wrangling over the use of race as an analytical category. It highlights the fact that racial identity remains meaningful, both politically and emotionally, even—and perhaps especially—among African Americans who recognize and grapple with the class divisions within black communities. Louie, like many of the participants in Bronzeville's redevelopment, understands that visions of racial identity are constructed. His comment nevertheless suggests that racial identity, although flawed, is an important political resource, in part because it provides a "story" that African Americans can use to help them see one another's humanity more clearly.

It is easy to imagine another story that might have been told about Bronzeville's history, one that included working-class men and women as equal contributors to the "greatness" of the migration era. And it is tempting that this new story could have provided the basis for a contemporary identity whose idea of authenticity derived from the everyday struggle against racialized forms of economic exploitation rather than the middle-class management of the institutional ghetto. Yet the question is not so much whether different notions of black identity can be constructed; it is whether a different story would help to avoid the pitfalls and limitations of appeals to racial identity. Can race-based politics accommodate a class analysis that prioritizes the conditions of poor and working-class blacks? Or are the appeals to racial identity rendered unworkable by black elites' tendency to name their own preferences as those of the race? The case of Bronzeville raises this question, rather than answers it. What it illustrates clearly, however, is that appeals to racial identity are both powerful and dangerous. They continue to resonate deeply with African Americans, despite and because of their underlying class dimensions. As a result, African American elites continue to rely on them to secure the support—or at least the quiescence—of their constituents. Those who advocate a race-based politics, then, can only continue to do so if they clarify how appeals to racial identity can serve poor and working-class blacks. If they do not, they help to maintain the pattern in which racial identity is used in the name of the many, but on behalf of the few.

Notes

Introduction

1. Group conflict theory has been used primarily to challenge the ideas of symbolic racism, which focuses on the relative effects of racism, self-interest, and group interests on whites (Kinder 1986; Kinder and Sanders 1996; Kinder and Sears 1981; McConahay 1982; McConahay and Hough 1976; Sears, Hensler, and Speer 1979; Sears, van Laar, Carillo, and Kosterman 1997; Sears, Lau, Tyler, and Allen 1980; Sears and Kinder 1985).

2. This conceptualization and measurement of racial identification has become the standard in racial attitude studies. See, for example, Simien (2004, 2005).

3. See Brubaker and Cooper (2000) for a useful exploration of the analytical confusions surrounding identity.

4. This discussion draws from the Chicago Fact Book Consortium's *Local Community Fact Book* (1990).

5. In Chicago, the North Side is generally understood as "white," while the South and West Sides are seen as "black." Although these interpretations reflect long-standing patterns of segregation and capture broad patterns, they gloss over the complexity introduced by black class mobility and immigration.

6. My greatest responsibility was a brief stint as the co-chair of Mid-South's economic development committee. My election to this position, which I was not skillful or experienced enough to prevent, was spurred in part by my consistent participation in neighborhood meetings.

7. When describing community organizations and their executive officers, I use correct names. I also identify and quote elected officials and their public

statements. However, when quoting informants, either from interviews or field notes, I use aliases.

1. The Way We Were

1. For more on client–patron relationships, see Kilson (1971) and Meier (1962).

2. At the same time that black leaders sought to establish this organization at the city level, a group of leaders sought to establish the Equal Rights and Protective League of Illinois, its state-level equivalent (Spear 1967, 85).

3. Meier (1962) and Meier and Lewis (1959) illustrate how these changes extended beyond Chicago to cities across the nation.

4. This distinction between "respectable" and illicit enterprises was often difficult to determine, as the same individual might own both types of businesses, or shift between one and the other. Robert Motts, for example, opened his more respectable theater with money he had earned working at the infamous John "Mush-mouth" Johnson's saloon (Blair forthcoming).

5. During the William Hale Thompson administration, blacks received far more patronage than they had in the past. During Thompson's third administration, "six assistant corporation counsels, five assistant city prosecutors, and one assistant city attorney were appointed. In addition there were law department investigators making the total number of colored appointees about 14 percent of all the employees of the department" (Gosnell 1935, 200). In addition to these material benefits, Thompson provided African Americans with symbolic support—publicly defending them, for example, against racism and declining to regulate the activities of black underworld figures (Gosnell 1935, 55–56).

6. Restrictive covenants are clauses in housing contracts that prevent the properties from being sold or rented to particular racial groups. For more on restrictive covenants, see Plotkin (1999).

7. Although as Drake and Cayton note, service jobs were not "negro jobs" (1993, 261).

8. Though oddly enough, the number of black-owned businesses actually reached a high of 2,464 in 1937, largely because Depression-era unemployment induced black residents to try their hand at business ownership (Drake and Cayton 1993, 434).

9. The majority of that growth occurred in Grand Boulevard, which lies to the south of Douglas.

10. The policy men, however, switched to the Democratic Party quickly because they needed political protection to shield their illegal activities from the law. See Drake and Cayton (1993, 352–53) and Biles (1984, 89–102).

11. "Policy" was the term used to describe the lottery games managed by independent gambling companies. For more on policy, see Drake and Cayton (1993, 470–94) and Thompson (2003).

12. While Pullman is the best-known employer of porters, others worked in elevators and at the train stations as Red Caps.

13. Strickland (2001, 130) reports that even when the league itself was not willing or able to provide material and symbolic support, staff members frequently participated in the left-wing activities of which Chicago Urban League funders disapproved.

14. This, despite the fact that the Republican candidate was the immensely popular Oscar DePriest.

15. See also J. Wilson (1960).

16. Although see Grimshaw (1992, 98) on black aldermen's response to urban renewal at the University of Chicago.

2. When We Were Colored

1. The commission was named the Mid-South Planning Group until 1993.

2. For more on neighborhood groups and resident participation, see Manley (1995) and L. Davis (2000).

3. According to community lore, the area to which they returned got its name from having been overlooked by developers during the age of urban renewal. Delia Chester, a member of the Douglas Development Corporation, claims that then Alderman William Barnett "named it that. We were looking at an aerial photo and he said, 'Lake Meadows, Prairie Shores, South Common, Stateway, Dearborn Homes, Ida B. Wells—this area in here is kinda like a gap in here.' . . . So he said 'This is the Gap.' So we named it the Gap."

4. Such a response was possible because of the advances of the civil rights movement and the context of economic prosperity. As Landry points out (1987, 73–78), both the 1950s and the 1970s witnessed either a strong movement or a strong economy. Only in the 1960s did these two combine to result in expanded social programs.

5. For example, Steven Gregory argues that War on Poverty programs distinguished the black poor and the black middle class by "differentiating the

institutional settings in which the needs and interests of the two groups were defined and addressed" (1998, 146). Where poor black residents were defined as social welfare dependents whose needs were addressed by service agencies, their middle-class counterparts were organized into community groups whose primary focus was neighborhood improvement and maintenance.

3. Back to the Future

1. Drake and Cayton (1993) argue that there were five hundred black businesses before migration, 5 percent of which were upper class (434, 522).

2. Timuel Black (2003) has recently completed the first in a two-volume set of oral histories that capture the lives and experiences of blacks whose families migrated to the neighborhood at the beginning of the twentieth century.

3. My assertion here is not that the blues itself is an invented tradition, but that the annual festival is, in part because it has purposes other than the practice of culture.

4. Ties and Chitlins

1. Schaffer and Smith (1986) predicted similarly that blacks in Harlem lacked the income and wealth to sustain their role in the neighborhood's gentrification.

2. One measure of the popularity and pervasiveness of these slang terms is their appearance and explanation on Wikipedia, http://en.wikipedia.org/wiki/Oreo_Cookie_(slang), accessed October 31, 2005.

3. Moore (2002) places a similar emphasis on collectivism as significant for middle-class black identity.

4. *Handkerchief-head* is a word for a black person perceived to be a race traitor.

5. We're All in This Mess Together

1. See Reed (1999a) for similar criticisms of work on racial group interests.

2. Dawson's work (1994) is devoted to describing the interactive mechanisms that link racial identity with the perception of racial group interests. My point here is that the concept itself presumes a link.

3. Chong and Rogers (2005) make a similar point.

4. One might question the use of the racial modifier with the concept of dividend when I stressed the importance of eliminating it when defining preferences. While preferences themselves cannot be racial because their relationship to a racial group is about perception, dividend—which is benefit and advantage—is

the result of categorization. Moreover, the concept of dividend as I have defined it here includes its intersection with other status categories.

5. The Chicago Housing Authority is notorious for its failure to follow through on commitments to residents, and the drawn-out, highly publicized battle between residents of Cabrini-Green and agency officials only served to exacerbate this perception (Bennett and Reed 1999).

Bibliography

Almada, Jeanette. 1997. "Students Draw Plans to Save S. Side Armory." *Chicago Sun-Times*, August 8.

Anderson, Alan B., and George W. Pickering. 1986. *Confronting the Color Line: The Broken Promise of the Civil Rights Movement in Chicago*. Athens: University of Georgia Press.

Anderson, Benedict. 1983. *Imagined Communities*. London: Verso.

Ashworth, Gregory J. 1994. "From History to Heritage, From Heritage to Identity: In Search of Concepts and Models." In *Building a New Heritage: Tourism, Culture and Identity in the New Europe*, ed. Gregory Ashworth and P. J. Larkham. London: Routledge.

Ashworth, Gregory J., and J. E. Tunbridge. 1990. *The Tourist Historic City*. London: Belhaven Press.

Baker, Houston A., Jr. 1980. *The Journey Back*. Chicago: University of Chicago Press.
———. 1984. *Blues, Ideology and Afro-American Literature: A Vernacular Theory*. Chicago: University of Chicago Press.

Bates, Beth Tompkins. 2001. *Pullman Porters and the Rise of Protest Politics in Black America, 1925–1945*. Chapel Hill, N.C.: University of North Carolina Press.

Bell, Derrick. 2004. *Silent Covenants: Brown v. Board of Education and the Unfulfilled Hopes for Racial Reform*. New York: Oxford University Press.

Bennett, Larry. 1989. "Postwar Redevelopment in Chicago: The Declining Politics of Party and the Rise of the Neighborhood." In *Unequal Partnerships: The Political Economy of Urban Redevelopment in Postwar America*, ed. Gregory D. Squires. New Brunswick, N.J.: Rutgers University Press.

———. 1993. "Harold Washington and the Black Urban Regime." *Urban Affairs Quarterly* 28, no. 3: 423–40.

———. 1999. "The Shifting Terrain of Neighborhood Politics." In *Community Politics and Policy*, ed. Gwenn Moore and J. Allen Whitt. Stamford, Conn.: JAI Press.

Bennett, Larry, and Adolph Reed Jr. 1999. "The New Face of Urban Renewal: The Near North Redevelopment Initiative and the Cabrini-Green Neighborhood." In *Without Justice for All: The New Liberalism and Our Retreat from Racial Equality*, ed. Adolph Reed Jr. Boulder, Colo.: Westview Press.

Bennett, Larry, Janet Smith, and Patricia Wright, eds. 2006. *Where Are Poor People to Live? Transforming Public Housing Communities*. Armonk, N.Y.: M. E. Sharple, Inc.

Betancur, John, Deborah Bennett, and Patricia Wright. 1991. "Effective Strategies for Community Economic Development." In *Challenging Uneven Development: An Urban Agenda for the 1990s*, ed. Philip Nyden and Wim Wiewel. New Brunswick, N.J.: Rutgers University Press.

Bey, Lee. 1996a. "Mayor Crafting Committee to Study Bronzeville." *Chicago Sun-Times*, May 16.

———. 1996b. "Face-lift for Bronzeville." *Chicago Sun-Times*, July 13.

———. 1996c. "King Drive Project Celebrated." *Chicago Sun-Times*, September 11.

Biles, Roger. 1984. *Big City Boss in Depression and War: Mayor Edward J. Kelly of Chicago*. DeKalb, Ill.: Northern Illinois University Press.

———. 1995. *Richard J. Daley: Politics, Race, and the Governing of Chicago*. DeKalb, Ill.: Northern Illinois University Press.

Black, Bob. 1996. "Bronzeville Contest." *Chicago Sun-Times*, May 2, p. 3.

Black, Timuel. 2003. *Bridges of Memory: Chicago's First Wave of Black Migration*. Evanston, Ill.: Northwestern University Press.

Blair, Cynthia. Forthcoming. *"We Must Live Anyhow": Race, Sexuality, and the Changing Landscapes of African American Women's Sex Work in Chicago, 1870–1930*. Chicago: University of Chicago Press.

Bobo, Lawrence. 1983. "Whites' Opposition to Busing: Symbolic Racism or Realistic Group Conflict?" *Journal of Personality and Social Psychology* 45, no. 6: 1196–1210.

———. 1998. "Race, Interests and Beliefs about Affirmative Action: Unanswered Questions and New Directions." *American Behavioral Scientist* 41, no. 7: 985–1005.

Bonilla Silva, Eduard. 2003. *Racism without Racists: Color-Blind Racism and the Persistence of Racial Inequality in the United States.* Lanham, Md.: Rowman and Littlefield.

Bowly, Devereux. 1978. *The Poorhouse: Subsidized Housing in Chicago, 1895–1976.* Carbondale, Ill.: Southern Illinois University Press.

Boyd, Michelle. 2000. "Reconstructing Bronzeville: Racial Nostalgia and Neighborhood Redevelopment." *Journal of Urban Affairs* 22, no. 2:107–22.

Boyer, M. Christine. 1992. "Cities for Sale: Merchandising History at South Street Seaport." In *Variations on a Theme Park: The New American City and the End of Public Space*, ed. Michael Sorkin. New York: Hill and Wang.

Branham, Charles. 1981. "The Transformation of Black Political Leadership in Chicago, 1864–1942." Ph.D. diss., University of Chicago.

Brashler, William. 1978. "The Black Middle Class: Making It." *New York Times*, December 3.

Bratt, Rachel G. 1997. "CDCs: Contributions Outweigh Contradictions, a reply to Randy Stoecker." *Journal of Urban Affairs* 19, no. 1:23–28.

Brown, Michael K., Martin Carnoy, Elliott Currie, Troy Duster, David B. Oppenheimer, Marjorie M. Schultz, and David Wellman. 2003. *Whitewashing Race: The Myth of a Color-Blind Society.* Berkeley and Los Angeles: University of California Press.

Brown, Michael K., and Steven P. Erie. 1981. "Blacks and the Legacy of the Great Society: The Economic and Political Impact of Federal Social Policy." *Public Policy* 29, no. 3: 299–330.

Browning, Rufus P., Dale Rogers Marshall, and David H. Tabb. 1984. *Protest Is Not Enough: The Struggle of Blacks and Hispanics for Equality in Urban Politics.* Berkeley and Los Angeles: University of California Press.

Brubaker, Rogers, and Frederick Cooper. 2000. "Beyond 'Identity.'" *Theory and Society* 29:1–47.

Burnham, Scott. 1994. "Political Fates Tied to CHA Projects." *Chicago Reporter*, May/June.

Campbell, Angus, Philip E. Converse, Warren E. Miller, and Donald E. Stokes. 1960. *The American Voter.* Chicago: University of Chicago Press.

Cannon, Lynn Weber. 1984. "Trends in Class Identification among Black Americans from 1952 to 1978." *Social Science Quarterly* 65, no. 1:112–26.

Cashin, Sheryll. 2004. *The Failures of Integration: How Race and Class Are Undermining the American Dream.* New York: Public Affairs.

Center for Urban Economic Development. 1980. *Grand Boulevard Revitalization: A Comprehensive Approach.* Chicago: University of Illinois at Chicago.

―――. 1986. *Greater Grand Boulevard Economic Development Study.* Chicago: University of Illinois at Chicago.

―――. 1993. *Forging Partnerships for a Healthy Viable Community: Provident Hospital, Urban Development Corporation and "North Washington Park" Area Residents.* Chicago: University of Illinois at Chicago.

Chapman, Richard. 1996. "Bronzeville Contest: Winners Find Path to Unknown Past." *Chicago Sun-Times,* May 28.

Chicago Commission on Race Relations. 1968. *The Negro in Chicago: A Study of Race Relations and a Race Riot in 1919.* New York: Arno Press.

Chicago Fact Book Consortium, ed. 1938. *Local Community Fact Book, Chicago Metropolitan Area.* Chicago: University of Illinois at Chicago.

―――. 1980. *Local Community Fact Book, Chicago Metropolitan Area.* Chicago: University of Illinois at Chicago.

―――. 1990. *Local Community Fact Book, Chicago Metropolitan Area.* Chicago: University of Illinois at Chicago.

Chicago Housing Authority. 2005. *The Plan for Transformation.* Chicago, Ill.

Chicago Historical Society. n.d. *Bronzeville: The Past and the Promise.* Chicago, Ill.

Chong, Dennis, and Reuel Rogers. 2005. "Racial Solidarity and Political Participation." *Political Behavior* 27, no. 4:347–74.

City of Chicago. 1984. *Black Metropolis Historic District.* Chicago, Ill.: Commission on Chicago Historical and Architectural Landmarks.

―――. 1987a. *Douglas Historic District.* Chicago, Ill.: Commission on Chicago Historical and Architectural Landmarks.

―――. 1987b. *The Gap Plan: New Promise for a Historic Neighborhood.* Chicago, Ill.: Department of Planning.

―――. 1994. *The Black Metropolis-Bronzeville District.* Chicago, Ill.: Department of Planning and Development.

―――. 1996. *A Guide to the Public Art of Bronzeville.* Chicago, Ill.: Department of Cultural Affairs.

―――. 1997. "Bronzeville Blue Ribbon Committee Report." Chicago, Ill.: Bronzeville Blue Ribbon Committee.

Clark, Kenneth. 1978. "No, No, Race, Not Class, Is Still at the Wheel." *New York Times,* December 3.

Clark, Kenneth, and C. Gershman. 1980. "The Black Plight: Race or Class?" *New York Times Magazine*, October 5.

Clavel, Pierre, and Wim Wiewel. 1991. *Harold Washington and the Neighborhoods: Progressive City Government in Chicago, 1983–1987.* New Brunswick, N.J.: Rutgers University Press.

Cohen, Cathy J. 1999. *The Boundaries of Blackness: AIDS and the Breakdown of Black Politics.* Chicago: University of Chicago Press.

Collens, Lew. 1995. *Illinois Institute of Technology: Serving the Economic Development Needs of the Community, the City, and the Region.* Presentation to the Economic Development Council, Chicago, Ill., November 29.

Collins, Patricia Hill. 1989. *Toward a New Vision: Race, Class and Gender as Categories of Analysis and Connection.* Memphis, Tenn.: Research Clearinghouse and Curriculum Integration Project, Center for Research on Women.

———. 2000. *Black Feminist Thought.* New York: Routledge.

Collins, Sharon M. 1997. *Black Corporate Executives: The Making and Breaking of a Black Middle Class.* Philadelphia: Temple University Press.

Conover, Pamela Johnston. 1984. "The Influence of Group Identifications on Political Perceptions and Evaluations." *American Journal of Political Science* 46, no. 3: 760–85.

———. 1989. "The Role of Social Groups in Political Thinking." *British Journal of Political Science* 18, no. 1:51–76.

Coontz, Stephanie. 1992. *The Way We Never Were: American Families and the Nostalgia Trap.* New York: Basic Books.

Dahl, Robert. 1961. *Who Governs?* New Haven, Conn.: Yale University Press.

Davis, Allison, Burleigh B. Gardner, and Mary R. Gardner. 1941. *Deep South: A Social Anthropological Study of Caste and Class.* Los Angeles: Center for Afro-American Studies, University of California, Los Angeles.

Davis, Leniece. 2000. "Restoring the Glory of Bronzeville: Communal Involvement, Political Efficacy, and Participation." Paper presented at the Midwest Political Science Association, April 27–30, Chicago, Ill.

Davis, Stephania. 1996. "Bronzeville's Golden Past Relies on City for Rebirth. *Chicago Tribune*, May 29.

Dawson, Michael C. 1994. *Behind the Mule: Race and Class in African-American Politics.* Princeton, N.J.: Princeton University Press.

del Barco, Mandalit. 2005. "Using the Black Panther Name to Market New Products." Radio broadcast on *All Things Considered*, National Public Radio, August 1.

Dickinson, Rachel. 1996. "Heritage Tourism Is Hot." *American Demographics* 18, no. 9 (September): 13–14.

Dillingham, Gerald L. 1981. "The Emerging Black Middle Class: Class Conscious or Race Conscious?" *Ethnic and Racial Studies* 4, no. 4:432–51.

Doggett, Leslie. 1993. "Multi-Cultural Tourism Development Offers a New Dimension in Travel." *Business America*, September 6, 8–10.

Dollard, John. 1957. *Caste and Class in a Southern Town.* 3d ed. Garden City, N.Y.: Doubleday.

Douglas Development Corporation. 1979. "Douglas Development and Planning Study: Creating Better Neighborhoods." Chicago, Ill.

Drake, St. Clair, and Horace R. Cayton. 1993 [1945]. *Black Metropolis: A Study of Negro Life in a Northern City.* Rev. ed. Chicago: University of Chicago Press.

Dubey, Madhu. 2003. *Signs and Cities: Black Literary Postmodernism.* Chicago: University of Chicago Press.

Dubois, W. E. B. 1899. *The Philadelphia Negro.* Philadelphia, Penn.: University of Pennsylvania Press.

Ehrenhalt, Alan. 1996. *The Lost City: Discovering the Forgotten Virtues of Community in the Chicago of the 1950s.* New York: Basic Books.

Eisinger, Paul. 1998. "City Politics in an Era of Federal Devolution." *Urban Affairs Review* 33, no. 3:308–25.

Emerson, Robert M., Rachel I. Fretz, and Linda L. Shaw. 1995. *Writing Ethnographic Fieldnotes.* Chicago: University of Chicago Press.

Eskridge, Ann E. 1998. "Discovering the Power of History." *American Visions* (October/November): 44–48.

Evans, Arthur S., Jr. 1992. "Black Middle Classes: The Outlook of a New Generation." *International Journal of Politics, Culture and Society* 6, no. 2:211–28.

Fairclough, Adam. 1987. *To Redeem the Soul of America: The Southern Christian Leadership Conference and Martin Luther King, Jr.* Athens: University of Georgia Press.

Farley, Reynolds, Charlotte Steeh, Maria Krysan, Tara Jackson, and Keith Reeves. 1994. "Stereotypes and Segregation: Neighborhoods in the Detroit Area." *American Journal of Sociology* 100, no. 3:750–80.

Favor, Martin. 1999. *Authentic Blackness: The Folk in the New Negro Renaissance.* Durham, N.C.: Duke University Press.

Fearon, James. 1999. "What Is Identity (As We Now Use the Word)?" Unpublished manuscript, November 3.

Feder, Barbara. 1994. "Plan Aims to Cure South Side Blues." *Chicago Reporter,* January.

Fenno, Richard. 2003. *Going Home: Black Representatives and their Constituents.* Chicago: University of Chicago Press.

Ferman, Barbara. 1996. *Challenging the Growth Machine: Neighborhood Politics in Chicago and Pittsburgh.* Lawrence, Kans.: University Press of Kansas.

Fields, Barbara Jean. 1982. "Ideology and Race in American History." In *Region, Race and Reconstruction,* ed. J. Morgan Kousser and James M. Macpherson. New York: Oxford University Press.

———. 1990. "Slavery, Race and Ideology in the United States of America," *New Left Review* (May/June): 95–118.

Fischer, Paul. 2004. "The Changing Nature of Federal Housing Policy in Bronzeville: A Declining Resource in a Growing Housing Market." Unpublished manuscript.

Fisher, Robert. 1994. "Community Organizing in the Conservative '80s and Beyond." *Social Policy* 25, no. 1:11–21.

Foner, Eric. 1990. *A Short History of Reconstruction, 1863–1877.* New York: Harper and Row.

Fossett, Mark A., and K. Jill Kiecolt. 1989. "The Relative Size of Minority Populations and White Racial Attitudes." *Social Science Quarterly* 70, no. 4:820–35.

Frazier, E. Franklin. 1957. *Black Bourgeoisie: The Rise of a New Middle Class in the United States.* New York: Free Press.

Gaines, Kevin. 1996. *Uplifting the Race: Black Leadership, Politics, and Culture in the Twentieth Century.* Chapel Hill, N.C.: University of North Carolina Press.

Garrett, Celeste. 1996. "Black Workers Left Out." *Chicago Sun-Times,* October 2.

Gates, Henry Louis, Jr. 1989. "Canon Formation, Literary History, and the Afro-American Tradition: From the Seen to the Told." In *Afro-American Literary Studies in the 1990s,* ed. Houston A. Baker Jr. and Patricia Redmond. Chicago: University of Chicago Press.

Gatewood, Willard B., Jr. 1988. "Aristocrats of Color: South and North, the Black Elite, 1880–1920." *The Journal of Southern History* 54, no. 1:249–66.

Gay, Claudine. 1994. "The Impact of Multiple Group Identities on the Policy Attitudes of Black Women." Paper presented at the American Political Science Association, New York, N.Y., September 1–4.

———. 2004. "Putting Race in Context: Identifying the Environmental Determinants of Black Racial Attitudes." *American Political Science Review* 98, no. 4:547–62.

Gieryn, Thomas F. 2000. "A Space for Place in Sociology." *Annual Review of Sociology* 26:463–96.

Gilliam, Franklin D., Jr. 1986. "Black America: Divided by Class?" *Public Opinion*, February, 53–57.

Gilliam, Franklin D., and Kenny J. Whitby. 1989. "Race, Class, and Attitudes toward Social Welfare Spending: An Ethclass Interpretation." *Social Science Quarterly* 70, no. 1: 88–100.

Gills, Douglas C. 1991. "Chicago Politics and Community Development." In *Harold Washington and the Neighborhoods: Progressive City Government in Chicago, 1983–1987*, ed. Pierre Clavel and Wim Wiewel. New Brunswick, N.J.: Rutgers University Press.

———. 2001. "Unequal and Uneven: Critical Aspects of Community-University Partnerships." In *Collaborative Research: University and Community Partnerships*, ed. Myrtis Sullivan and Marilyn Willis. Washington, D.C.: American Public Health Association.

Glanton, Dahleen. 1997. "Drawing on History." *Chicago Tribune*, March 31.

Glaser, James. 1994. "Back to the Black Belt: Racial Environment and White Racial Attitudes in the South." *The Journal of Politics* 56, no. 1:21–43.

Glizzio, Charles A. 1975. *John Jones and the Repeal of the Illinois Black Laws*. Duluth: University of Minnesota Social Science Research Publications.

Goffman, Erving. 1974. *Frame Analysis*. Cambridge: Harvard University Press.

Gosnell, Harold F. 1935. *Negro Politicians: The Rise of Negro Politics in Chicago*. Chicago: University of Chicago Press.

———. 1937. *Machine Politics: Chicago Model*. Chicago: University of Chicago Press.

Grazian, David. 2003. *Blue Chicago: The Search for Authenticity in Urban Blues Clubs*. Chicago: University of Chicago Press.

Green, Kenneth. 1983. "Greening of the Gap." *Chicago Defender*, September 26.

Greenberg, Cheryl Lynn. 1991. *"Or Does it Explode?": Black Harlem in the Great Depression*. New York: Oxford University Press.

Greenstone, J. David, and Paul Peterson. 1973. *Race and Authority in Urban Politics: Community Participation and the War on Poverty*. New York: Russell Sage Foundation.

Gregory, Steven. 1992. "The Changing Significance of Race and Class in an African-American Community." *American Ethnologist* 19, no. 2:255–74.

———. 1998. *Black Corona: Race and the Politics of Place in an Urban Community*. Princeton, N.J.: Princeton University Press.

Grimshaw, William J. 1992. *Bitter Fruit: Black Politics and the Chicago Machine, 1931–1991.* Chicago: University of Chicago Press.

Grossman, Ron. 1985. "The Gap: Old Neighborhood Reclaimed by New Black Generation." *Chicago Tribune,* February 24.

Hayes, Bernetta J. 1997. "Claiming Our Heritage Is a Booming Industry." *American Visions* (October/November): 43–46.

Hays, R. Allen. 1985. *The Federal Government and Urban Housing: Ideology and Change in Public Policy.* Albany, N.Y.: State University of New York Press.

Hill, James. 1997. "Heartbeat of Bronzeville Grows Stronger." *Chicago Tribune,* May 6.

Hirsch, Arnold R. 1983. *Making the Second Ghetto: Race and Housing in Chicago, 1940–1960.* Cambridge: Cambridge University Press.

———. 1995. "Martin H. Kennelly: The Mugwump and the Machine." In *The Mayors: The Chicago Political Tradition,* ed. Paul M. Green and Melvin G. Holli. Carbondale, Ill.: Southern Illinois University Press.

Hirsch, Arnold R., and Raymond A. Mohl, eds. 1993. *Urban Policy in Twentieth-Century America.* New Brunswick, N.J.: Rutgers University Press.

Hobsbawm, Eric, and Terence Ranger, eds. 1983. *The Invention of Tradition.* Cambridge: Cambridge University Press.

Hoffman, Lily M., and Jiri Musil. 1999. "Culture Meets Commerce: Tourism in Postcommunist Prague." In *The Tourist City,* ed. Dennis R. Judd and Susan S. Fainstein. New Haven, Conn.: Yale University Press.

Holcomb, Briavel. 1993. "Revisioning Place: De- and Re-constructing the Image of the Industrial City." In *Selling Places: The City as Cultural Capital, Past and Present,* ed. Gerry Kearns and Chris Philo. Oxford: Pergamon.

———. 1999. "Marketing Cities for Tourism." In *The Tourist City,* ed. Dennis R. Judd and Susan S. Fainstein. New Haven, Conn.: Yale University Press.

Holt, Glen, and Dominic A. Pacyga. 1979. *Chicago, A Historical Guide to the Neighborhoods: The Loop and South Side.* Chicago: Chicago Historical Society.

Huckfeldt, Robert. 1986. *Politics in Context: Assimilation and Conflict in Urban Neighborhoods.* New York: Agathon Press.

Hunt, Scott, and Robert Benford. 1994. "Identity Talk in the Peace and Justice Movement." *Journal of Contemporary Ethnography* 22, no. 4:488–517.

Jackson, John, Jr. 2001. *Harlemworld: Doing Race and Class in Contemporary Black America.* Chicago: University of Chicago Press.

———. 2005. *Real Black: Adventure in Racial Sincerity.* Chicago: University of Chicago Press.

Jasper, James M. 1997. *The Art of Moral Protest.* Chicago: University of Chicago Press.

Jennings, James. 1982. "Race, Class and Politics in the Black Community of Boston." *The Review of Black Political Economy* 12, no. 1:47–63.

Jordan, Jennifer. 1986. "Cultural Nationalism in the 1960s: Politics and Poetry." In *Race, Politics and Culture: Critical Essays on the Radicalism of the 1960s,* ed. Adolph Reed Jr. New York: Greenwood Press.

Judd, Dennis R., and Margaret Collins. 1979. "The Case of Tourism: Political Coalitions and Redevelopment in Central Cities." In *The Changing Structure of the City: What Happened to the Urban Crisis,* ed. Gary Tobin. Beverly Hills, Calif.: Sage.

Judd, Dennis R., and Susan S. Fainstein, eds. 1999. *The Tourist City.* New Haven, Conn.: Yale University Press.

Kantowicz, Edward R. 1995. "Carter H. Harrison II: The Politics of Balance." In *The Mayors: The Chicago Political Tradition,* ed. Paul M. Green and Melvin G. Holli. Carbondale, Ill.: Southern Illinois University Press.

Kaufmann, Karen. 1998. "Racial Conflict and Political Choice: A Study of Mayoral Voting Behavior in Los Angeles and New York." *Urban Affairs Review* 33, no. 5:655–85.

———. 2004. *The Urban Voter: Group Conflict and Mayoral Voting Behavior in American Cities.* Ann Arbor: University of Michigan Press.

Kearns, Gerry, and Chris Philo, eds. 1993. *Selling Places: The City as Cultural Capital.* Oxford: Pergamon.

Key, V. O., Jr. 1949. *Southern Politics.* New York: Random House.

Kilson, Martin. 1971. "Political Change in the Negro Ghetto, 1900–1940s." In *Key Issues in the Afro-American Experience,* ed. Nathan I. Huggins, Martin Kilson, and Daniel M. Fox. New York: Harcourt Brace Jovanovich.

———. 1983. "The Black Bourgeoisie Revisited: From E. Franklin Frazier to the Present." *Dissent* 30, no. 1:85–96.

Kim, Claire. 2000. *Bitter Fruit: The Politics of Black–Korean Conflict in New York City.* New Haven, Conn.: Yale University Press.

Kinder, Donald R. 1986. "The Continuing American Dilemma: White Resistance to Racial Change 40 Years after Myrdal." *Journal of Social Issues* 42, no. 2: 151–71.

Kinder, Donald R., and David O. Sears. 1981. "Prejudice and Politics: Symbolic Racism Versus Racial Threats to the Good Life." *Journal of Personality and Social Psychology* 40, no. 3:414–31.

Kinder, Donald R., and Lynn Sanders. 1996. *Divided by Color.* Chicago: University of Chicago Press.

King, Deborah. 1989. "Multiple Jeopardy, Multiple Consciousness: The Context of a Black Feminist Ideology." *Signs* 14, no. 1:42–72.

Kleppner, Paul. 1985. *Chicago Divided: The Making of a Black Mayor.* DeKalb, Ill.: Northern Illinois University Press.

Knoke, David, and Natalie Kyriazis. 1977. "The Persistence of the Black-Belt Vote: A Test of Key's Hypothesis." *Social Science Quarterly* 57, no. 4:900–906.

Knupfer, Anne Meis. 1996. *Toward a Tenderer Humanity and a Nobler Womanhood: African American Women's Clubs in Turn-of-the-Century Chicago.* New York: New York University Press.

Kotler, Philip, Donald H. Haider, and Irving Rein. 1993. *Marketing Places.* New York: Free Press.

Kretzmann, John. 1991. "The Affirmative Information Policy." In *Harold Washington and The Neighborhoods: Progressive City Government in Chicago, 1983–1987,* ed. Pierre Clavel and Wim Wiewel. New Brunswick, N.J.: Rutgers University Press.

Kretzmann, John, John L. McKnight, and Nicol Turner. 1996. *Voluntary Associations in Low-Income Neighborhoods: An Unexplored Community Resource.* Institute for Policy Research Northwestern University, Evanston, Ill.

Landry, Bart. 1987. *The New Black Middle Class.* Berkeley and Los Angeles: University of California Press.

Law, Christopher M. 1992. "Urban Tourism and its Contribution to Economic Regeneration." *Urban Studies* 29, no. 3/4:599–618.

Lipsitz, George. 1998. *The Possessive Investment in Whiteness: How White People Profit from Identity Politics.* Philadelphia: Temple University Press.

Logan, John R., and Harvey L. Molotch. 1987. *Urban Fortunes: The Political Economy of Place.* Berkeley and Los Angeles: University of California Press.

Long, Jerome. 1996. "The Urban Campus: Realizing the Promise." *Catalyst* (Spring). http://www.iit.edu/publications/catalyst/spring96/spring96.cover.html.

Longini, Mario. 2000. "Family Mobility and Childcare at the End of a Public Housing Era." *Perspectives on Civic Activism and City Life* 1:1–15.

Lucas, Harold. 1997. "Historic Summary of Black Metropolis Bronzeville and Its Significance." *South Street Journal,* February 28–March 13.

MacKuen, Michael, and Courtney Brown. 1987. "Political Context and Attitude Change." *American Political Science Review* 81, no. 2:471–90.

Main, Frank. 2004. "Bridgeport Man Accused of Bat-Wielding Hate Crime." *Chicago Sun-Times*, March 11.

Manley, Theodoric, Jr. 1995. *The Black Metropolis Revisited: The Strength and Resilience of African-American Community Organizations*. Chicago, Ill.: DePaul University, Center for African American Research.

Marable, Manning. 1981. "Beyond the Race-Class Dilemma." *The Nation*, April 11, 428–29.

Marks, Carole. 1989. *Farewell—We're Good and Gone: The Great Black Migration*. Bloomington, Ind.: Indiana University Press.

Massey, Douglas, and Nancy Denton. 1993. *American Apartheid: Segregation and the Making of the Underclass*. Cambridge: Harvard University Press.

Matthews, Donald R., and James W. Prothro. 1966. *Negroes and the New Southern Politics*. New York: Harcourt, Brace, and World.

McBride, David, and Monroe H. Little. 1981. "The Afro-American Elite, 1930–1940: A Historical and Statistical Profile." *Phylon* 42, no. 2:105–19.

McCaul, Robert L. 1987. *The Black Struggle for Public Schooling in Nineteenth-Century Illinois*. Carbondale, Ill.: Southern Illinois University Press.

McConahay, John B. 1982. "Self-Interest Versus Racial Attitudes as Correlates of Anti-Busing Attitudes in Louisville: Is it the Buses or the Blacks?" *The Journal of Politics* 44, no. 3:692–720.

McConahay, John B., and Joseph C. Hough, Jr. 1976. "Symbolic Racism." *Journal of Social Issues* 32, no. 2:23–45.

McIntosh, Peggy. 1988. "White Privilege and Male Privilege: A Personal Account of Coming to See Correspondences through Work in Women's Studies." Wellesley, Mass.: Center for Research on Women, Wellesley College.

Meier, August. 1962. "Negro Class Structure and Ideology in the Age of Booker T. Washington." *Phylon* 23, no. 3:258–66.

Meier, August, and David Lewis. 1959. "History of the Negro Upper Class in Atlanta, Georgia, 1890–1958." *Journal of Negro Education* 28, no. 2:128–39.

Mele, Chistopher. 1996. "Globalization, Culture, and Neighborhood Change: Reinventing the Lower East Side of New York." *Urban Affairs Review* 32, no. 1:3–22.

———. 2000. *Selling the Lower East Side: Culture, Real Estate, and Resistance in New York City*. Minneapolis: University of Minnesota Press.

Mid-South Planning and Development Commission. 1993. "Mid-South Strategic Development Plan: Restoring Bronzeville." Chicago, Ill.

Miller, Arthur H., Patricia Gurin, Gerald Gurin, and Oksana Malanchuk. 1981. "Group Consciousness and Political Participation." *American Journal of Political Science* 25, no. 3:494–511.

Miller, Sabrina I. 1996. "Black History Was Born, Nurtured Here." *Chicago Tribune.* February 1.

Miller, Warren E. 1956. "One-Party Politics and the Voter." *The American Political Science Review* 50, no. 3:707–25.

Mills, Caroline. 1993. "Myths and Meanings of Gentrification." In *Place/Culture/Representation,* ed. James Duncan and David Ley. London: Routledge.

Mitchneck, Beth. 1998. "The Heritage Industry Russian Style: The Case of Yaroslavl." *Urban Affairs Review* 34, no. 1:28–51.

Mollenkopf, John H. 1983. *The Contested City.* Princeton, N.J.: Princeton University Press.

Moore, Kesha S. 2002. "Creating the Black American Dream: Race, Class and Community Development." Ph.D. diss., University of Pennsylvania.

———. 2005. "What's Class Got to Do with It?: Community Development and Racial Identity." *Journal of Urban Affairs* 27, no. 4:437–51.

Morris, Aldon D. 1984. *The Origins of the Civil Rights Movement: Black Communities Organizing for Change.* New York: The Free Press.

Morrison, Toni, ed. 1992. *Race-ing Justice, En-gendering Power: Essays on Anita Hill, Clarence Thomas, and the Construction of Social Reality.* New York: Pantheon Books.

Muñiz, Vicky 1998. *Resisting Gentrification and Displacement: Voices of Puerto Rican Women of the Barrio.* New York: Garland Publishing.

Nagel, Joane. 1994. "Constructing Ethnicity: Creating and Recreating Ethnic Identity and Culture." *Social Problems* 41, no. 1:152–76.

Ogletree, Charles J. 2004. *All Deliberate Speed: Reflections on the First Half Century of Brown v. Board of Education.* New York: W.W. Norton and Company.

Omi, Michael, and Howard Winant. 1994. *Racial Formation in the United States: From the 1960s to the 1990s.* New York: Routledge.

Owens, Michael Leo. 1997. "Renewal in a Working-Class Black Neighborhood." *Journal of Urban Affairs* 19, no. 2:183–205.

Parent, Wayne, and Paul Stekler. 1985. "The Political Implications of Economic Stratification in the Black Community." *Western Political Quarterly* 38, no. 4:521–38.

Pérez, Gina. 2002. "The Other 'Real World': Gentrification and the Social

Construction of Place in Chicago." *Urban Anthropology* 3, no. 1:37–68. Berkeley and Los Angeles: University of California Press.

Philpott, Thomas. 1991. *The Slum and the Ghetto. Immigrants, Blacks, and Reformers in Chicago, 1880–1930.* Belmont, Calif.: Wadsworth Publishing Co.

Pierce, Bessie Louise. 1957. *A History of Chicago.* Vol 3. Chicago: University of Chicago Press.

Pinderhughes, Dianne. 1987. *Race and Ethnicity in Chicago Politics: A Re-Examination of Pluralist Theory.* Urbana, Ill.: University of Illinois Press.

Plotkin, Wendy. 1999. "Deeds of Mistrust: Race, Housing, and Restrictive Covenants in Chicago: 1900–1953." Ph.D. diss., University of Illinois at Chicago.

Pogge, Jean. 1992. "Reinvestment in Chicago Neighborhoods: A Twenty-Year Struggle." In *From Redlining to Reinvestment: Community Responses to Urban Disinvestment,* ed. Gregory D. Squires. Philadelphia, Penn.: Temple University Press.

Polletta, Francesca. 1998. "'It Was Like a Fever . . . ': Narrative and Identity in Social Protest." *Social Problems* 45, no. 2:137–59.

Polletta, Francesca, and James M. Jasper. 2001. "Collective Identity and Social Movements." *Annual Review of Sociology* 27:283–305.

Preston, Michael B. 1979. *Black Machine Politics in the Post-Daley Era.* Evanston, Ill.: Northwestern Center for Urban Affairs.

Prince, Sabiyha. 2002. "Changing Places: Race, Class and Belonging in the 'New Harlem.'" *Urban Anthropology* 31, no. 1:5–35.

Putnam, Robert D. 1966. "Political Attitudes and the Local Community." *The American Political Science Review* 60, no. 3:640–54.

Quintanilla, Ray. 1994. "Aldermen Keep Firm 'Hold' on Bronzeville." *Chicago Reporter,* January.

Ralph, James. 1993. *Northern Protest: Martin Luther King, Jr., Chicago, and the Civil Rights Movement.* Cambridge: Harvard University Press.

Rast, Joel. 1999. *Remaking Chicago: The Political Origins of Urban Industrial Change.* DeKalb, Ill.: Northern Illinois University Press.

Reardon, Kenneth. 1990. "Local Economic Development in Chicago 1983–1987: The Reform Efforts of Mayor Harold Washington." Ph.D. diss., Cornell University.

Reed, Adolph, Jr. 1988. "The Black Urban Regime: Structural Origins and Constraints." *Comparative Urban and Community Research* 1:138–89.

———. 1995. "Demobilization in the New Black Political Regime: Ideological

Capitulation, and Radical Failure in the Post-Segregation Era." In *The Bub-bling Cauldron*, ed. Michael Peter Smith and Joe R. Feagin. Minneapolis: University of Minnesota Press.

———. 1996. "Romancing Jim Crow: Black Nostalgia for a Segregated Past." *The Village Voice*, April 16.

———. 1999a. *Stirrings in the Jug: Black Politics in the Post-Segregation Era*. Min-neapolis: University of Minnesota Press.

———, ed. 1999b. *Without Justice for All: The New Liberalism and our Retreat from Racial Equality*. Boulder, Colo.: Westview Press.

Robnett, Belinda. 1997. *How Long? How Long?: African-American Women in the Strug-gle for Civil Rights*. New York: Oxford University Press.

Rodkin, Dennis, Charles Whitaker, and Deborah Wilk. 2004. "The New South Side: A Special Report on the Remarkable Boom That's Transforming a Historic Slice of the City." *Chicago*, March, 70–85.

Rustin, Bayard. 1965. "From Protest to Politics: The Future of the Civil Rights Movement." *Commentary* 39:25–31.

Schaffer, Richard, and Neil Smith. 1986. "The Gentrification of Harlem?" *Annals of the Association of American Geographers* 76, no. 3:347–65.

Schlay, Anne, and Robert Giloth. 1987. "The Social Organiztion of a Land-Based Elite: The Case of the Failed Chicago 1992 World's Fair." *Journal of Urban Affairs* 9:305–24.

Sears, David O., Carl P. Hensler, and Leslie K. Speer. 1979. "Whites' Opposition to 'Busing': Self-Interest or Symbolic Politics?" *American Political Science Review* 73, no. 2:369–84.

Sears, David O., Richard R. Lau, Tom R. Tyler and Harris M. Allen, Jr. 1980. "Self-Interest vs. Symbolic Politics in Policy Attitudes and Presidential Voting." *American Political Science Review* 74, no. 3:670–84.

Sears, David O., and Donald R. Kinder. 1985. "Whites' Opposition to Busing: On Conceptualizing and Operationalizing Group Conflict." *Journal of Person-ality and Social Psychology* 48, no. 5:1141–47.

Sears, David O., Colette van Laar, Mary Carillo, and Rick Kosterman. 1997. "Is It Really Racism? The Origins of White Americans' Opposition to Race-Targeted Policies." *Public Opinion Quarterly* 61, no. 1:16–57.

Seligman, Amanda. 2005. *Block by Block: Neighborhoods and Public Policy on Chicago's West Side*. Chicago: University of Chicago Press.

Severinsen, Kay. 1995. "A Rebirth in Bronzeville." *Chicago Sun-Times*, May 26.

Simien, Evelyn. 2004. "The Intersection of Race and Gender: An Examination of Black Feminist Consciousness, Race Consciousness, and Policy Attitudes" *Social Science Quarterly* 85, no. 3:793–810.

———. 2005. "Race, Gender and Linked Fate." *Journal of Black Studies* 35, no. 5:529–50.

Simpson, Andrea Y. 1998. *The Tie That Binds: Identity and Political Attitudes in the Post–Civil Rights Generation.* New York: New York University Press.

Simpson, William. 1996. "Bronzeville's Tarnished Past." *Chicago Sun-Times*, July 24.

Sites, Paul, and Elizabeth I. Mullins. 1985. "The American Black Elite, 1930–1978." *Phylon* 46, no. 3:269–80.

Smedley, Audrey. 1993. *Race in North America: Origin and Evolution of a Worldview.* Boulder, Colo.: Westview Press.

Smith, Gavin. 1991. "The Production of Culture in Local Rebellion." In *Golden Ages, Dark Ages: Imagining the Past in Anthropology and History,* ed. William Roseberry and Jay O'Brien. Berkeley and Los Angeles: University of California Press.

Smith, Neil. 1992. "New City, New Frontier: The Lower East Side as Wild, Wild West." *In Variations on a Theme Park: The New American City and the End of Public Space,* ed. Michael Sorkin. New York: Hill and Wang.

———. 1996. *The New Urban Frontier: Gentrification and the Revanchist City.* London: Routledge.

Smith, Preston. 2000. "The Quest for Racial Democracy: Black Civic Ideology and Housing Interests in Postwar Chicago." *Journal of Urban History* 26, no. 2:131–57.

Smith, Robert C. 1981. "Black Power and Transformation from Protest to Politics." *Political Science Quarterly* 96, no. 3:431–43.

Smith, Rogers. 2003. *Stories of Peoplehood: The Politics and Morals of Political Membership.* Cambridge: Cambridge University Press.

Snow, David A., E. Burke Rochford Jr., Steven K. Worden, and Robert D. Benford. 1986. "Frame Alignment Processes, Micromobilization, and Movement Participation." *American Sociological Review* 51, no. 4:464–81.

Sorkin, Michael. 1992. *Variations on a Theme Park: The New American City and the End of Public Space.* New York: Hill and Wang.

South Side Partnership. 1999. "Rebuilding Bronzeville: Challenges and Opportunities for the South Side Partnership, a Position Paper." Photocopy. Chicago, Ill.

Spear, Allan H. 1967. *Black Chicago: The Making of a Negro Ghetto, 1890–1920*. Chicago: University of Chicago Press.

Squires, Gregory, Larry Bennett, Katherine McCourt, and Phillip Nyden. 1987. *Chicago: Race Class and Urban Decline*. Philadelphia: Temple University Press.

Stein, Judith. 1989. "Defining the Race, 1890–1930." In *The Invention of Ethnicity*, ed. Werner Sollors. New York: Oxford University Press.

Steinberg, Stephen. 1995. *Turning Back: The Retreat from Racial Justice in American Thought and Policy*. Boston, Mass.: Beacon Press.

Stevens, Michelle. 1982. "Douglas Area Comes Back to Life." *Chicago Sun-Times*, April 30.

Stevenson, Angela. 1996. "Lost Treasures of Bronzeville." *Chicago Sun-Times*, May 28.

Stoecker, Randy. 1997. "The CDC Model of Urban Redevelopment: A Critique and an Alternative." *Journal of Urban Affairs* 19, no. 1:1–22.

Strickland, Arvah. 2001 [1966]. *History of the Chicago Urban League*. Urbana, Ill.: University of Illinois Press.

Swain, Carol. 1995. *Black Faces, Black Interests: The Representation of African-American in Congress*. Cambridge: Harvard University Press.

Tate, Katherine. 1994. *From Protest to Politics: The New Black Voters in American Elections*. New York: Russell Sage Foundation.

———. 2003. *Black Faces in the Mirror: African-Americans and their Representatives in the U.S. Congress*. Princeton, N.J.: Princeton University Press.

Taylor, Monique. 2002. *Harlem between Heaven and Hell*. Minneapolis: University of Minnesota Press.

Thomas, Jerry, and Gary Marx. 1997. "Bishop Vows to Fight Racism in His Schools." *Chicago Tribune*, March 25.

Thompson, Nathan. 2003. *Kings: The True Story of Chicago's Policy Kings and Numbers Racketeers*. Chicago: The Bronzeville Press.

Urry, John. 1999. "Sensing the City." In *The Tourist City*, ed. Dennis Judd and Susan Fainstein. New Haven, Conn.: Yale University Press.

Valocchi, Steve. 1996. "The Emergence of the Integrationist Ideology in the Civil Rights Movement." *Social Problems* 43, no. 1:116–30.

Van den Berghe, Pierre L., and Charles F. Keyes. 1984. "Tourism and Re-Created Ethnicity." *Annals of Tourism Research* 11, no. 3:343–52.

Venkatesh, Sudhir. 2000. *American Project: The Rise and Fall of a Modern Ghetto*. Cambridge, Mass.: Harvard University Press.

Waite, Lori G. 2001. "Divided Consciousness: The Impact of Black Elite Consciousness on the 1966 Chicago Freedom Movement." In *Oppositional Consciousness: The Subjective Roots of Social Protest*, ed. Jane Mansbridge and Aldon Morris. Chicago: University of Chicago Press.

Warner, Edwin, and Sarah Bedell. 1974. "America's Rising Black Middle Class." *Time*, June, 26–27.

Washburn, Gary. 1983. "'Rehab Fever' Fills the Gap with New Possibilities." *Chicago Tribune*, August 28.

Washington, Betty. 1977. "For a Far-Out House, They Decided to Buy Close In." *Chicago Daily News*, March 18–20.

Weatherford, M. Stephen. 1982. "Interpersonal Networks and Political Behavior." *American Journal of Political Science* 26, no. 1:117–43.

Weir, Margaret. 1999. "Power, Money, and Politics in Community Development." In *Urban Problems and Community Development*, ed. Ronald Ferguson and William T. Dickens. Washington D.C.: Brookings Institution Press.

Welch, Susan, and Michael W. Combs. 1985. "Intra-Racial Differences in Attitudes of Blacks: Class Cleavages or Consensus?" *Phylon* 46, no. 2:91–97.

Welch, Susan, and Lorn Foster. 1987. "Class and Conservatism in the Black Community." *American Politics Quarterly* 15, no. 4:445–70.

West, Cornel. 1993. *Race Matters*. Boston, Mass.: Beacon Press.

Whitby, Kenny. 1997. *The Color of Representation*. Ann Arbor: University of Michigan Press.

Williams, Brett. 1988. *Upscaling Downtown: Stalled Gentrification in Washington, D.C.* Ithaca, N.Y.: Cornell University Press.

———. 1999. "The Great Family Fraud of Postwar America." In *Without Justice for All: the New Liberalism and Our Retreat from Racial Equality*, ed. Adolph Reed Jr. Boulder, Colo.: Westview Press.

———. 2002. "Gentrifying Water and Selling Jim Crow." *Urban Anthropology* 31, no. 1:93–121.

Wilson, James Q. 1960. *Negro Politics: The Search for Leadership*. New York: The Free Press.

Wilson, William J. 1980. *The Declining Significance of Race: Blacks and Changing American Institutions*. 2d ed. Chicago: University of Chicago Press.

———. 1996. *When Work Disappears: The World of the New Urban Poor*. New York: Alfred A. Knopf.

Wood, Robert E. 1984. "Ethnic Tourism, the State and Cultural Change in Southeast Asia." *Annals of Tourism Research* 11, no. 3:353–74.

Wright, Gerald C. 1977. "Contextual Models of Electoral Behavior: The Southern Wallace Vote." *American Political Science Review* 71, no. 2:497–508.

Young, Michelle. 1980. "Blacks Filling in the 'GAP.'" *Chicago Defender*, July 26.

Index

Michelle R. Boyd is assistant professor of African American studies and political science at the University of Illinois at Chicago.